Architecture of Consoles: The Sprite Decade

A Practical Analysis

Rodrigo Copetti

https://www.copetti.org

To my family, friends and supporters

Contents

1

Introduction

1.1 The architecture of consoles series

Looking at the evolution of video game consoles is fascinating. While conventional PCs tend to evolve 'incrementally', new generations of consoles introduce completely new ways of working. The writings you see here are part of a series aimed at uncovering the rationale behind the latest trends in technology. They will also demonstrate why each system can't be summarised by its 'bits', megahertz, amount of RAM and whatnot.

Basic knowledge of computing is preferable, however, I try really hard to adapt my content for wider audiences, so please don't be afraid to give it a try! But if that's not enough, you may want to look at the supporting readings[1] or read previous articles[2] first.

1.1.1 About this edition

Thank you for purchasing this book! This edition originates from the content initially published on my personal website[3], it's been re-styled and optimised to take advantage of the capabilities of physical documents.

While similar in content, this edition is free from the digital limitations of the web, such as storage and bandwidth constraints. As a result, diagrams and photography are imported from raw files at full resolution, enabling to publish the best quality that the printer allows. Additionally, extra chapters are provided to assist in the navigation of this book and to acknowledge those who helped build its content.

[1] https://www.copetti.org/writings/consoles/readings
[2] https://www.copetti.org/writings/consoles/
[3] https://www.copetti.org/writings/consoles/

1.1.2 Open to feedback

As always, the original manuscripts of the articles are available on Github[4] to enable readers to report mistakes or propose changes. Likewise, if you have any comments and/or issues regarding this edition, please get in touch through there.

1.2 The Sprite Decade (1983-1990)

Before consoles embraced the third dimension, marketshare in the 2D arena was highly contested. Selling in a saturated market meant that both manufacturers and developers had to push boundaries — sometimes out of ambition, other times by necessity. Companies like Sega and SNK opted for off-the-shelf hardware for their consoles, providing developers comfortable tools to implement their games. Others such as Nintendo and Hudson Soft, constrained by budget, relied on ingenuity, leading to a surge of unconventional techniques and creative workarounds.

For this volume, I wanted to compare how 2D rivals navigated the challenges of that era, from CPU designs that pushed beyond 8-bit limitations, to graphics chips that leveraged the CRT beam for groundbreaking visual effects. Alongside these, a vibrant array of sound synthesisers, I/O, copy protection techniques, and expansion options.

Now, without further ado, here they are!

[4] https://github.com/flipacholas/Architecture-of-consoles

2

NES / Famicom Architecture

More than a 6502 machine

2.1 A quick introduction

At first glance, the NES appears to be just another 6502 computer, with a sophisticated case and a controller.

And while this is *technically* true, let me show you why the CPU is not the *central* part of this system.

2.2 Models and variants

Nintendo ended up shipping lots of different variants of the same console across the world [1] and even though they all share the same architecture, many look dramatically different and some may include built-in accessories. So, to keep it simple for this article, I'll focus on the two most popular revisions:

- The **Family Computer** (known as *Famicom*) was the first incarnation, but was only released in Japan. This toy-looking design features two non-removable controllers (from which the second controller bundles an internal microphone), a front socket for the light gun (called *Zapper*), RF video out (using NTSC-J signal) and extra pins in the cartridge slot to expand the audio capabilities.
- The **Nintendo Entertainment System** (known as *NES*) was the redesigned edition for western audiences living in North America, Europe and Oceania; with a look and mechanism that matches the common VHS/Betamax player. On the technical side,

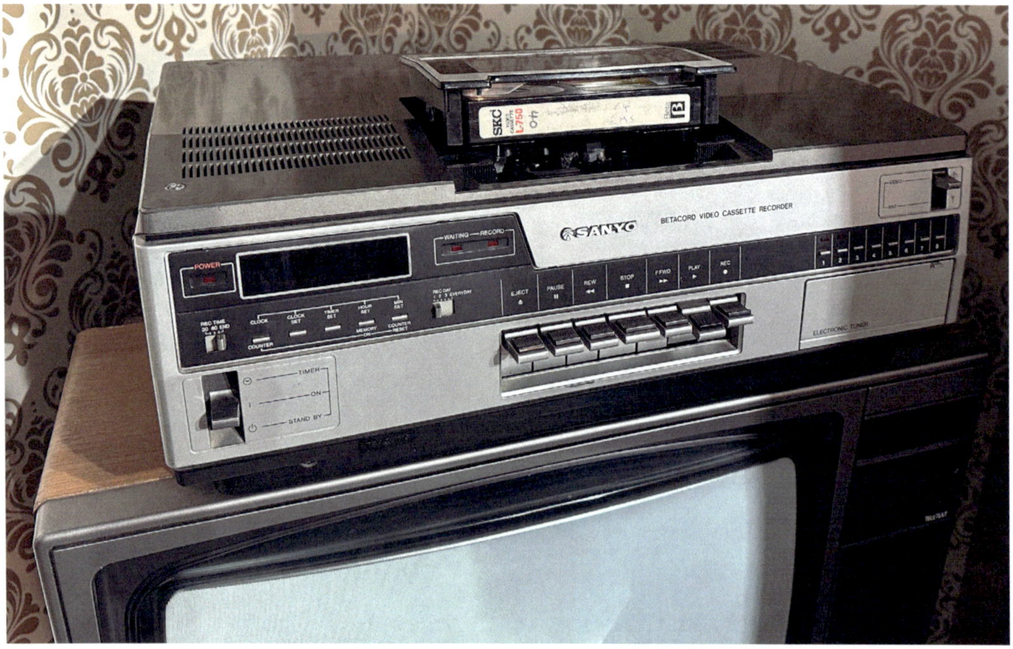

Figure 2.1: *A typical Betamax recorder. This and similar appliances influenced the international design of the NES. I spotted this particular one at The Centre for Computing History (Cambridge, UK) when I visited in August 2024.*

> the controllers are now detachable (and microphone-lacking) and the video out has been improved with extra NTSC/PAL composite RCA connectors, although the audio expansion has been replaced with an anti-piracy subsystem. To top it off, the bottom of the case seals an 'expansion port' that was left unused, along with extra cartridge pins that communicate to that port [2].

Because the author grew up with the 'NES' name, I will default to using that term to refer to the console in general, but I will switch to 'Famicom' when referring to unique capabilities only found in the Japanese variant.

2.3 Supporting Imagery

Figure 2.2: *The Nintendo Entertainment System (NES). Released on 18/10/1985 in America and 01/09/1986 in Europe. [3]*

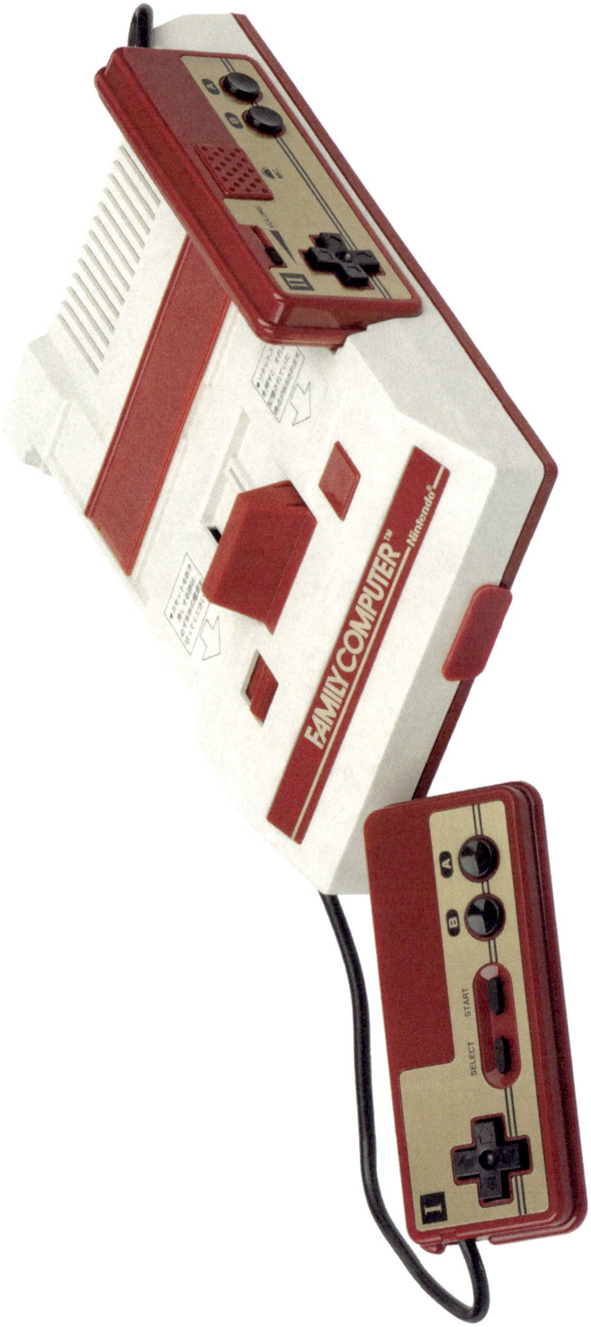

Figure 2.3: *The Famicom. Released on 15/07/1983 in Japan. [3]*

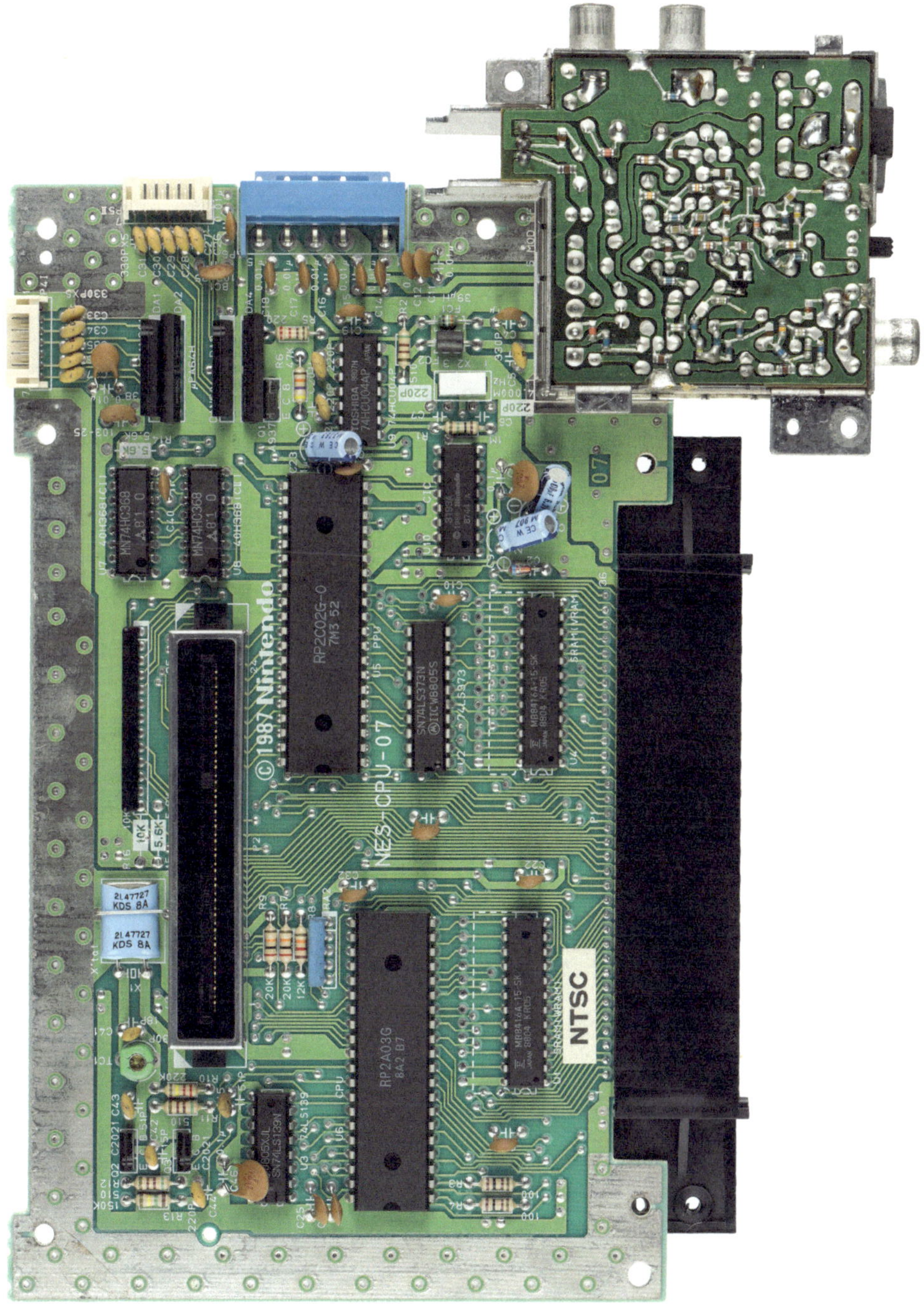

Figure 2.4: *Motherboard [3]. Showing the 'NES' variant.*

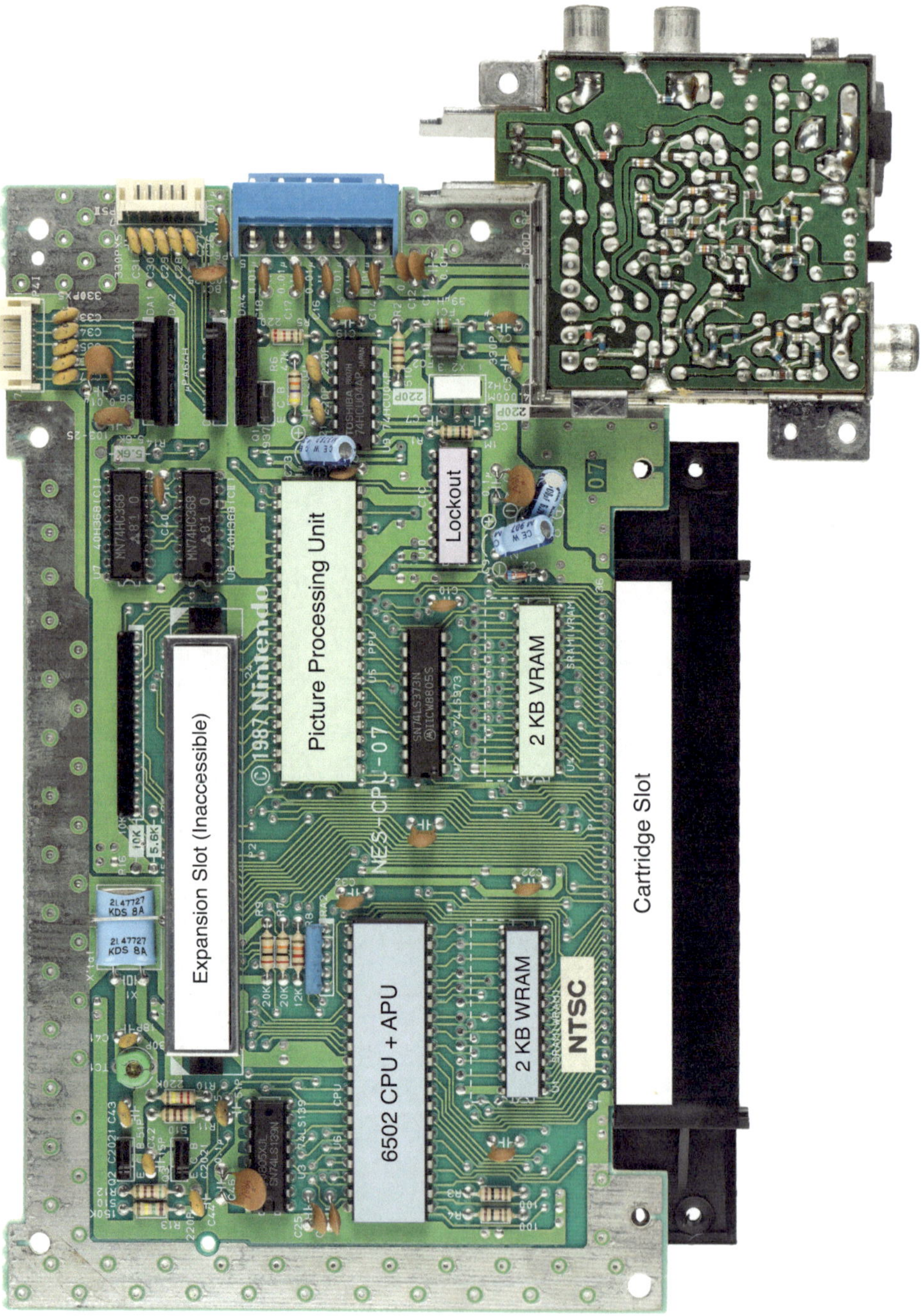

Figure 2.5: *Motherboard with important parts labelled.*

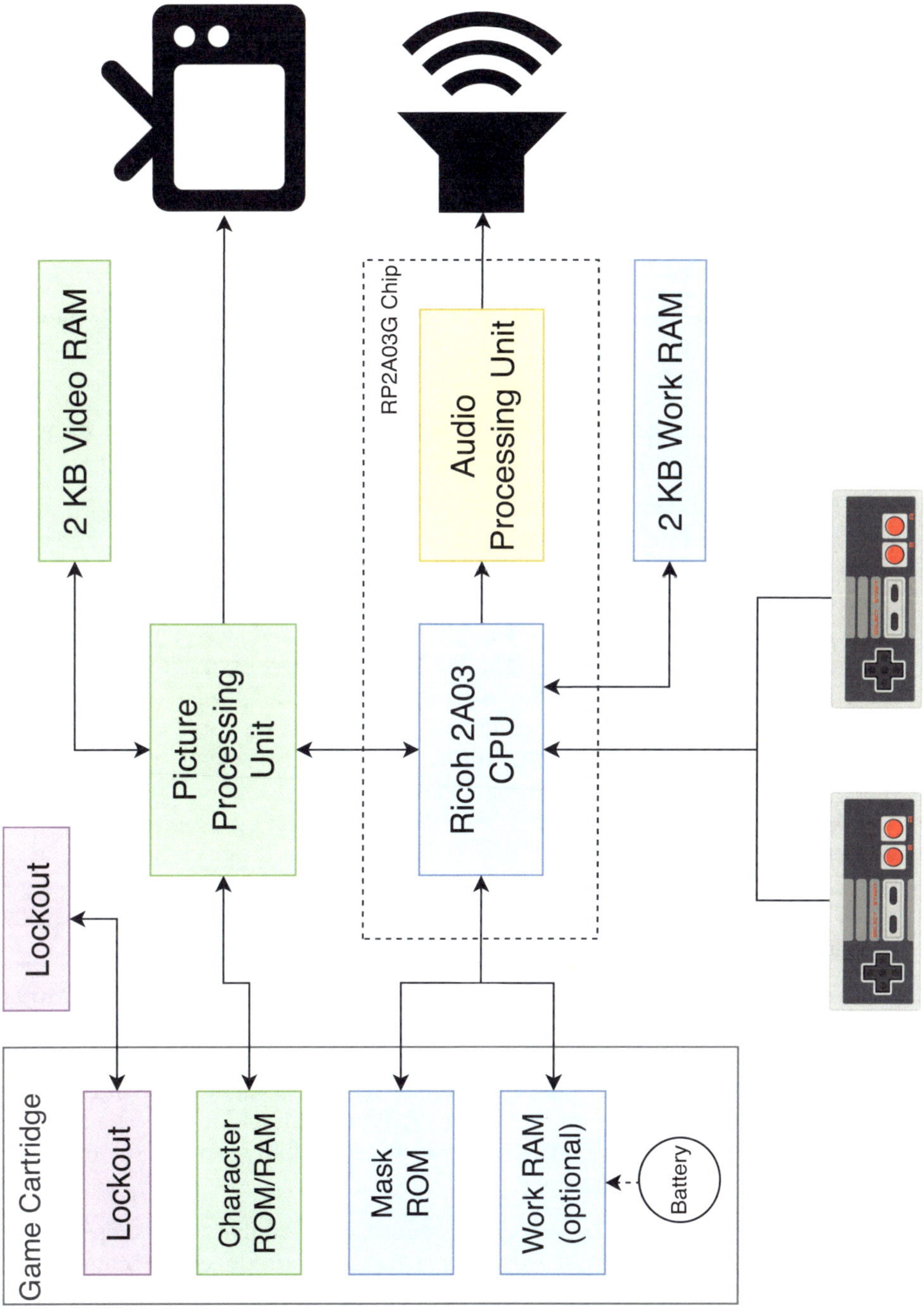

Figure 2.6: *Main architecture diagram.*

2.4 CPU

The NES's CPU is a **Ricoh 2A03** [4], which is based on the popular 8-bit **MOS Technology 6502** and runs at **1.79 MHz** (or 1.66 MHz in PAL systems). This is the central component that executes the code inside the game cartridge.

2.4.1 A bit of context

To understand the circuitry residing inside the NES' motherboard, we must first take a look at the state of the industry at the time. Interestingly, the CPU market in the late 70s and early 80s was quite diverse.

If you were a startup aiming to build an affordable microcomputer for the western world, you had plenty of options available:

- The **Intel 8080** (1974): A popular CPU featured in the MITS Altair 8800, the first 'personal' computer. It comes with a modest 8-bit data bus, a 16-bit address bus (enough to handle the necessary memory), and seven 8-bit registers. With capabilities like this, a line was drawn between the simple calculator and an actual computer.
- The **Zilog Z80** (1976): Displeased with Intel's direction and lack of investment in their CPU division, former engineers of the 8080 started their own company to produce an 'unofficial' successor, enhanced with more instructions, registers, and internal components. To top it off, it was sold at a lower price and could still execute 8080 programs [5, p. 86]. The new CPU was well received by British firms Amstrad and Sinclair, as well as the Japanese Sega[1], among others.
- The **Motorola 6800** (1974): Another 8-bit CPU designed around the same time. While a direct competitor of the 8080, the 6800 was programmed using a more sophisticated instruction set, albeit running at a slower clock speed [6]. Nevertheless, many do-it-yourself computer kits, synthesisers, and all-in-one computers included the 6800.

Faced with similar setbacks that Intel's employees went through, engineers at Motorola grew frustrated with the company's lack of interest in capitalising on the potential of the 6800 [7]. So, they joined a small but ambitious silicon firm, **MOS**, where they worked on a redesigned version of the 6800 - the **MOS 6502**. While incompatible with the rest, the new chip was much, *much* cheaper to produce [8] [9, p. 76], and it was only a matter of time before iconic computer makers (Commodore, Tandy, Apple, Atari, Acorn, and so forth) chose the 6502 to power their machines.

Back in Japan, Nintendo needed something inexpensive yet familiar to develop for, so they selected the 6502. **Ricoh**, their CPU supplier, successfully produced a 6502-compatible clone.

[1] See "Sega Master System Architecture"

(a) *A Commodore PET, carrying a 6502 CPU.*

(b) *A Tandy TRS-80, carrying a Z80 CPU.*

Figure 2.7: *The panorama of late-70s computers, also provided by The Centre for Computing History (Cambridge, UK).*

2.4.2 Core functionality

To understand how capable this console is, let's first check what the original MOS 6502 offers:

- The **6502 ISA**: MOS wanted to offer drastic improvements at the cost of compatibility with third-parties (especially Motorola) [6]. Thus, the 6502 instruction set still handles **8-bit** words like the 6800 and others, but its programming is not cross-compatible.
- An **8-bit data bus** and a **16-bit address bus**. This was the typical combination for microprocessors of that era. Basically, it allows to operate data in chunks of eight bits without running out of memory locations (at least, too quickly).
  - On paper, 16-bit addresses means the 8-bit CPU will need extra cycles to process the extra size. However, thanks to MOS's new addressing modes (explained further down), these penalties were alleviated without requiring too much circuitry.
- **Three general-purpose registers** (`X`, `Y` and `A`), which may look constrained when compared to larger register files[2]. This decision reduces costs but also means the CPU would need to move memory around more frequently. With the 6502, `X` and `Y` are called 'index registers' and are used to address memory, while `A` is directly connected to the ALU and dedicated to arithmetic operations.
  - By comparison, the Motorola 6800 has two accumulator registers and only one index register, which allows for a simpler instruction set.
- An **8-bit Arithmetic Logic Unit** (ALU), which comes as no surprise for an 8-bit CPU, but it's worth pointing out that others like the Zilog Z80 came with an 4-bit ALU instead[3].
- An **8-bit stack pointer**: This is usually beyond the scope of this analysis, but I wanted to highlight it due to its significant deviation from Motorola's design. As mentioned before, the address bus is 16-bit, so a memory-dependent component like the stack pointer should ideally match that size. However, MOS opted to halve the requirement and store the stack within a fixed memory range. Nevertheless, it was a clever cost-saving measure, as it encouraged developers to adopt efficient programming techniques to maximise the stack space.
- **13 addressing modes**. Thanks to the inclusion of two index registers, programs can choose between many formats for accessing memory. Some are optimised for zero-page addressing (the first 256 bytes of memory), while others encode a lookup address to retrieve the actual address dynamically. In the end, this helped save as many memory cycles as possible, at the cost of complexity.
  - By comparison, the 6800 and its single index register only offer seven addressing modes, with no equivalent for the flexible types.

As you can see, the remarkable engineering behind the 6502 allowed MOS to sell a compelling product at an extremely affordable price.

---

[2]See "Sega Master System Architecture" - Section 4 "CPU"

[3]See "Sega Master System Architecture" - Section 4 "CPU"

2.4.2.1 Ricoh's licensing enigma

How Ricoh managed to clone the 6502 isn't clear to this day. One would expect MOS to have licensed the chip design to Ricoh, but there are many contradictions to this:

- Both Ricoh's and MOS's variants feature the same layout, but Ricoh's contains severed buses (disabling certain functions) [10]. I go into more detail later.
- A document explicitly stating that MOS licensed the 6502 to Ricoh is yet to be found.
- An article published in 2008 by Nikkei Trendy states that Ricoh licensed from Rockwell, an authorised chip manufacturer [11]. However, it's debatable whether a second source was able to provide IP to a third party, much less with MOS's approval.
- It wouldn't be the first time Nintendo got away with circumventing IP rights, as *Ikegami Tsushinki v. Nintendo* ruled in Japan that Nintendo didn't own the code of the original Donkey Kong [12].

2.4.2.2 Scrapped functions

The Ricoh 2A03 omits the **Binary-Coded Decimal** (BCD) mode originally included in the 6502 [13]. BCD encodes each decimal digit of a number as a separate 4-bit binary. The 6502 uses 8-bit 'words' - meaning that each word stores two decimal digits.

As an example for the curious, the decimal number `42` is represented as:

- `0010 1010` in binary.
- `0100 0010` in BCD.

We could go on and on talking about it, but to give an outline: BCD is useful for applications that require treating each decimal place separately (for instance, a digital clock). However, it requires more storage since each 8-bit word can only encode up to the decimal number `99` - whereas traditional binary can encode up to `255`.

In any case, Ricoh deliberately broke BCD mode in its chip by severing the control lines that activate it. This was presumably done to avoid paying royalties to MOS, since BCD was patented by them (and the legislation that enabled copyrighting integrated circuit layouts in the United States wasn't enacted until 1984 [14]).

2.4.3 Memory

Both Ricoh 2A03 and MOS 6502 feature an **8-bit data bus** and a **16-bit address bus**, which allow them to access up to **64 KB of memory**. So, how did Nintendo fill that memory space?

On one side, the motherboard contains a chip providing **2 KB of Static RAM** (SRAM) [15]. Nintendo calls this area 'Work RAM' (WRAM) and can be used to store:

- Variables for handling the game state and/or to look up information.
- The 'stack', which temporarily saves register values while the CPU is executing subroutines.

- A 'buffer area' so the CPU can copy large data between two locations.

On the other side, the components of the system are **memory-mapped** [16], meaning that they are accessed using memory addresses and therefore occupy part of the CPU's address space. Consequently, the Ricoh 2A03's memory space is filled with addresses pointing to the game cartridge, WRAM, the PPU, the APU and two controllers (don't worry about each component, as they are explained throughout this article).

2.4.3.1 Segmentation Fault

Inherited from MOS' design, this console also features a special 'anomaly' called **Open Bus**: If an instruction tries to read from an unmapped or invalid address, the last value read is supplied instead [17]. If this goes unhandled by the program, execution may continue in an unpredictable state.

2.4.3.2 Cartridge/game data

Just in case you don't know, NES games are distributed in the form of **cartridges**, and the cartridge's buses connect directly to the CPU.

Nintendo wired up the cartridge lines in a way that only 49120 Bytes ($\sim$ 49.97 KB) of cartridge data can be accessed [16]. Now, what do I mean by 'cartridge data'? Well, any chip connected to those buses, for instance:

- A **Program ROM** where the game's program resides. This excludes the graphics data, as you'll later see in the 'Graphics' section. Naturally and unlike the other chips, this one is mandatory.
- **RAM chips** to extend WRAM.
- A **battery-packed RAM chip** to store saves.

The existence of different combinations stems from the fact that the CPU doesn't care about what kind of component it is reading from; it only sees memory locations. So, it is up to game studios to choose (or devise) a feasible layout to fit in their game.

For example, Nintendo's 'Super Mario Bros' used a layout they call *NES-NROM-256* and consists of 32 KB of program ROM and 8 KB of 'Character ROM' for graphics (we'll see more about it in the 'Graphics' section) [19]. *NES-NROM-256* was also prepared to house up to 3 KB of extra WRAM, though the game doesn't make use of it.

Figure 2.8: *PCB of Super Mario Bros [18].*

Figure 2.9: *The same PCB with important parts labelled. The meaning of the 'Lockout' chip is explained in the 'Anti-piracy' section.*

2.4.3.3 Going beyond existing capabilities

One of the major limitations of 16-bit address buses (affecting 3rd and 4th-generation consoles) is their compact address space. Nowadays, 32-bit computers can address up to 4 GB of memory (and 64-bit machines lavishly enjoy up to 16 exabytes), so this is no longer a concern, but back then, the NES only had a 64 KB address space, and a significant portion was consumed by the memory-mapped hardware (something competitors avoided[4]).

So, did this mean that game studios could only develop games that stayed within the 49.97 KB limit? Absolutely not! If history has taught us anything, it is that there's always a clever solution to a challenging problem, and this issue was tackled with a **Mapper**.

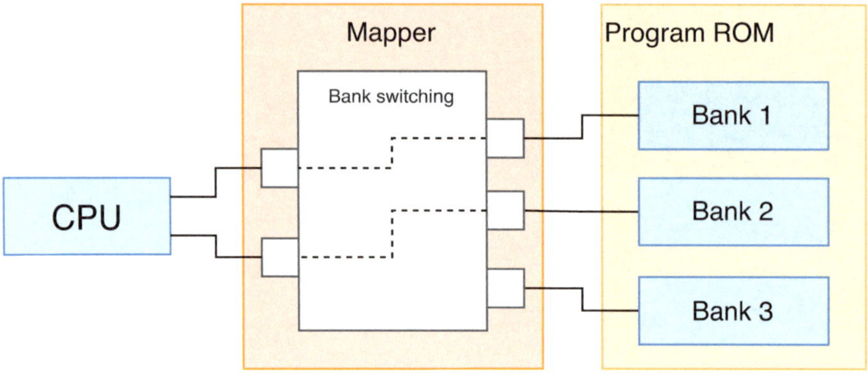

Figure 2.10: *Simplified representation of how a mapper extends the addressing capabilities of the CPU. With the inclusion of a mapper, the CPU can access extra banks (groups of addresses) of a large Program ROM. Although the game/program has the new task of manually switching between banks whenever needed.*

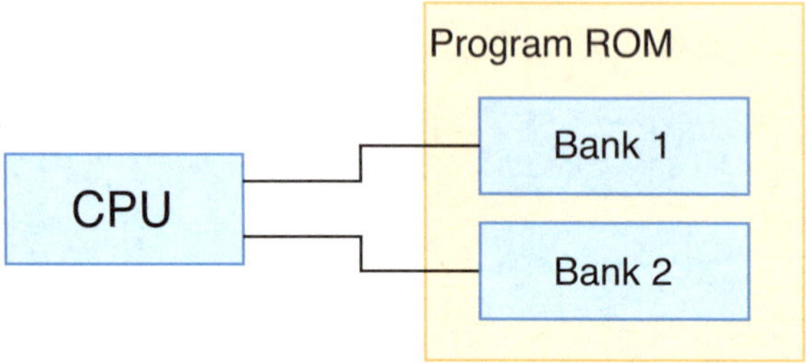

Figure 2.11: *The same setup but without a mapper installed. While simpler and inexpensive, the CPU can only access a finite number of banks.*

A mapper is an extra chip included in the cartridge that sits between the memory chips and the console's address lines. Its primary job is to extend the address space, allowing

[4]See "Sega Master System Architecture" - Section 4.3 "Accessing the rest of the components"

developers to fit more chips. This is achieved through **bank switching**: memory addresses are grouped into banks, and the mapper provides switches (controlled via memory addresses) to alternate between them. Now, the CPU still perceives the same amount of memory, so it is the game (programmed with a mapper present) in charge of operating it. Due to their cost-effectiveness, mappers were the order of the day in 80s-to-early-90s technology.

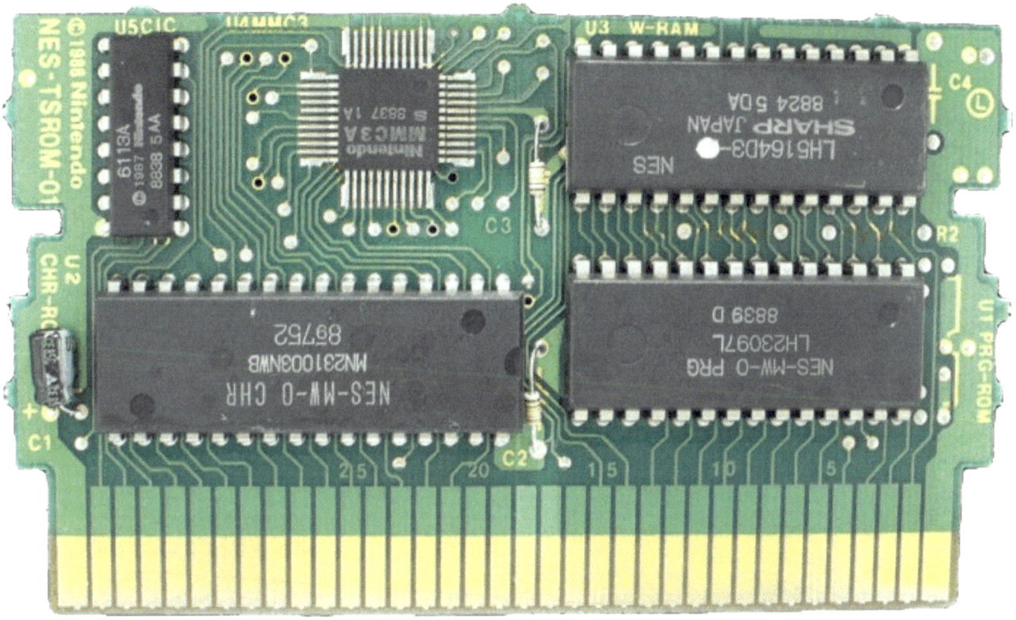

Figure 2.12: *PCB of Super Mario Bros 2 [20]. Super Mario Bros 3 also uses this layout but bundles a 256 KB Program ROM instead.*

Back to the NES, games like 'Super Mario Bros 2' and 'Super Mario Bros 3' shipped with the 'MMC3' mapper (made by Nintendo) in their cartridges. For comparison, MMC3 provided up to 512 KB of space for the Program ROM, up to 256 KB for Character memory and up to 8 KB for extra WRAM [21]. You can now see why 'Super Mario Bros 3' differs significantly in quality compared to the first instalment.

All in all, while this console may appear limited while examining its internal features, Nintendo made sure it could adapt as technology evolves. On the other side, while this technique helped to keep the costs down of the console, it shifted part of the burden to the game cartridge. So, game quality and cartridge costs were two concerns game studios had to balance.

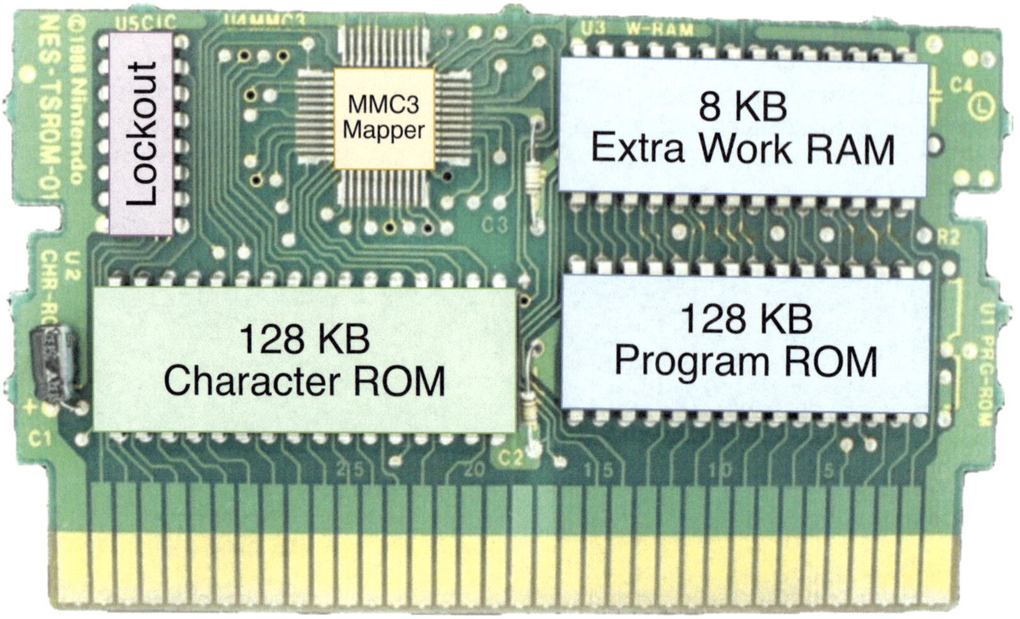

Figure 2.13: *The same picture with important parts labelled. At first, I thought the extra WRAM was for storing saves, but then I realised there are no saves in this game (and there isn't a battery either). In reality, that RAM chip is used to store a decompressed level.*

2.5 Graphics

Graphics are generated by a proprietary chip called the **Picture Processing Unit** (PPU). This is one of the chips that gives the NES an *identity*. To put it another way, since anyone could pick up a 6502 at a hardware store, why is the NES any different from, say, an Apple II or a Commodore 64? Well, what distinguishes the NES from other machines are the chips that surround the CPU: the PPU and the APU. These make up the NES' unique graphics and audio capabilities, respectively.

That being said, the PPU renders 2D graphics called **sprites** and **backgrounds**, outputting the result to the video signal.

Figure 2.14: *The European PPU chip on my NES' motherboard.*

2.5.1 Organising the content

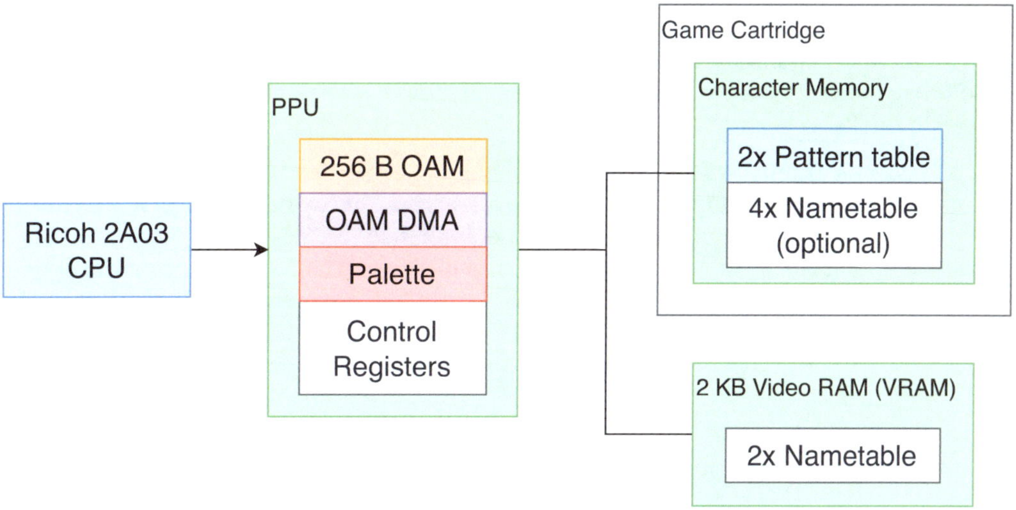

Figure 2.15: *Memory architecture of the PPU.*

To render something on the screen, the PPU must know *which* graphics to draw, *where* on the screen to place them, and *how* to draw them (i.e., which palette to use).

To answer these questions, the PPU came pre-programmed with a different memory layout that looks for specific types of data:

- Graphics data is pulled from the game cartridge, which contains a dedicated chip

called **Character memory** that stores the 2D drawings (called **tiles**) organised into a data structure named **Pattern table**. Character memory materialises in the form of 'Read-Only Memory' (ROM) or 'Random-Access Memory' (RAM), depending on whether the game ships with an immutable set of graphics or the CPU must intervene, respectively.
  - The PPU addresses **up to 8 KB** of Character memory organised into two groups of 4 KB each.
- Meta-data telling the PPU 'where' and 'how' to draw graphics is found in other areas:
  - The motherboard houses **2 KB of SRAM** specifically for graphics-related data. Nintendo calls this space **Video RAM** (VRAM), and it stores two data structures called **Nametables**.
  - The PPU embeds **256 bytes** of DRAM to store the **Object Attribute Memory** (OAM).
  - Lastly, the PPU also bundles **4 bytes** of memory to define colour palettes.

Don't worry about the new terminology; the meanings of these data structures are discussed step by step in the following paragraphs.

2.5.2 Constructing the frame

As with its contemporaries, this chip is designed for the behaviour of a CRT display. There is no frame buffer as such: **the PPU will render in step with the CRT's beam**, building the image on the fly.

The PPU draws frames with a fixed dimension of **256x240 pixels** [22]. Alas, due to the discrepancies in analogue video standards across the world, the image will differ in appearance depending on the region of the appliance (NTSC or PAL) from which it is displayed. In a nutshell, NTSC televisions will crop the top and bottom edges to accommodate overscan (only ~224 scan-lines are visible), so these edges are considered 'danger zones' by developers when deciding where to place elements in the game. On the other hand, PAL tellies won't crop the edges but will show extra black bars to fill the taller signal (PAL uses 288 scan-lines).

Behind the scenes, the frame output by the PPU is composed of two different layers. For demonstration purposes, let's use *Super Mario Bros.* to show how this works:

2.5.2.1 Tiles

To begin with, the PPU uses **tiles** as a basic ingredient for producing sprites and backgrounds.

The NES defines tiles as basic **8x8 pixel maps**, these are stored in **Character memory** (residing in the game cartridge) and organised into a big data structure called **Pattern Table** [23]. Each tile occupies 16 bytes, and a Pattern table houses 256 tiles [24]. Since the PPU addresses up to 8 KB of Character memory, it can access up to two Pattern tables.

Inside a tile, each of its pixels is encoded using a 2-bit value, which references one of four colours from a palette. Programmers can define up to eight palettes (four for the background and four for sprites). The colours referenced on each palette point to a 'master palette' consisting of 64 colours [25], representing all the colours that this console can produce. Each palette is made of four colours, with one reserved for `transparent`.

To start drawing something on the screen, games populate a set of tables with references to tiles stored in Character memory. Each table is responsible for one layer (sprite or background) of the frame. Then, the PPU reads from those tables and composes the scan-lines that will be beamed by the CRT gun.

I will now explain how each layer/table works and how they differ in terms of functionality.

(a) *Two pattern tables with multiple tiles squashed together.*

(b) *A single tile.*

Figure 2.16: *Tiles Found in Character ROM (for demonstration purposes a default palette is being used).*

2.5.2.2 Background Layer

Figure 2.17: *Visualised background with selected area marked.*
This background map is set up with vertical mirroring, which enables smooth horizontal scrolling. However, only the top half can be used.

The background layer is a 512x480 pixel map containing static tiles [26]. You may recall that the viewable frame is much smaller, so the game decides which part of the layer is selected for display. Games can also shift the viewable area during gameplay; that's how the **scrolling effect** is accomplished.

To save memory, groups of four tiles are combined into 16x16-pixel maps called **blocks**, in which all tiles share a colour palette.

Nametables (stored in VRAM) specify which tiles to display in the background layer. The PPU looks for four 1024-byte Nametables, each one corresponding to a quadrant of the layer. However, only 2 KB of VRAM is available! Meaning that only two Nametables can be stored without additional hardware provided by the cartridge. Yet, the remaining two still have to be addressed somewhere: most games simply point the remaining two where the first two are (this is called **mirroring**).

Although this architecture may seem flawed at first, it was designed to minimise costs while ensuring simple **expandability**: if the game requires a wider background, just fit extra VRAM in the cartridge.

Moving on, the last bytes of each Nametable store a 64-byte **Attribute table** that specifies which colour palette is assigned to each block [27].

2.5.2.3 Sprite Layer

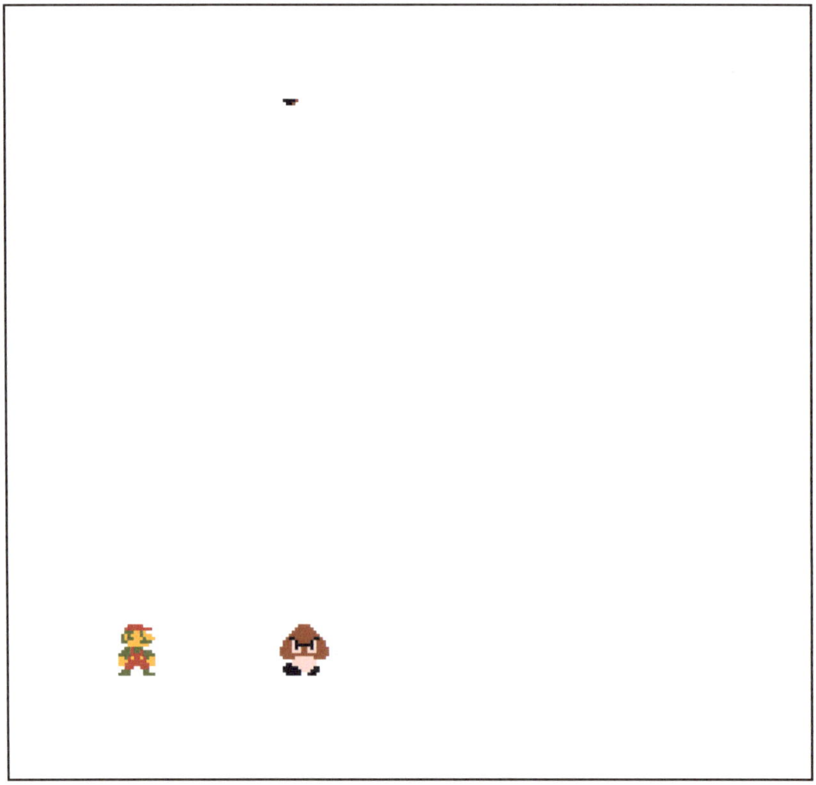

Figure 2.18: *Rendered sprite layer.*

Sprites are tiles that can move around the screen. They can also overlap one another, or appear behind the background. The viewable graphic is determined by its priority value (similar to the concept of 'layers' in traditional graphic design software).

The **Object Attribute Memory** (OAM) table specifies which tiles will be used as sprites [28]. In addition to the tile index, each entry includes an (x,y) position and several attributes (colour palette, priority and flip flags). This table resides in a 256-byte DRAM located within the PPU chip.

The CPU can populate the OAM table, but this process can be slow in practice and risks corrupting the frame if not timed correctly. As a result, the PPU contains a small component called **Direct Memory Access** or 'DMA' which can be programmed (by altering the PPU's registers) to fetch the table from WRAM. With DMA, the table is guaranteed to be uploaded when the next frame is drawn; however, the CPU will be halted during the transfer!

The PPU is limited to **eight sprites per scan-line** and up to **64 sprites per frame**. Luckily, the scan-line limit can be partially circumvented thanks to a technique called 'OAM order rotation', in which the game manually alters the order of entries in OAM. This makes the PPU render a different sprite set at each frame, and the speed of the CRT beam will trick the user into seeing more sprites than allowed. However, they will also appear to flicker on-screen.

2.5.2.4 Background Split

Before we move on, there's an additional detail worth mentioning. If you play Super Mario Bros, you'll notice that when Mario moves, the scene scrolls without a hitch. However, you'll also observe that the top area (where the stats are) remains static **even though both portions belong to the same background layer!** So, what is happening here? Well, the game is altering the scrolling values mid-frame to show the overworld and the stats (residing in a fixed portion of the background) at the same time. The NES doesn't provide this feature natively, but the game deduces the timings by observing the state of the PPU (manifested through its status register [29]).

To accomplish this, games use a technique called **Sprite 0 Hit**. Super Mario Bros instructs the PPU to render a dummy sprite behind the coin, this happens to be the first sprite drawn within the frame. After the PPU beams it, it updates its status register with a flag to indicate that the first sprite (a.k.a 'sprite 0') has been drawn. Meanwhile, the game continuously checks mid-frame whether the sprite 0 status has been flagged (a.k.a 'hit'). When this occurs, the game updates the scrolling value of the background table to align it with Mario's position.

Overall, 'Sprite 0 Hit' is a very delicate procedure, as it's easy to mess up the timings (sprite 0's flag is not cleared after polling it, which leads to 'duplicated' positives [30]). Furthermore, as this routine repeats indefinitely, it can be quite costly (in terms of CPU cycles) to execute. On the bright side, later mappers took over this function by employing automatic interrupts that are triggered whenever an arbitrary scan-line is hit [31] (a much more efficient technique), which significantly improved the visual capabilities of Super Mario Bros 3, for instance.

Figure 2.19: *Rendered background layer highlighting the two portions with different scrolling values defined. Only the second portion scrolls as Mario moves.*

2.5.2.5 Result

Once the frame is finished, it's time to move on to the next one!

However, the CPU can't modify any table currently in use by the PPU, otherwise, artefacts may show up on the screen. So, when all scan-lines are completed, the PPU triggers the **Vertical Blank** (V-Blank) interrupt on the CPU [32]. This notifies the game that it can start updating the tables without tearing the picture currently displayed. At that moment, the CRT's beam is pointing below the visible area of the screen, into the overscan (or bottom border area).

Only a handful of PPU registers can be updated outside the V-Blank window [33], which explains the ability to scroll the background layer mid-frame.

Figure 2.20: *Tada!*

2.5.3 Secrets and limitations

If you're thinking that a frame-buffer system with memory allocated to store the full frame would have been preferable: RAM costs were prohibitively high, and the console's goal was to be affordable. Let me now show you why this design still proved to be both efficient and flexible.

2.5.3.1 Multi-Scrolling

Some games require the main character to move vertically; therefore, the nametable is set up with **horizontal mirroring**. Other games need their character to move left and right, and so implement **vertical mirroring** instead.

Either type of mirroring allows the PPU to update background tiles without the user noticing, as there is ample of space to scroll while new tiles are being rendered at a distance.

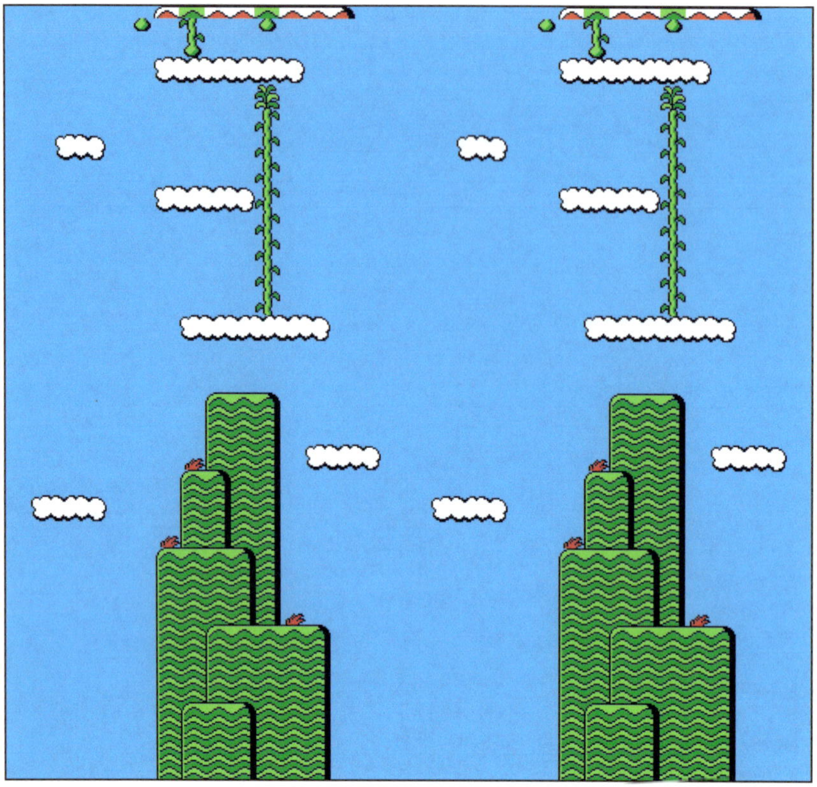

Figure 2.21: *In this level of Super Mario Bros. 2, the Nametable is set up for vertical scrolling (horizontal mirroring).*

But what happens if the character needs to move diagonally? The PPU can scroll in any direction; however, without extra VRAM, the edges are forced to share the same colour palette (remember that tiles are grouped in blocks).

This explains why some games like *Super Mario Bros. 3* show strange graphics at the right edge of the screen while Mario moves (the game is set up for vertical scrolling) [34]. It's possible that they needed to minimise the hardware cost per cartridge, as this game already bundles a powerful mapper.

As an interesting *fix*: the PPU allowed developers to apply a vertical mask on top of tiles, effectively concealing part of the glitchy area.

Figure 2.22: *With Super Mario Bros. 3, Mario can run and fly. Thus, the PPU needs to scroll diagonally. Notice the right edge is showing the wrong colour palette, and the left edge has a mask applied.*

2.5.3.2 Tile-Swapping

Another remarkable feature of Super Mario Bros. 3 is the number of graphics it can display.

This game displays more background tiles than strictly permitted. How does it achieve this? By taking two screen captures at different times while the display is generated, we can see that the final frame is actually composed of *two* distinct frames.

This is another wizardry of the MMC3 mapper, which not only addresses extra space in the Program ROM, but also extends the Character ROM space by connecting **two separate Character chips**. By determining which part of the screen the PPU is requesting, the mapper redirects to one chip or the other, thereby allowing more unique tiles on-screen than was originally supported [35].

(a) *Early scan lines.*

(b) *Late scan lines.*

(c) *Actual frame displayed to the user.*

Figure 2.23: *Hypothetical frames rendered using tiles available during specific scan lines.*

2.5.3.3 Curious behaviour

Throughout my research, I came across many interesting articles that explain unusual behaviour of the PPU, so I thought to mention a few here:

- Unlike the Master System's VDP[5], which generates RGB colours that are subsequently encoded into NTSC/PAL signals for broadcasting, the **NES' PPU does all at once** [25]. Hence, there isn't a one-to-one correspondence between the colours of the PPU master palette and the standard RGB colourspace (widely adopted by present technology). This leaves some room for interpretation and, as a consequence, various emulators may display a different palette.
  - The discrepancies between RGB palettes can be observed using Tim Worthington's DIY kit, which adds RGB signal output to the NES. This also houses a switch to choose between three predefined palettes [36].
- The master palette contains a **'cursed' colour** (`$0D`), which might disrupt the NTSC TV signal [37]. Well, what happens is that some TVs mistake the signal for displaying that colour as the blanking signal, which may cause flickering.
- The PPU relies on DRAM to store its Object Attribute Memory (OAM). Now, unlike SRAM, DRAM must be refreshed constantly to prevent data loss. Conversely, **the PPU doesn't refresh DRAM when it's not rendering the frame** [28]. This typically occurs during vertical blanking. For this reason, it is advised to always update OAM during vertical blanking, since the non-refreshing period (happening during V-blank) will have corrupted part of the table.
  - The PPU variant for PAL systems is unaffected by this, as it does refresh during V-Blank (which lasts longer on PAL systems).

2.6 Audio

A dedicated component called **Audio Processing Unit** (APU) provides this service [38]. Ricoh embedded it inside the CPU chip, presumably to prevent unlicensed cloning of both the CPU and APU.

2.6.1 Functionality

This audio circuitry is commonly referred to as a **Programmable Sound Generator** (PSG), which vaguely implies that it can only produce a predefined set of waveforms. This is *mostly* true in this case.

The APU sequences audio data across **five channels**, each reserved for a specific waveform or signal. The channels contain different properties that alter the waveform's pitch, sound,

[5] See "Sega Master System Architecture" - Section 5 "Graphics"

volume and duration. They are continuously mixed and transmitted through the output audio signal.

The APU's functionality is exposed through memory addresses. The CPU reads the music-related data found in the Program ROM and programs the APU accordingly.

Furthermore, the Famicom model implements extra cartridge pins that send the mixed audio signal to the cartridge, so the latter can mix it with **extra channels** (requiring additional chips) [2].

Let's now review the five channels the APU provides [39]:

2.6.1.1 Pulse

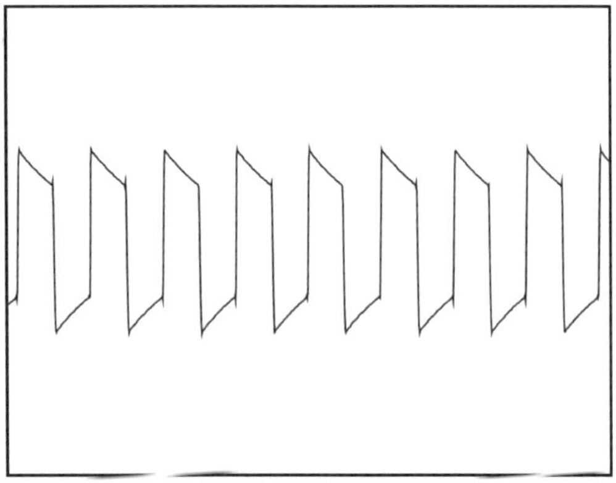

(a) *Pulse 1 channel.*

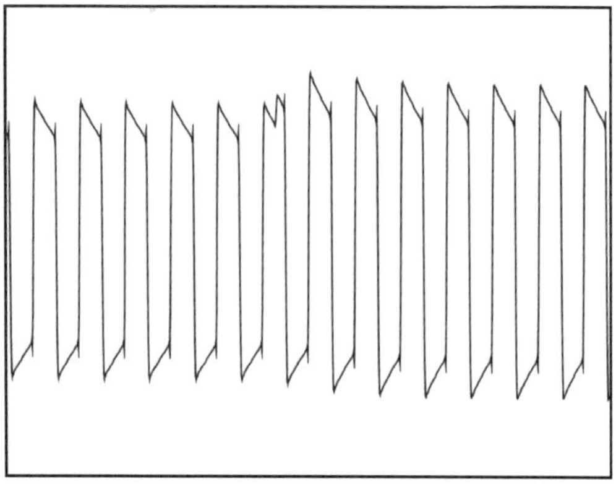

(b) *Pulse 2 channel.*

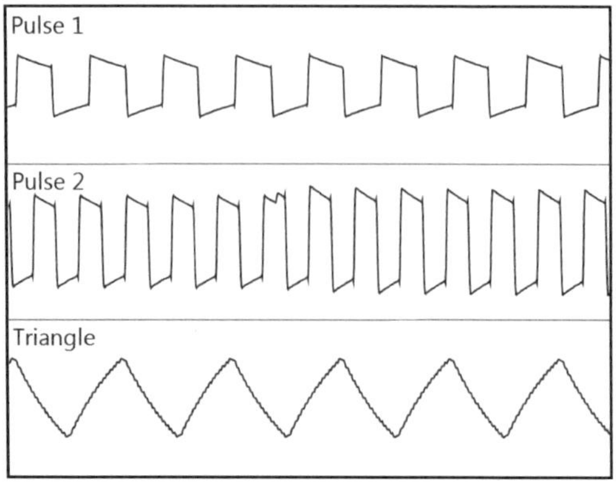

(c) *All audio channels.*

Figure 2.24: *Oscilloscope display of a music score from Mother (1989).*

The first **two channels** produce **pulse waves** [40]. When heard, they exhibit a very distinct *beep* sound that is mainly used for **melody or sound effects**. By varying the pulse width (also known as the **duty cycle**), the respective sequencer can generate three types of pulse waves. The circuits are also connected to a **sweep unit** (allowing to bend the pitch) and an **envelope generator** to lower the volume over time (commonly referred to as **decay**).

Most games use one pulse channel for melody and the other for accompaniment. You'll often find that when a game needs to play a sound effect, the accompaniment channel is temporarily switched to play the effect before returning to its original role. This prevents interrupting the melody during gameplay.

I believe it's fair to say that pulse waves are one of the emblems of this generation of consoles. I assume their adoption was primarily driven by cost-effectiveness: the (limited) CPU can only process a finite amount of data at a time, and pulse waves are ideal because they require few parameters to play simple melodies (which, in turn, frees up CPU cycles for other operations).

2.6.1.2 Triangle

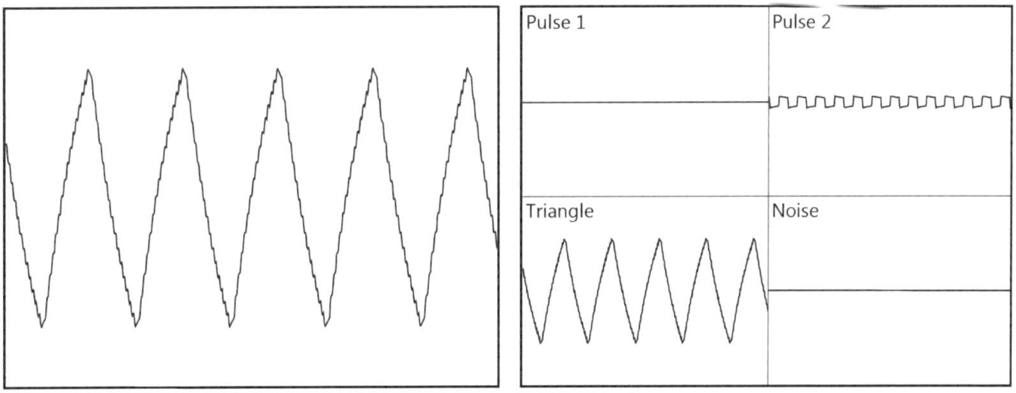

(a) *Triangle channel.* **(b)** *All audio channels.*

Figure 2.25: *Oscilloscope display of a music score from Mother (1989).*

One of the specialities of the APU, when compared to the competition, is its ability to produce **triangle waves**. These are often used as a **bassline** for melodies. Additionally, by dramatically modifying its pitch, it can also be used for **percussion**.

The APU has one channel reserved for this type of wave. Behind the scenes, a dedicated sequencer takes 32 cycles to generate a triangle signal [41]; this limitation causes the resulting triangle waveform to resemble a step ladder.

On the other side, the respective circuitry does not provide volume control. In any case, some games discovered alternative methods by fiddling with the mixer's volume control.

2.6.1.3 Noise

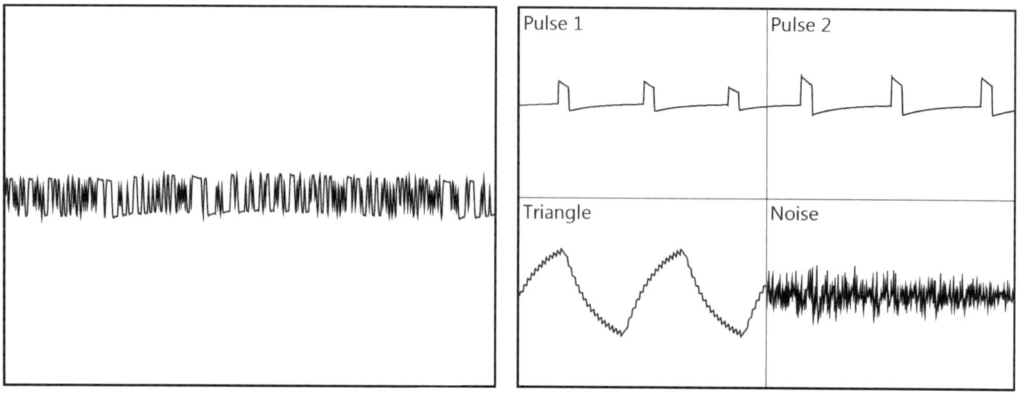

(a) *Noise channel.* **(b)** *All audio channels.*

Figure 2.26: *Oscilloscope display of a music score from Mother (1989).*

The concept of 'Noise' refers to a series of waveforms that lack any discernible pattern or order. In turn, our ears interpret it as white static. That said, the APU allocates one channel to play different kinds of noise.

Behind the scenes, the noise generator relies on an envelope generator (similar to the Pulse channel) that is randomly muted by an OR gate [42]. The condition for muting is determined by the value of a 15-bit shift register connected to a feedback loop. All in all, this makes the circuitry output a signal with *pseudo-unpredictable* patterns, resulting in noise.

For control, four bits adjust the period of the envelope generator, while one bit modifies the 'Mode' of the shift register. This layout provides 32 noise presets. Half (16) of these presets generate **clean static**, and the other half produce **robotic static**.

Generally speaking, games utilise the noise channel for percussion or ambient effects.

2.6.1.4 Sample

Samples are recorded pieces of music that can be replayed. As you can see, samples are not confined to a single waveform, but they consume a lot more storage space.

The APU has one channel dedicated to samples. Here, samples are limited to **7-bit resolution** (encoded with values from `0` to `127`) and a **~15.74 kHz sampling rate** [43]. To program this channel, games can either stream 7-bit values (which steals significant cycles and storage) or use **delta modulation** to encode only the variation between consecutive samples.

The delta modulation system in the APU only accepts 1-bit values, meaning games can only indicated whether the sample increments or decrements by `1` each time the counter kicks

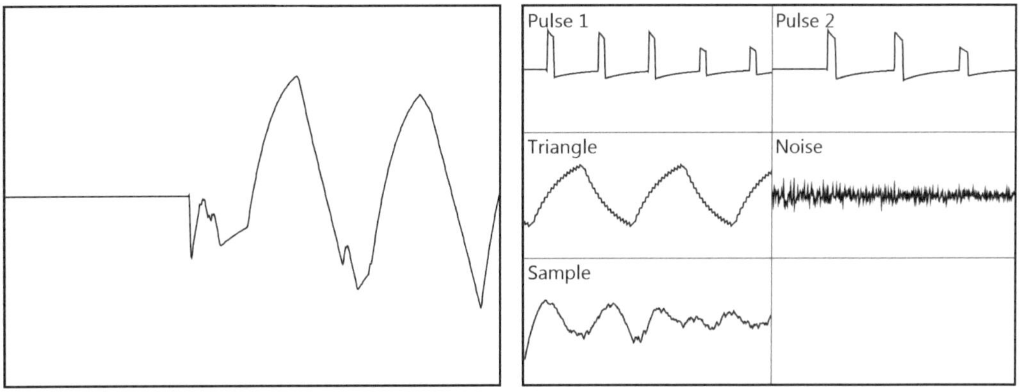

(a) *Sample channel.* **(b)** *All audio channels.*

Figure 2.27: *Oscilloscope display of a music score from Mother (1989).*

in. Thus, at the cost of fidelity, delta modulation can save games from having to stream continuous values to the APU.

Since programming this channel takes longer space and CPU cycles, games typically store small pieces (like drum sounds) that can be replayed repeatedly. Be as it may, throughout the NES' lifespan, numerous developers have come up with clever uses for this channel.

2.6.2 Secrets and limitations

While the APU could not match the audio quality of vinyl, cassette or CD, programmers did find ways to extend its capabilities, largely thanks to the modular architecture of the NES.

2.6.2.1 Extra Channels

Remember that the Famicom provided exclusive cartridge pins available for sound expansion? Well, games like *Castlevania 3* took advantage of this feature by incorporating an additional chip called **Konami VRC6**, which introduced **two extra pulse waves and a sawtooth wave** to the mix.

The two examples (Figure 2.28) illustrate the difference between the Japanese and the American versions of the game. The Japanese variant, running on the Famicom, benefits from the enhanced audio capabilities, while the American version, designed for the NES, is constrained by the five predefined channels.

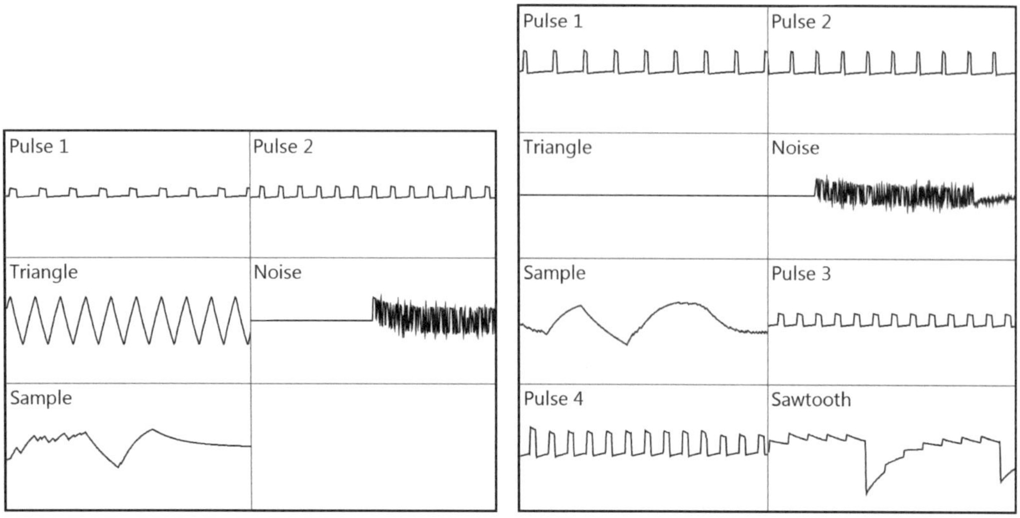

(a) *Castlevania III (USA/Europe, 1989).* **(b)** *Akumajō Densetsu (Japan, 1989).*

Figure 2.28: *Oscilloscope display of the same music score across the two regions.*

2.6.2.2 Tremolo

Rather than increasing cartridge costs, some games prioritised creativity over technology to simulate additional channels.

For instance, Final Fantasy III came up with the idea of using tremolo effects to create the illusion of extra channels.

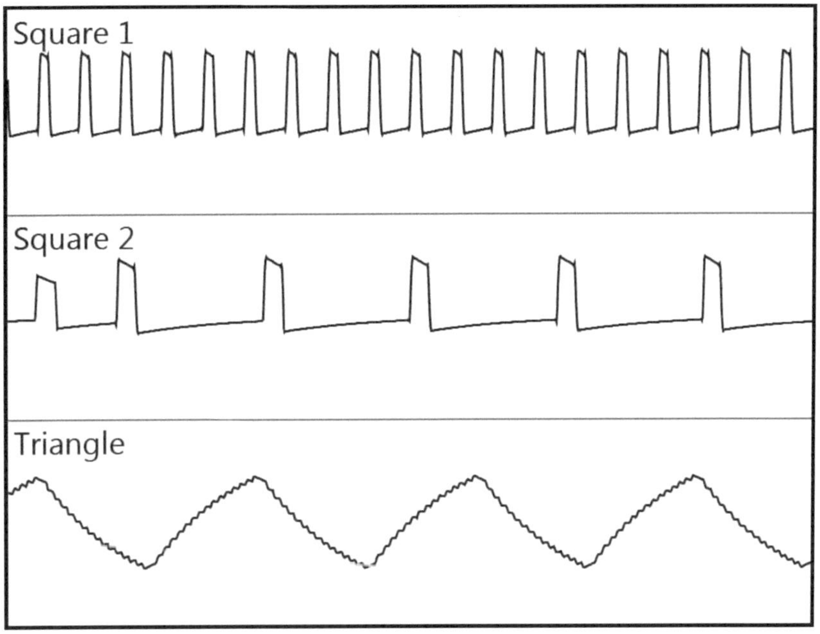

Figure 2.29: *Oscilloscope view of Final Fantasy III (1990).*

2.6.3 A more refined observation

Now that you've had a glimpse of what the APU is capable of, let me show you a more precise method for observing how its sound behaves. This will not only complement what you already know about the APU but also provide a more objective examination.

First things first, let's start with a brief introduction to sound theory.

Thanks to the principles of **Fourier Analysis**, we can decompose every single sound we hear into a **sum of sine waves** with different frequencies and amplitudes [44]. The lowest-frequency sine wave is called the **fundamental**, while the others are referred to as **overtones**. If you add the fundamental wave and its overtones, you get the original sound back. Having said that, with sounds that have a recognisable pitch, you'll find most (if not all) overtones have frequencies that are multiples of the fundamental frequency. Thus, these overtones are called **harmonics** [45].

Harmonics will be a recurring topic in this section, as waveforms such as pulses, triangles, and sawtooths adhere to a formula that determines the harmonics they must contain. Otherwise, these waveforms might deviate from their 'perfect' shape.

2.6.3.1 Introduction to spectrograms

As sine waves are now the key ingredient that can make up any sound, we can now analyse the sounds that we hear by their sine waves. Now, for any kind of data analysis, there's nothing more convenient than plotting a graph to organise vast amounts of information. Well, in the case of sound analysis, we've got **Spectrograms**. These encode all the information from an audio sample in a single plot. The X-axis denotes time (in seconds), the Y-axis denotes the frequencies (in Hz) of sine waves produced during that time, and the Z-axis (intensity of each dot) denotes the power/loudness (in decibels) of each frequency.

As you can observe from this example (Figure 2.30), each horizontal line (a.k.a. sequences of dots) corresponds to a sine wave (the lowest is the fundamental, while the rest are the harmonics) and their intensity indicates the amplitude. With this in mind, we can extract the following information:

- Over time, horizontal lines tend to drastically displace. That's the pitch of the Pulse channel changing.
- The start of each note is loud (the dots are vibrant) followed by a quick quell. That's the APU's envelope control in action.
  - Moreover, at the end of the decay period, a vertical line shows up. It's quite brief so it's not easily audible but, in any case, that's noise (a short popping sound) and I suspect it's a deficiency of the APU.
- Holding a note for more than 0.25 seconds makes **vibrato** emerge (continuous fluctuations in the Y-axis). I'm not sure if that's intentional (using the sweep function) or an adverse effect of the APU.

Notice how most of these observations are not easily derived by just listening to an audio sample; this is the reason for writing this section.

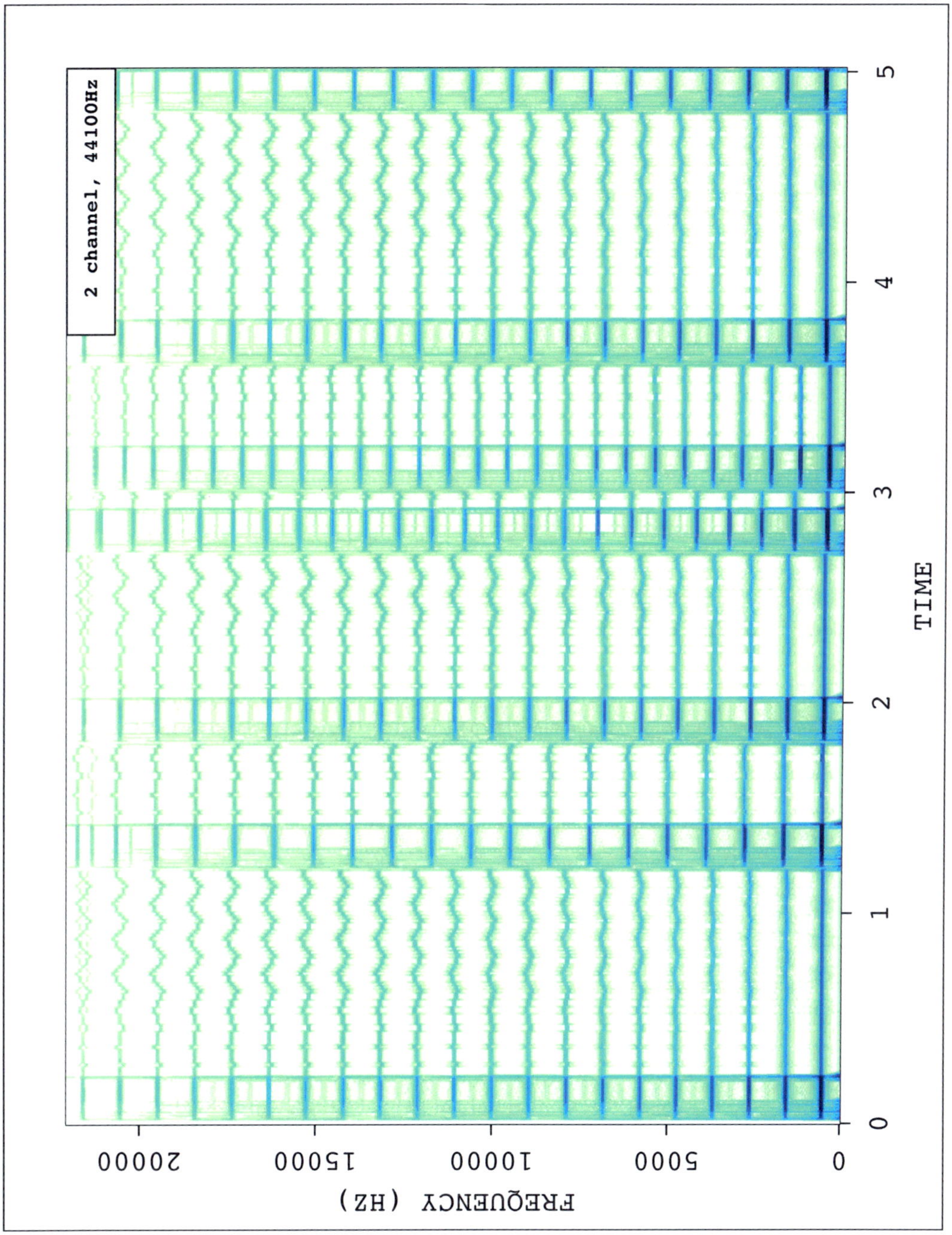

Figure 2.30: *Example of spectrogram visualising one Pulse channel.*

2.6.3.2 Plotting the APU

To study the NES' APU, I've compiled five spectrograms, each corresponding to one of the APU's channels, using the previous examples. Alongside them, you'll find my attempt at unravelling what the data is exhibiting.

Before we start, I must confess that, to gather the data without inaccuracies (such as extra noise), some compromises were made. The recordings were obtained using a Windows program called 'towave', which uses **band-limited synthesis** to solve a fundamental problem with the emulation of PSG-based audio chips. Essentially, pulses, triangles and sawtooths consist of **infinite harmonics**. However, this doesn't mix well with modern sound cards which are limited to 44.1 kHz samples. Thus, a technique called 'band-limited synthesis' is employed to select the right harmonics within the sound card's limitations. All in all, this technique provides a feasible balance between performance, accuracy, and aliasing prevention. However, the data may not be 100% identical to its analogue counterpart (which, by contrast, would also introduce other issues, like noise from the recording equipment), but I believe it is to an acceptable degree and, most importantly, does the job for this section of the article.

That being said, let's get on with the analysis.

2.6.3.2.1 Pulse The theory says that a pulse tone only contains odd harmonics. In other words, the fundamental is combined with its third harmonic, fifth and so forth. Moreover, each harmonic decreases its amplitude the further it is from the fundamental. The amplitude formula is `amplitude = 1 ÷ harmonic number` [46].

Hence, notice how the intensity of each harmonic on the spectrogram dims the higher it is on the Y-axis. However, the APU's pulse waves also seem to exhibit the aforementioned vibrato effect which intensifies at each harmonic number. Moreover, areas of the spectrogram that should be empty of any sound contain hushed overtones (possibly the result of noise and other imperfections).

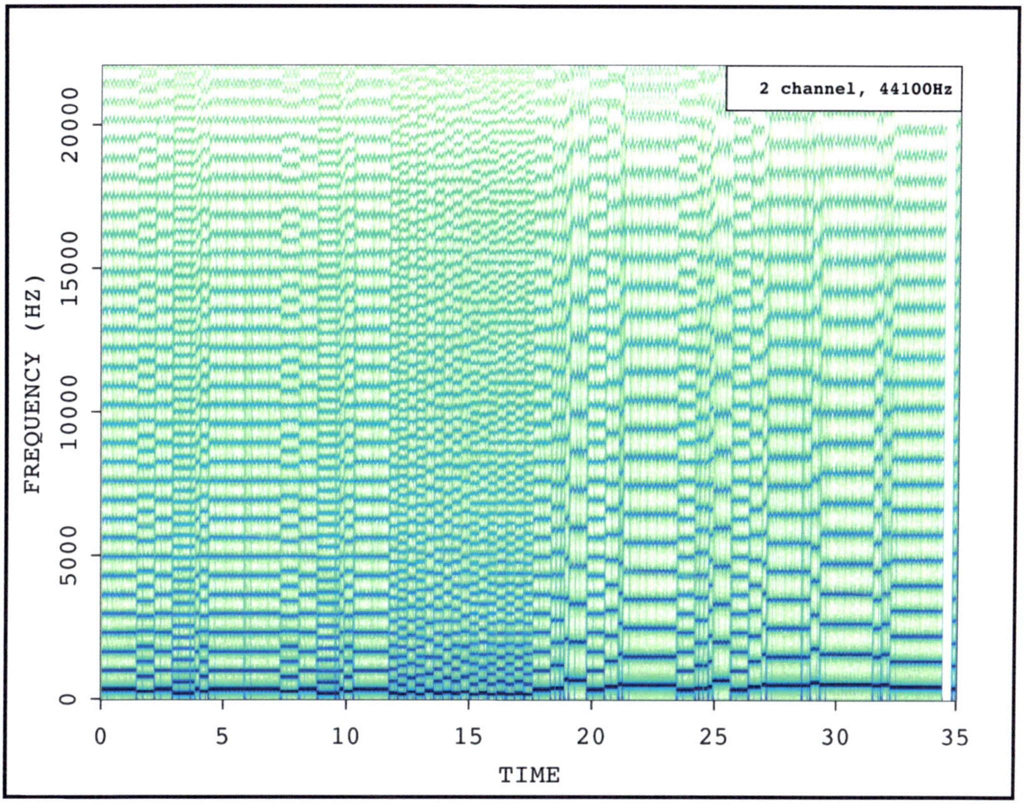

Figure 2.31: *Spectrogram of the Pulse 1 channel.*

2.6.3.2.2 Triangle A triangle wave is also made of odd harmonics, but their amplitude decreases more rapidly (following the formula `amplitude = 1 ÷ harmonic number`^{2} [47]).

However, this is not what is shown here. The step-ladder-shaped triangle that the APU produces introduces additional harmonics and increased amplitudes.

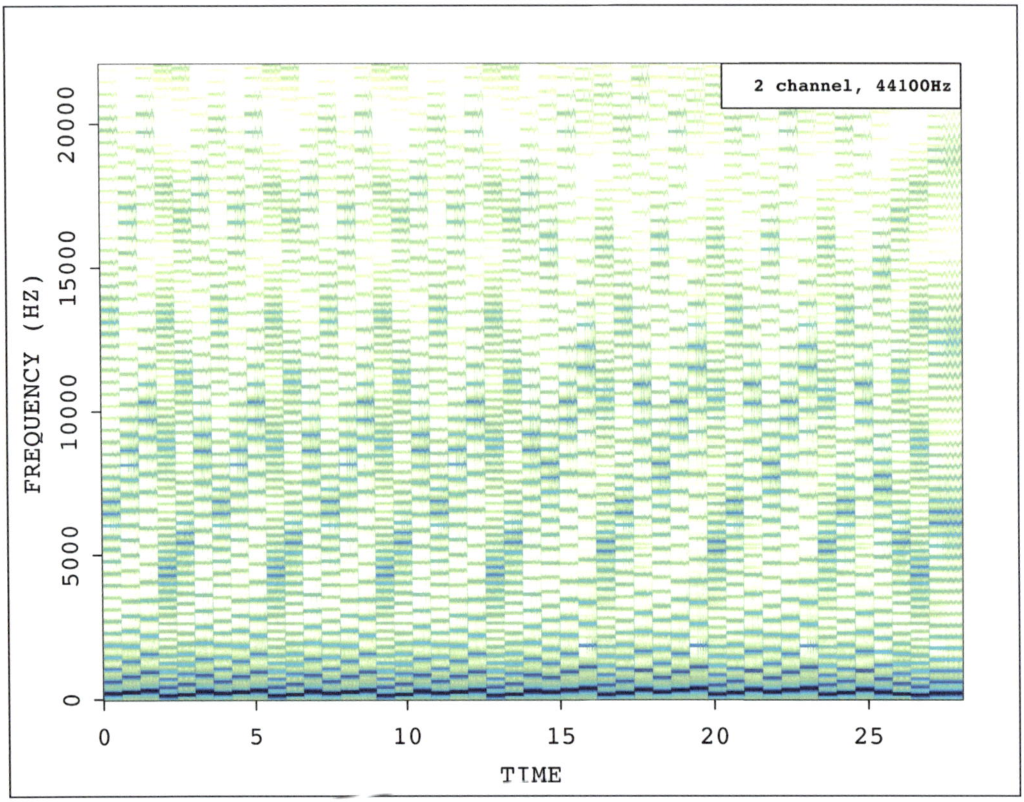

Figure 2.32: *Spectrogram of the Triangle channel.*

2.6.3.2.3 Noise Naturally, noise doesn't abide by the rules of harmonics and may randomly fill the entire frequency spectrum, hence the absence of a clearly recognisable pitch.

Although, by observing the timeline, you can distinguish between the various noise presets provided by the APU, each exhibiting a unique set of overtones.

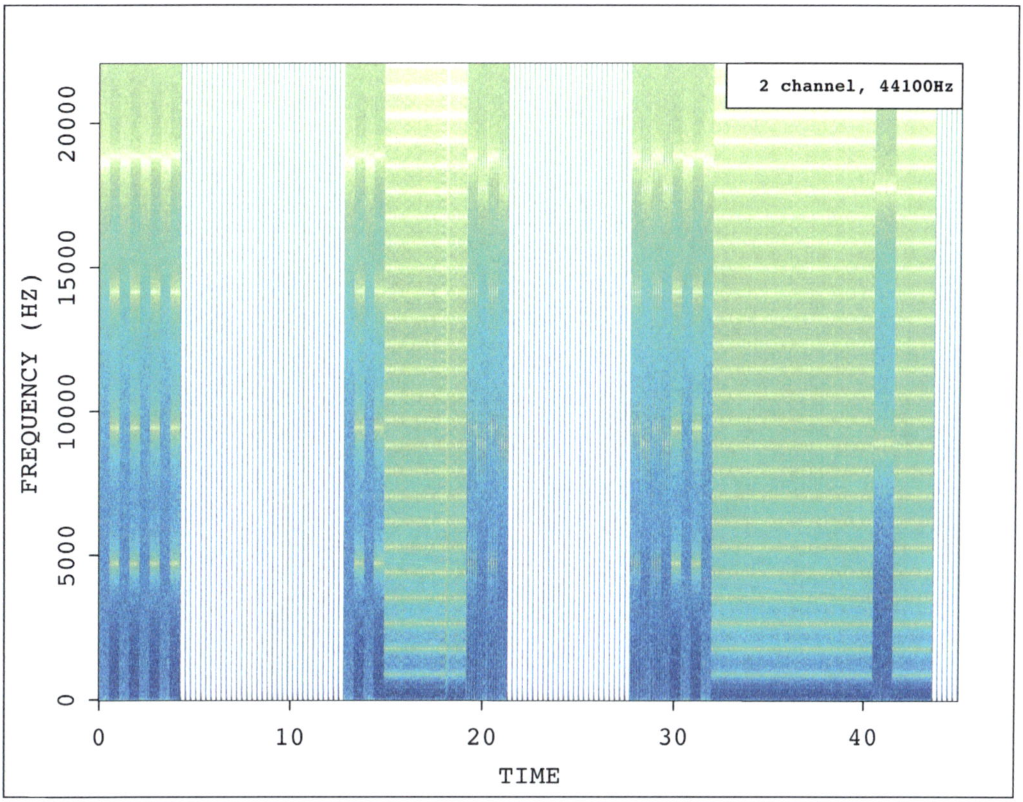

Figure 2.33: *Spectrogram of the Noise channel.*

2.6.3.2.4 Sample Unlike the previous channels, the sample channel only plays back whatever low-resolution recording the developer feeds to the APU. Considering the example played a drum kit, I can't see any identifiable treats on the spectrogram (apart from similarities to white noise).

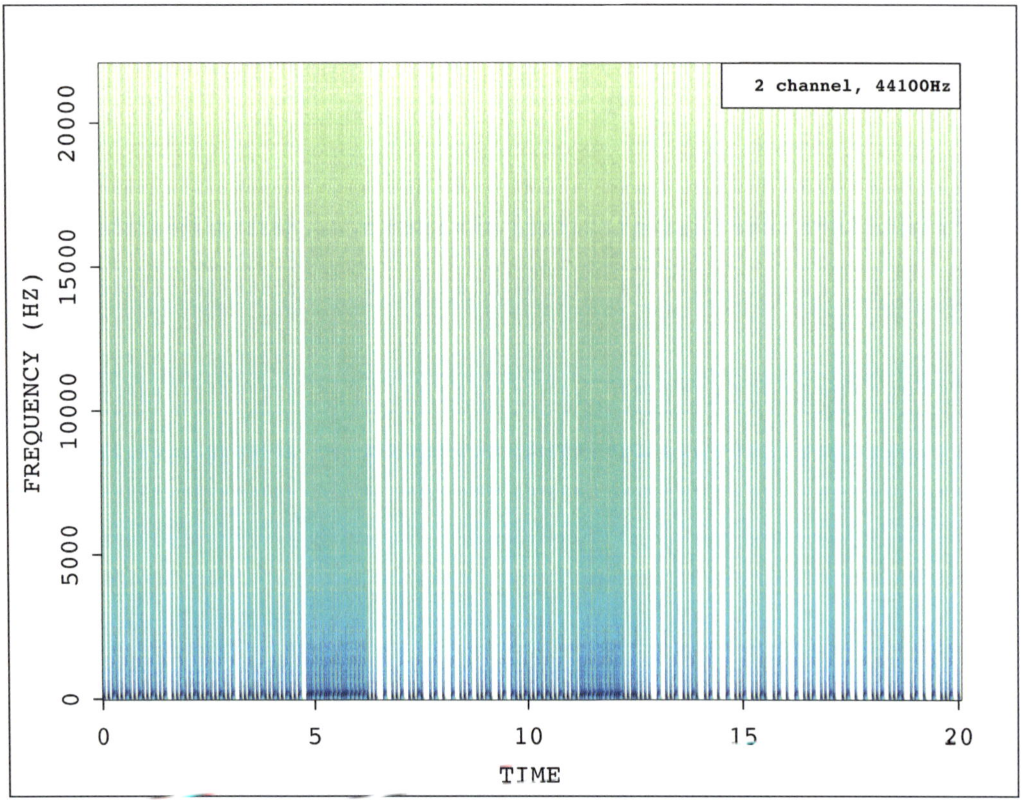

Figure 2.34: *Spectrogram of the Sample channel.*

2.6.3.2.5 Sawtooth As a bonus, let's also check out the Sawtooth channel from the VRC6 expansion (Figure 2.35). To begin with, a perfect Sawtooth wave is made of all the harmonics and each exhibits decreasing amplitudes (where `amplitude = 1 ÷ harmonic number` [48]).

This is quite a requirement for digital equipment and is naturally unaffordable for a game cartridge (which may not even need such perfection!). So, similarly to the APU's triangle waves, the VRC6 sequences Sawtooth waves in 7 cycles (and thus produces similar step-ladder effects).

Consequently, the respective spectrogram appears very cluttered, as the VRC6's approximation techniques fill the wave with extra harmonics in various places.

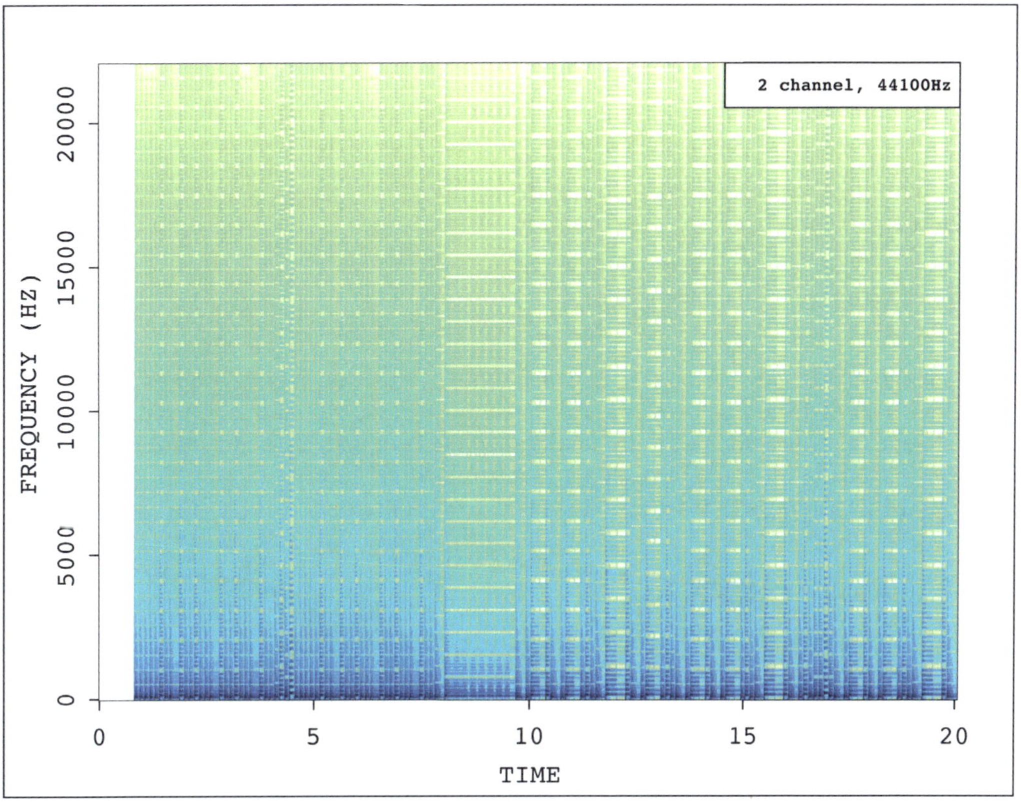

Figure 2.35: *Spectrogram of the VRC6's Sawtooth channel.*

2.6.3.3 Conclusion

Well, it seems that the NES' synthetic waveforms are nowhere near shaped as the theory dictates. Does this mean the APU is flawed? Not at all! The design of the APU ultimately gave this console its unique and identifiable sounds - these characteristics, whether intentional or not, made the spectrograms display unusual patterns.

As a side note, while perfect geometry may be visually appealing, our ears are surprisingly less receptive to waveforms with excellent edges! (you may start hearing popping noises).

Looking ahead, sound analysis using spectrograms will prove useful in other articles, whether for simple analysis or for comparing different systems. However, it is important to note that these graphs are not *the mother lode* tool by all means, especially with sound samples that have been mixed with too many channels or instruments, which can complicate their decomposition. Nevertheless, they provide a solid foundation for any kind of objective study.

2.7 Games

NES games are mainly written in the 6502 assembly language and reside in the **Program ROM**, while the game's graphics (tiles) are stored in **Character memory**.

Furthermore, games were sold (or rented out) at retail stores **under the approval of Nintendo**.

2.7.1 The alternative medium

Even though it was only released in Japan, I thought this would be a good opportunity to introduce a short-lived but peculiar add-on that, just like the mappers, brought in more capabilities to this console. This peripheral, called the **Famicom Disk System** (FDS), shipped in 1986 (~3 years after the Famicom). It resembled an external floppy drive and came bundled with an oddly shaped cartridge called the 'RAM adapter'.

(a) *The drive [3], where floppies are inserted (the photo shows a cardboard floppy inserted for protection). It either runs on six C batteries (1.5 V each) or a 3.6 W AC adapter.*

(b) *The RAM adapter [3], fitted on the cartridge slot of the Famicom and connected to the drive via a cable.*

Figure 2.36: *The two components that make up the Famicom Disk System (FDS).*

The Famicom Disk System added the following functionality to the console:

- A new medium of distribution for games called **Famicom Disk** [49]. Based on the 'Quick Disk' by Mitsumi, it offers **~64 KB of data** per side and is re-writable.
- An **extra audio channel** that uses wavetable synthesis[6] [50].

[6] See "Game Boy / Color Architecture" - Section 5.1.2 "Wave"

Figure 2.37: *FDS equipment mounted onto the Famicom [3].*

Unlike multi-chip cartridges, the floppy is a simple medium. Hence, all game data needs to be squashed inside, though it is organised with the use of a proprietary **file system**.

Nonetheless, the architecture of the Famicom/NES strictly enforces segregated Program and Character memory. The 'RAM adapter', which came with the box, addresses this by housing **32 KB of Program RAM** and **8 KB of Character RAM** to buffer the game data read from the floppy disk. In doing so, this setup enables the console to read data as if it were reading from a cartridge-based game.

To operate the drive, the RAM adapter embeds an additional 8 KB ROM to store a **BIOS** [51]. This program performs the following tasks:

- Displays a splash animation.
- Bootstraps the game from the floppy disk. Behind the scenes, the BIOS contains routines to copy the floppy's contents to the appropriate memory chip, allowing the console to read them.

- Provides I/O APIs for games to use, such as traversing the disk's file system.

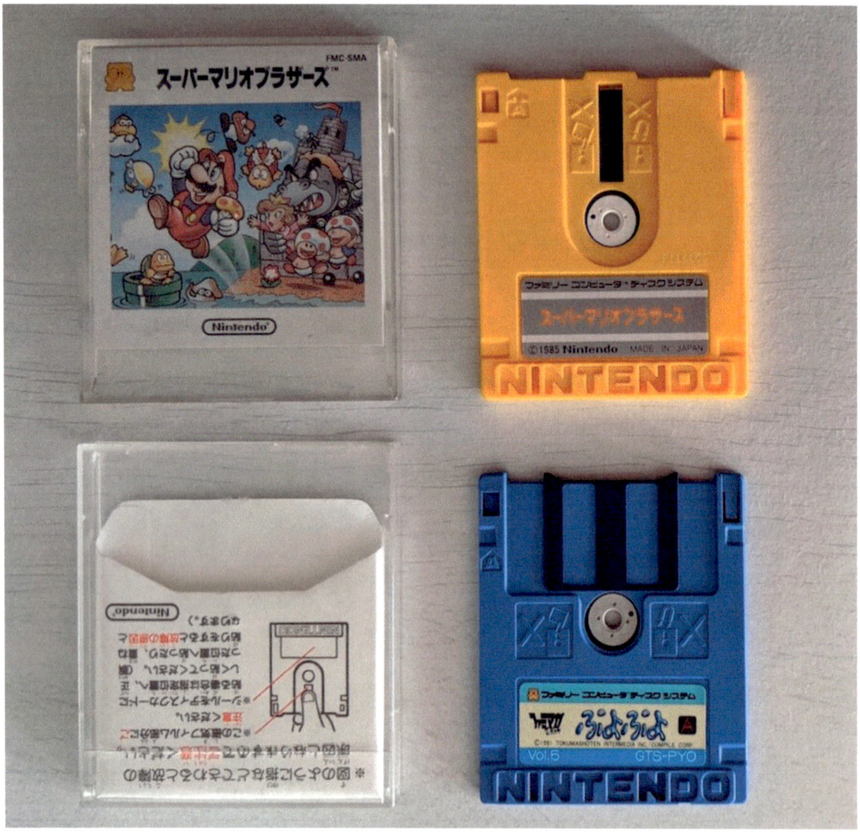

Figure 2.38: *Example of two retail games for the FDS. The blue 'flavour' of the disc is dust proof.*

During that era, Nintendo deployed some 'kiosks' at retail stores, so users could bring their floppies and overwrite them with a new game at a reduced price.

Unfortunately, after a few years of lifespan, the Famicom Disk System was discontinued. Consequently, subsequent games reverted to the cartridge medium. On the bright side, new mappers were introduced with similar (or better) capabilities compared to the FDS' functions.

Figure 2.39: *The FDS splash animation, waiting for the user to... uhm... insert a game.*

2.8 Anti-piracy and region lock

Nintendo was able to block unauthorised publishing by including a proprietary **lockout** chip called the **Checking Integrated Circuit** (CIC) [52]. It is located on the console's motherboard and connected to the reset signal, making it difficult to remove.

The CIC runs **10NES**, an internal program that verifies the presence of another lockout chip in the game cartridge. If the verification fails, the console enters an infinite reset loop.

Both lockout chips are in constant communication during the console's uptime. Nonetheless, this system can be bypassed by cutting one of the pins on the console's lockout chip, which places it in an idle state. Alternatively, sending a -5V signal can halt it.

The CIC exists in response to the video game crash of 1983. Nintendo's then-president, Hiroshi Yamauchi, decided that to ensure high-quality games, the company would take responsibility for approving every single title [53].

You'll notice that the Japanese model of the console, the Famicom, was released before the 1983 crash. That's why neither game cartridges nor the console includes CIC circuitry [54]. Instead, the pins are used for optional sound expansion.

2.9 That's all folks

This article was originally published on January 25, 2019 and last updated on June 7, 2025. See the online repository[7] for the complete changelog.

[7] https://github.com/flipacholas/Architecture-of-consoles

3

Sega Master System Architecture

Competent straight out of the box

3.1 A quick introduction

The Master System comes from a long line of succession. What began as a collection of off-the-shelf components has now acquired a new identity thanks to Sega's engineering.

3.2 Models and variants

I was a bit confused at first when reading about the different models that Sega eventually shipped. So, here is a summary of the main models to clarify any potential confusion:

- **Sega Mark III**: The first console featuring this architecture, released exclusively in Japan.
- **Sega Master System** (Europe and America): A rebranded Mark III with a new case, a BIOS ROM chip, and a different cartridge slot.
- **Sega Master System** (Japan): A European/American Master System with the Mark III's cartridge slot, a new FM chip, and a jack port for '3D glasses'. However, it lacks the `RESET` button.

From now on, I'll use the term 'Master System' or 'SMS' to collectively refer to these models, except when discussing features exclusive to a specific variant.

3.3 Supporting Imagery

Figure 3.1: *The Sega Master System. Released on 20/10/1985 in Japan, 09/1986 in America and 06/1987 in Europe [3]*

Figure 3.2: *Motherboard [3]. The sound chip is embedded in the video display processor.*

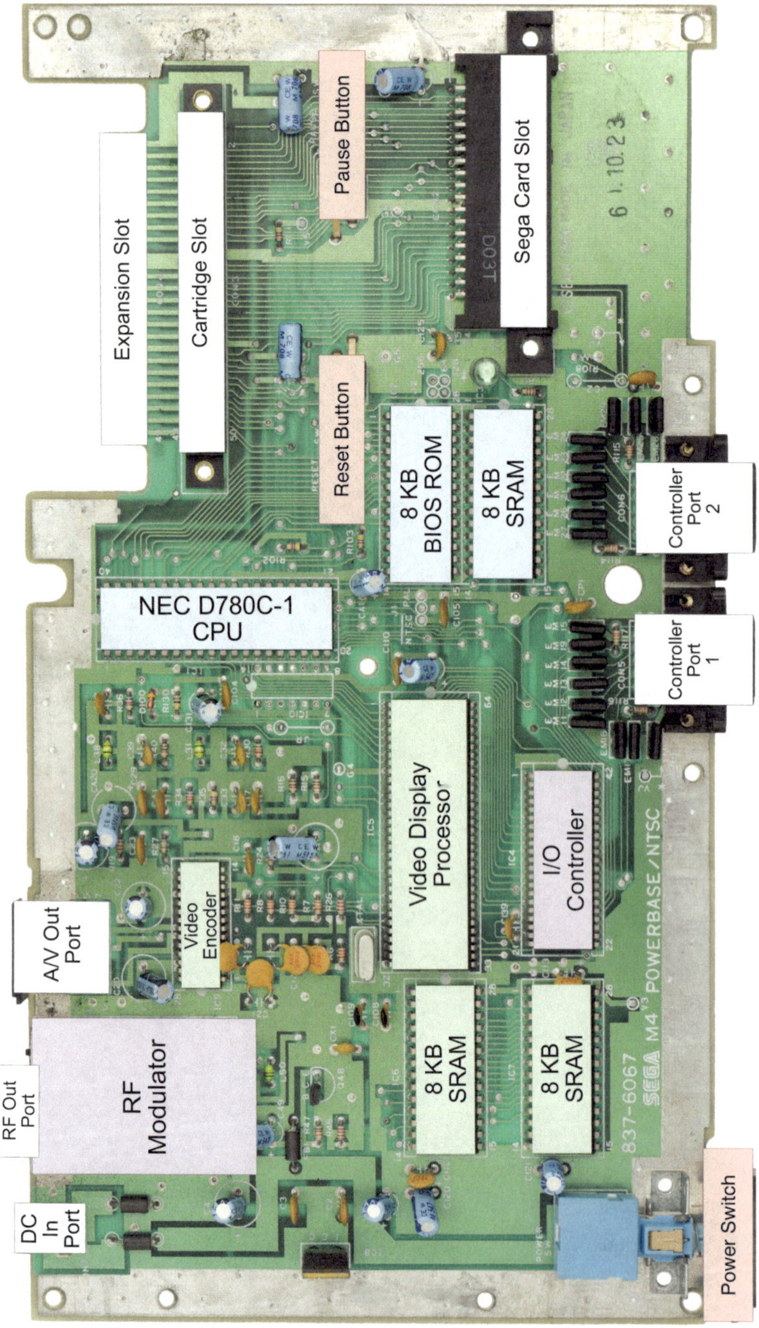

Figure 3.3: *Motherboard with important parts labelled.*

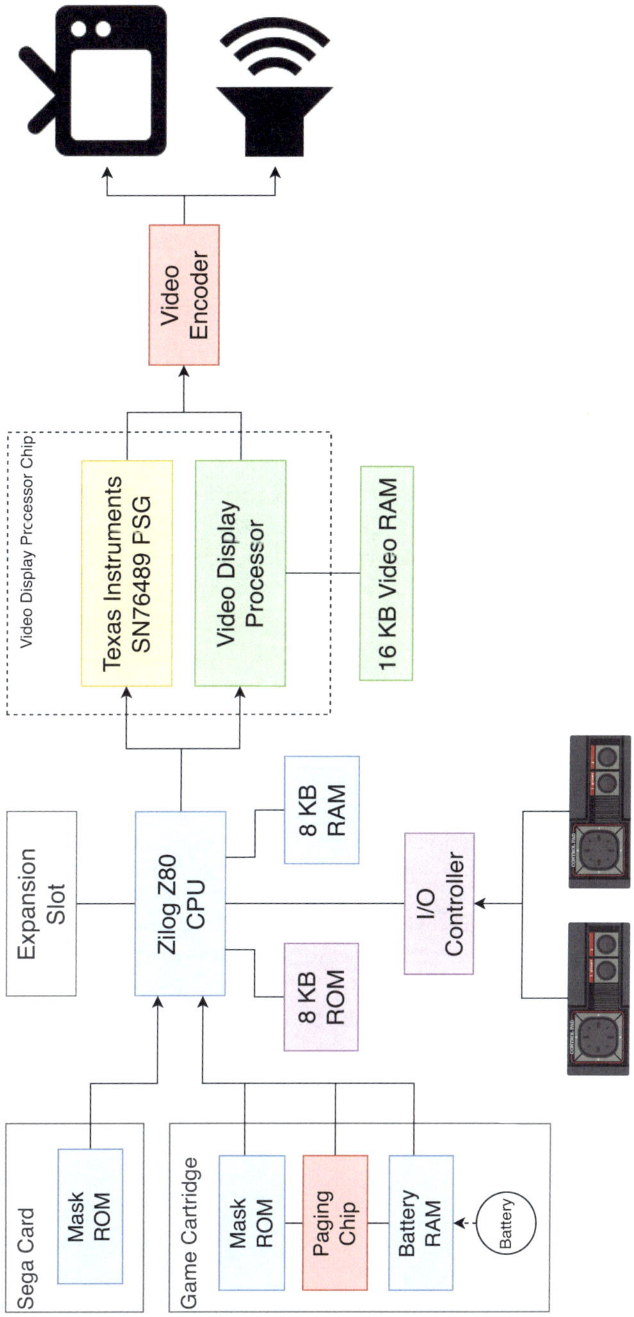

Figure 3.4: *Main architecture diagram.*

3.4 CPU

Sega opted for a fully-fledged **Zilog Z80** CPU running at **~3.58 MHz**, a popular choice among computer manufacturers such as Sinclair, Amstrad, and Tandy.

The Z80 CPU has an interesting background, as it was designed by none other than the authors of the Intel 8080 (Federico Faggin and Masatoshi Shima), who became disenchanted with Intel's direction and decided to start their own silicon company, Zilog, in 1974.

Their debut product can be considered an unofficial successor to the Intel 8080, now featuring:

- The **Z80 ISA**: An instruction set compatible with the Intel 8080 but expanded with lots more instructions. It handles **8-bit** words.
- An **8-bit data bus**, ideal for moving 8-bit data around. Larger values will consume extra CPU cycles.
- **Fourteen 8-bit general-purpose registers** [56]: This is quite a lot, considering the Intel 8080 features half and the MOS 6502 only three[1]. However, the Z80's register file exhibits some caveats (or advantages, depending on how you see it):
  - Only **seven registers are accessible at a time**, the other seven are called 'Alternative Registers' and must be swapped with the first set to be able to access them. This aligns with the principle of bank switching[2]. Also, the Z80 provides specialised instructions like `EX` and `EXX` to transfer the contents between each set.
  - Within each set, six 8-bit registers may also be paired together to provide up to **three 16-bit registers**, allowing the manipulation of larger values.
- A **16-bit address bus**, its consequences are explained in the next section.
- A **4-bit ALU**: This may be a bit shocking, but it simply means that operations on 8-bit values take twice as many cycles to compute.

The motherboard picture at the start of the article shows an NEC D780C-1 CPU, which is simply SEGA second-sourcing the chip to different manufacturers. Other revisions even included the chip manufactured by Zilog. But for this article, it doesn't matter who fabricated the CPU, as the internal features remain the same.

[1] See "NES / Famicom Architecture" - Section 4.2 "Core functionality"

[2] See "NES / Famicom Architecture" - Section 4.3.3 "Going beyond existing capabilities"

(a) *The American Tandy TRS-80 (1977). I found it in the Computer History Museum (Mountain View, California), during my visit in June 2019.*

(b) *The British Sinclair ZX80 (1980), it is way smaller than it looks! This is part of Christopher Rivett's collection [55].*

Figure 3.5: *Popular computers across the world carrying a Z80 CPU.*

Figure 3.6: *The Z80 chip on the Master System's motherboard*

3.4.1 Relative comparison

Notice how the 6502 CPU (featured in the NES[3]) runs at a mere ~2 MHz, which is about half the speed of the Master System's chip. Combined with the Z80's larger register file, one might assume the Master System would outperform the NES without a doubt.

Conversely, if we dig deeper, we see that the 6502 houses a larger (8-bit) ALU. Thus, arithmetic operations that may only take two cycles in the 6502, **will consume four** on the Z80. Ultimately, this shows that relative qualities like CPU clock speed or register file size, when analysed in isolation, may be deceiving. Both the Z80 and 6502 excel and struggle at different tasks; it all comes down to the skills of the programmer.

3.4.2 Memory available

As mentioned earlier, the Z80 has a 16-bit address bus, so the CPU can find up to **64 KB worth of memory**. Now, in the Master System's memory map, you'll find **8 KB of RAM** for general-purpose use [57], this is mirrored in another 8 KB block. Finally, **up to 48 KB of game ROM** are mapped as well.

[3] See "NES / Famicom Architecture" - Section 4.2 "Core functionality"

3.4.3 Accessing the rest of the components

As you may have read in the previous paragraph, only the main RAM and some cartridge ROM are found in the address space. So, how does the program access other components? Well, unlike Nintendo's Famicom/NES[4], not all the hardware in the Master System is mapped to memory locations. Instead, certain peripherals are accessed through the **I/O space**.

This is because the Z80 family contains an interesting feature called **I/O ports**, which enable the CPU to communicate with other hardware without exhausting memory addresses. To achieve this, there is a separate address space for 'I/O devices' called **ports**, and both share the same data and address bus. The difference, however, is that ports are read from and written to using `IN` and `OUT` instructions, respectively, as opposed to the traditional load/store instruction (`LD`).

When an `IN` or `OUT` instruction is executed, the Z80 sets up the address lines to point to the peripheral (which could be, for instance, a keyboard), flags its `IORQ` pin to indicate that an I/O request has been initiated, and finally flags the `RD` pin or the `WR` pin depending on whether it's an `IN` or `OUT` instruction, respectively. Consequently, the addressed peripheral must manually monitor the address bus and the I/O pins and perform the required operation. In the case of an `IN` instruction, the CPU stores the received value in a predefined register.

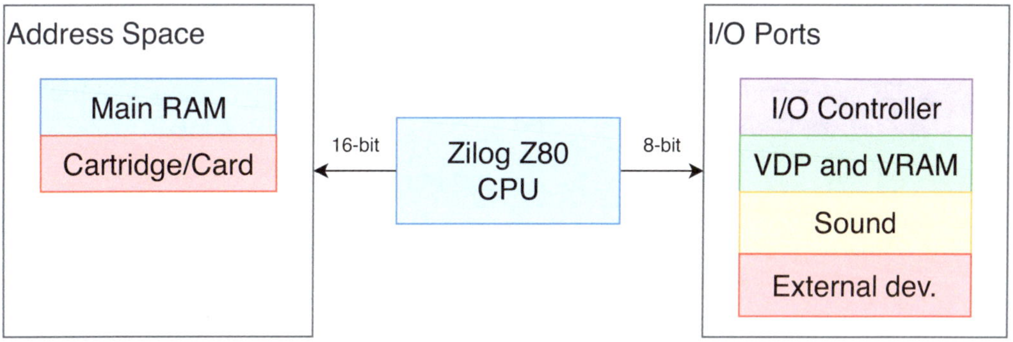

Figure 3.7: *SMS' Addressing layout.*

The way SEGA interconnected the CPU with the rest of the components enables it not only to access values but also to expose or conceal certain components from the memory map.

Interestingly, the Game Boy[5] housed a Z80 'variant' that completely omitted the I/O ports. Thus, it had to fit everything into the memory map.

---

[4] See "NES / Famicom Architecture"

[5] See "Game Boy / Color Architecture" - Section 3 "CPU"

3.4.4 Backwards compatibility

The architecture of this console is very similar to its predecessor, the **Sega SG-1000**. This allowed the Master System to gain backwards compatibility with the SG-1000. Although, this only applies to the Japanese variant, as others feature a different cartridge slot.

3.5 Graphics

The drawings on the screen are produced by a proprietary chip called **Video Display Processor** or 'VDP'. Internally, it shares the same design as the Texas Instrument TMS9918 (used in the SG-1000) [58], though it has been enhanced with features which we will discuss in the following sections.

3.5.1 Organising the content

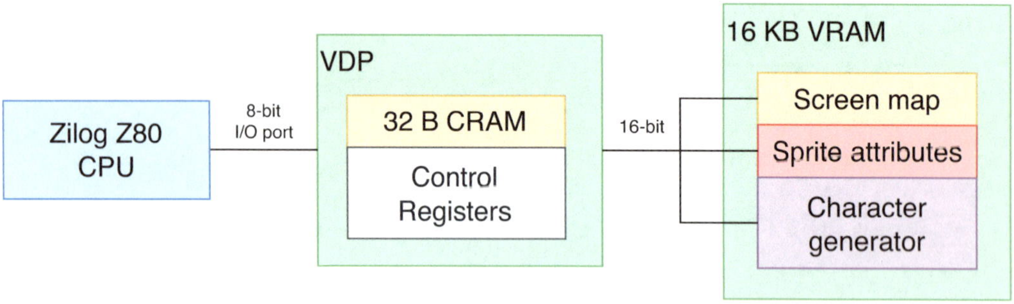

Figure 3.8: *Memory architecture of the VDP.*

Connected to the VDP are **16 KB of VRAM**, which only the VDP can access using a **16-bit data bus** (Sega modified the original design to access two memory chips with 8-bit buses simultaneously [59]). If you look at the motherboard picture again, you'll notice that both RAM and VRAM chips are roughly the same, except that VRAM uses the chip model ending in '20', which offer lower latency [60].

For the Master System, VRAM houses everything the VDP requires for rendering (except Colour RAM). The CPU fills VRAM by writing to specific VDP registers, which in turn forward the values to VRAM. Since the VDP is accessed through I/O ports, the CPU must use `IN` and `OUT` instructions.

3.5.2 Constructing the frame

The VDP renders frames with a resolution of **up to 256x192 pixels**. Later revisions added support for 256x224 px and 256x240 px. However, to maintain compatibility with all models, developers adhered to the standard resolution. This chip has the same *modus operandi* as Nintendo's PPU[6]; in other words, graphics are rendered on the spot.

Furthermore, the VDP has four different modes of operation. These alter the characteristics of the frame (colour depth and resolution):

- **Mode 0 to III**: Inherited from the TMS9918 found on the SG-1000. They are included for backwards compatibility, although any SMS game can use them.
- **Mode IV**: The native mode of the Master System, which enables access to all the state-of-the-art features of the VDP. For this analysis, we will focus on this mode!

Let us now examine how a frame is drawn step by step. For this, I'll borrow *Sonic The Hedgehog*'s assets. Also, to make explanations easier, this analysis will focus on the standard memory layout that Sega suggests for organising the graphics content (just remember that the VDP is very flexible, allowing games to optimise the layout).

3.5.2.1 Tiles

Mode IV is based on the **tile system**. To recall previous explanations[7] about tile engines, tiles are just **8x8 pixel bitmaps** that the renderer retrieves to draw the game's graphics. In the case of the VDP, the frame consists of two planes: the background layer and the sprite layer.

Inside VRAM, there is an area dedicated to tiles called **Character generator** (Sega refers to tiles as 'Characters'), and it's set to be **14 KB long**. Each tile occupies 32 bytes, so we can store up to 448 tiles.

Each tile contains 64 pixels, and the VDP rules that each pixel must use 4 bits, allowing **16 colours can be chosen**. These bits reference a single entry in **Colour RAM** or 'CRAM', which is located within the VDP and stores the colour palettes. Colour palette systems reduce the size of tiles in memory and enable programmers to alternate their colours without storing multiple copies.

Colour RAM stores **two palettes of 16 colours each**. Each entry is 6 bits wide, with each 2-bit set defining one colour from the RGB model. This provides a total of 64 colours to choose from.

[6] See "NES / Famicom Architecture" - Section 5.2 "Constructing the frame"
[7] See "NES / Famicom Architecture" - Section 5.2.1 "Tiles"

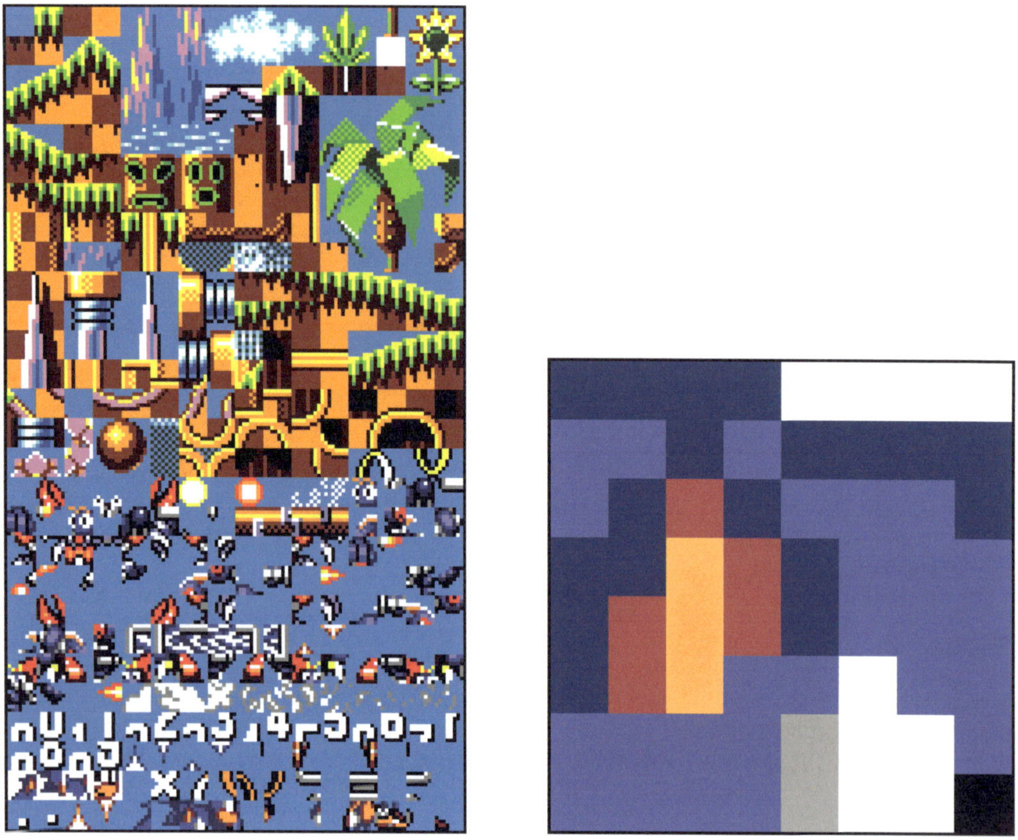

(a) *All tiles.* **(b)** *A single tile.*

Figure 3.9: *Tiles Found in VRAM.*

3.5.2.2 Background Layer

The background layer is a large plane where static tiles are drawn. To place something here, there is another area in VRAM called **Screen map**, which takes 1.75 KB.

This allows developers to build a layer of 896 tiles (32x28 tiles) [61], but if we do the math, we see that this layer is larger than the display resolution of the console. The reality is, only 768 tiles (32x24 tiles) are visible, so the visible area is manually selected at the programmer's will. Also, by slowly alternating the X and Y coordinates of the selected area, a **scrolling effect** is achieved.

Each entry in the map is 2 bytes wide (matching the width of the VDP's data bus) and contains the address of the tile in the Character generator, along with the following attributes:

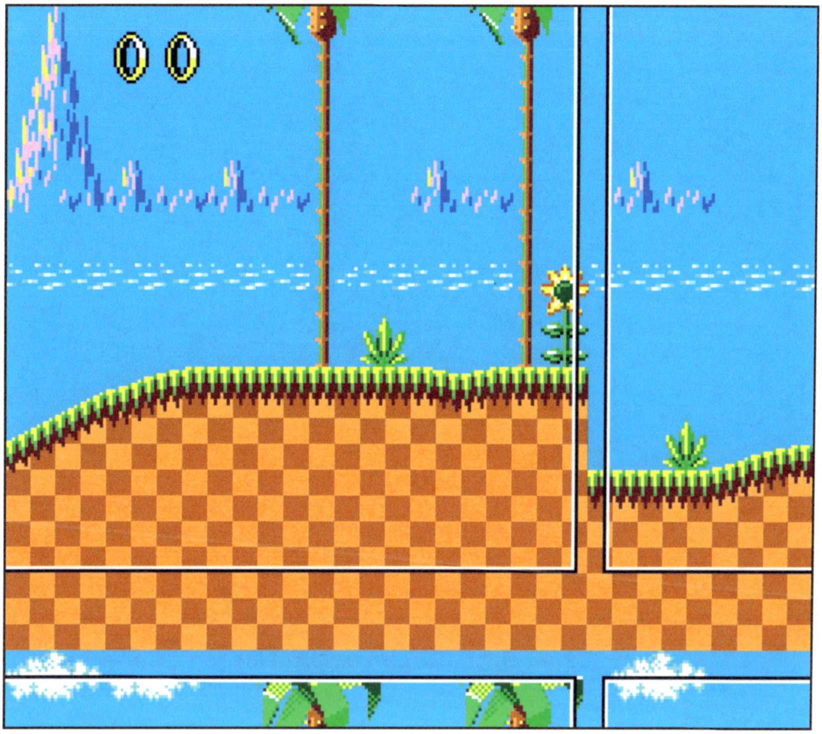

Figure 3.10: *Allocated Screen map with selected area marked.*

- **Horizontal and Vertical flip**.
- The **priority bit** (determines whether to draw some or all the tile in front of sprites).
- The **colour palette** used.

Curiously enough, there are three unused bits in the entry that the game can use for other purposes (e.g., extra flags to assist the game engine).

3.5.2.3 Sprites

Sprites are essentially tiles that can move freely. The VDP can raster **up to 64 sprites** using a single tile (8x8 px) or two tiles stacked vertically (8x16 px).

The **Sprite Attribute Table** is a 256-byte area in VRAM that contains an array of all the defined sprites. Its entries are similar to those of the background layer, except that each sprite contains two additional values representing the X/Y coordinates.

The VDP is limited to **a maximum of eight sprites per horizontal scan-line** [62]. Also, if multiple sprites overlap, the first one in the list is displayed.

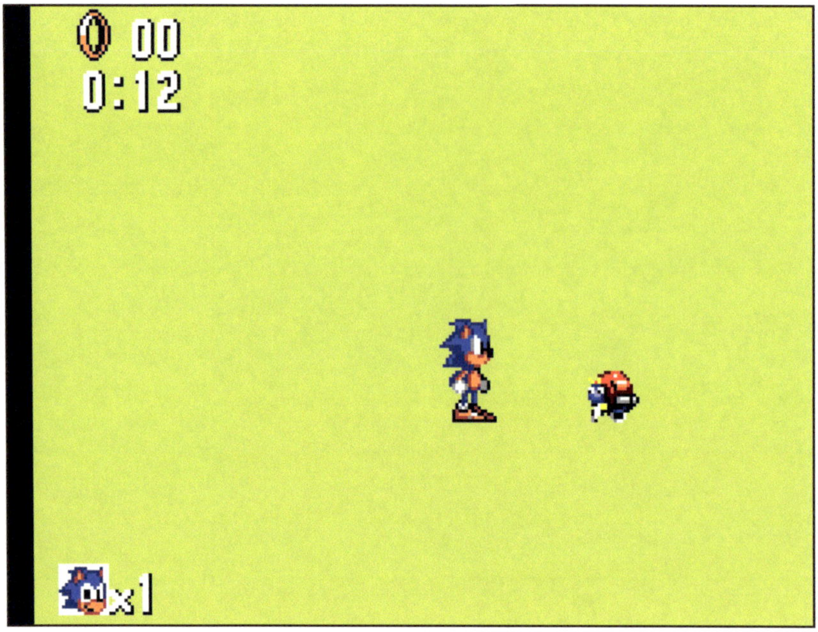

Figure 3.11: *Rendered Sprite layer.*

3.5.2.4 Result

The VDP automatically blends the two layers to form the final frame. The rendering process is performed scan-line by scan-line, so the VDP doesn't really know how the frame will look; that's only visible to the user once the picture is constructed on the TV.

If you examine the example image (Figure 3.12), you may notice a vertical column at the left side of the frame. This occurs because the screen map is tall enough to provide vertical scrolling without producing artefacts, **but not wide enough for horizontal scrolling**. To address this, the VDP can **mask** the left-most side with an 8 px column to prevent intermediate tiles from being displayed.

To update the graphics for the next frame without disrupting the image currently being displayed, the VDP sends two types of **interrupts** to the CPU. One notifies that the CRT TV has finished beaming a chosen number of scan-lines (called **horizontal interrupt**), while the other signals that the CRT has completed drawing the final scan-line (called **vertical interrupt**), indicating the frame is finished. During these events, the CRT's beam is repositioning to draw the next scan-line (**blanking interval**), so any alteration of the VDP's state won't tear the image. Horizontal blanking has a shorter time-frame than vertical blanking, yet it still allows to change, let's say, the colour palette. This still can produce certain effects.

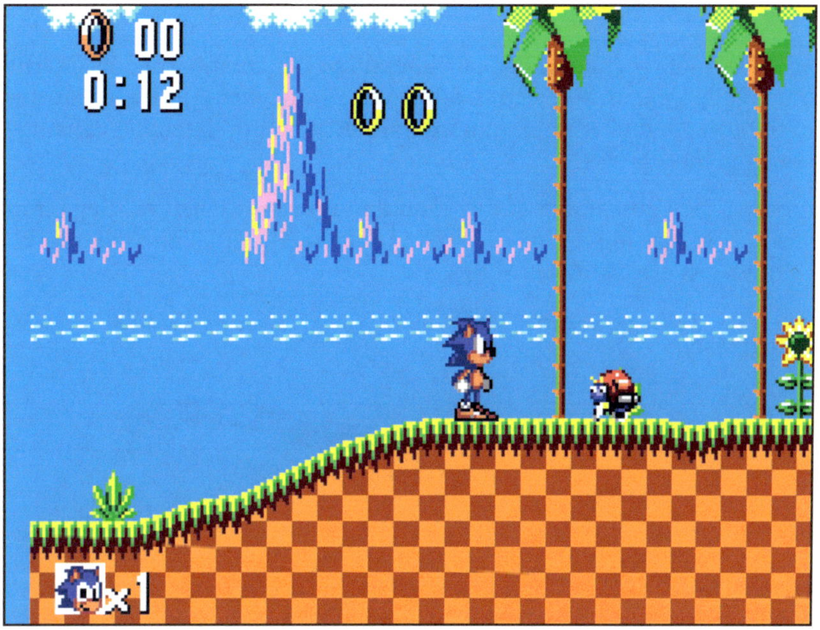

Figure 3.12: *Tada!*

3.5.3 Secrets and limitation

At first glance, the VDP may seem like another chip with minimal functionality that we now take for granted. Although, it still managed to draw significant attention away from Nintendo's offering at the time. Why was that?

3.5.3.1 Collision detection

First of all, the VDP could **tell if two sprites were colliding**. This was done by checking its `status` register [63]. While it could not identify which sprites in particular were colliding, developers could 'triangulate' the location by reading other registers as well, such as the `scan-line counter`.

This feature was not new, actually, as the TMS9918 also included it. Thus, the SG-1000 also had collision detection.

3.5.3.2 The need for modularity

When I previously analysed the design of Nintendo's PPU, I emphasised its internal memory architecture. While limited, some constraints were somewhat beneficial[8] as they enabled the system to be expanded with extra hardware included in the game cartridge, keeping the costs down in the process.

The VDP doesn't take advantage of this modular approach. Instead, Sega implemented a different solution that in turn saves cartridge costs. The smaller background layer and horizontal interrupts are examples of this.

3.5.3.3 3D glasses

Figure 3.13: *Sega 3-D glasses [3]. The American variant connected through the card port.*

It turns out Sega also shipped **'3D glasses'** as an official accessory! The glasses worked in sync with the CRT. During gameplay, the game alternates the position of objects between frames. Each lens contains an LCD screen that turns black to block your vision. The correct combination of graphics flickering and alternating shutters eventually creates a stereoscopic image in your head, resulting in a '3D' effect.

The shutters are controlled via several memory addresses, but none of them indicate whether the glasses are actually plugged in. Therefore, games that support this accessory include a settings option to manually activate this feature.

The LCD controllers are interfaced with a jack cable, which plugs into the console. The European and American versions did not include the jack input, so they rely on the card port to connect an adaptor (we'll see more about the card slot later on).

[8] See "NES / Famicom Architecture" - Section 5.3 "Secrets and limitations"

3.5.4 Video Output

The video-out connector of this system is *incredibly* versatile. It exposes both **composite** and **RGB** signals, which can be considered the two 'extremes' of video quality.

The downside, however, is that it doesn't carry 'composite sync', so using the RGB output requires capturing the sync signal from composite, and its quality isn't optimal.

3.6 Audio

The audio capabilities of this console are pretty much aligned with other 80s equipment. Inside the VDP chip, we find a slightly-customised version of the **Texas Instruments SN76489** [64], which is a **Programmable Sound Generator** or 'PSG'. This is the same type used in the NES/Famicom, albeit having different functions.

3.6.1 Functionality

A PSG can only synthesise a limited set of waveforms, with each channel allocated to a single waveform. I previously introduced some PSGs in the NES[9] and the Game Boy[10] article, if you are interested in this type of sound synthesis.

In the SMS, the PSG is programmed by altering its set of registers through the aforementioned I/O ports.

Let us now examine each type of waveform the SN76489 can synthesise:

3.6.1.1 Pulse

Pulse/Tone waves produce that iconic sound of the 8-bit generation. The sound wave is generated by latching up the voltage, holding it steady, and then dropping it. Repeating this at a constant rate produces a tone.

The period of the wave defines the frequency of the sound (musical note), while its duty cycle affects the timbre.

The SN76489, in particular, can produce **three pulse waves at the same time**. It also exposes a 10-bit counter on each channel that is used internally to latch the output, resulting in pulse waves with programmable frequencies.

[9] See "NES / Famicom Architecture" - Section 6 "Audio"
[10] See "Game Boy / Color Architecture" - Section 5 "Audio"

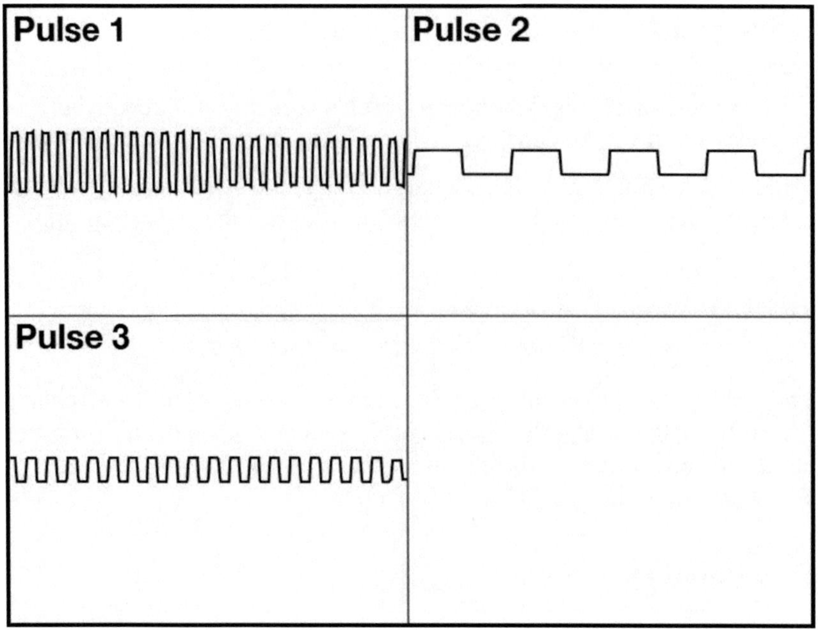

Figure 3.14: *Oscilloscope display of Sonic The Hedgehog (1991), showing the pulse channels.*

3.6.1.2 Noise

Noise is a type of signal associated with interference. When outputted to a speaker, it sounds like static.

The SN76489 contains a Linear Feedback Shift Register (LFSR) which is fed with some input and cycled through to generate a pseudo-random signal. It can alternate between **white noise** and **periodic noise**.

The oscillator offers three frequencies to choose from, which alter the pitch of the noise [65]. There's also a fourth option where the output of the third pulse channel modulates the noise channel. Some games used this option, combined with the periodic mode, to produce bass-like sounds (similar to a pulse at four octaves lower).

Overall, games typically use the noise channel for **percussion or sound effects**.

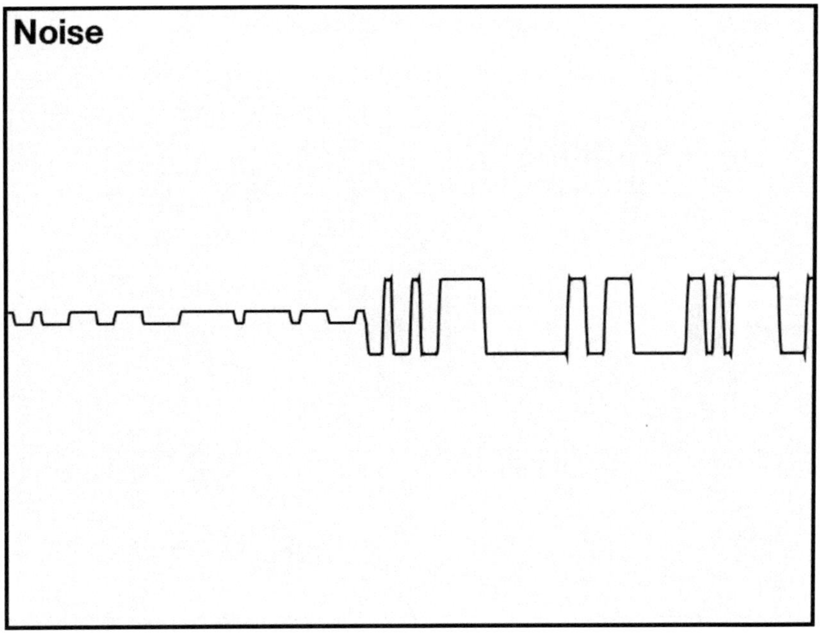

Figure 3.15: *Oscilloscope display of Sonic The Hedgehog (1991), showing the noise channel.*

3.6.1.3 Mixed

So far we have discussed what each channel does individually. In practice, the TV receives a mono signal with all the channels mixed by the PSG.

Finally, the chip also contains programmable attenuators that lower the decibels of each channel, effectively acting as a **volume control**.

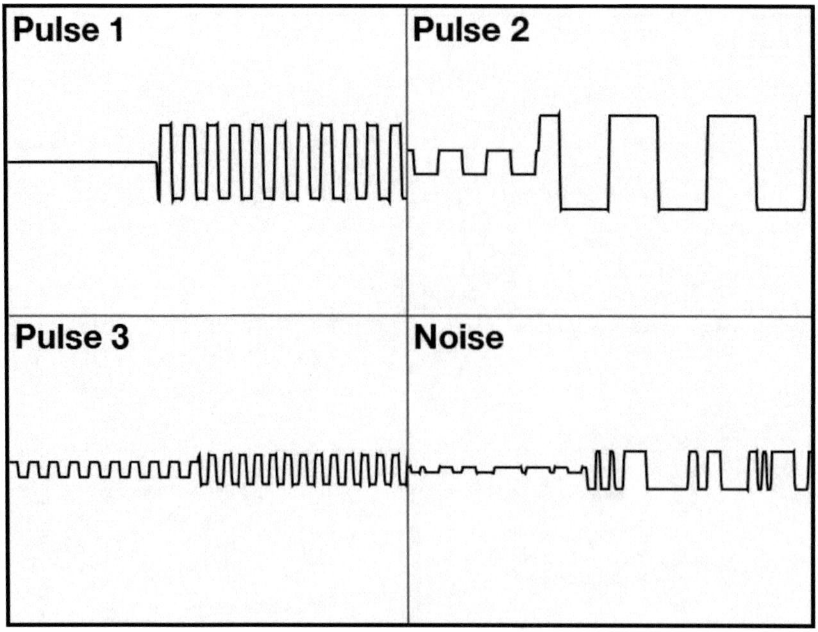

Figure 3.16: *Oscilloscope display of Sonic The Hedgehog (1991), showing all audio channels.*

3.6.2 Secrets and limitations

Just like the VDP, the PSG is a no-brainer, but it does hide some interesting functionality:

3.6.2.1 FM Expansion

The Japanese version of the Master System embedded an extra chip made by Yamaha called **YM2413**. It is drastically different from the PSG, as it uses **frequency modulation** to generate sound. I briefly explained how this works in the Mega Drive article[11], in case you are interested.

This chip adds **nine audio channels**. Each channel can either select one of the 16 preset instruments, or define a custom one by programming the carrier and modulator. Unfortunately, only one custom instrument is allowed at a time. On the other hand, the custom instrument offers interesting functions, such as ADSR envelope controls and feedback.

The YM2413 also has a second mode of operation called **Rhythm mode**, which instead provides **six channels** supplemented with **five additional channels** for rhythm instruments only.

[11] See "Mega Drive / Genesis Architecture" - Section 5.1.1 "Yamaha YM2612"

The final sound output is generated by the YM2413, which mixes its channels with those of the PSG.

The Mark III variant did not include this chip, but FM functionality was available as an expansion unit called the **FM Sound Unit**. The European and American Master Systems, however, had to stick with the PSG, although some third-party modifications eventually appeared.

3.6.2.2 Sample play

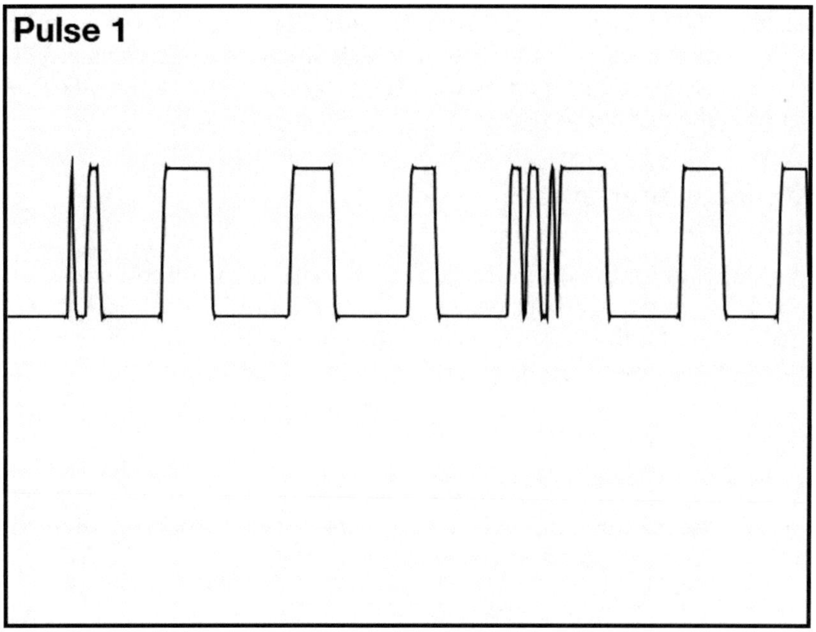

Figure 3.17: *Oscilloscope display of Alex Kidd - The Lost Stars (1986), showing the 1-bit PCM sample.*

While the SN76489 lacks a PCM channel[12] for reproducing samples, there are some tricks that can be used to simulate this functionality.

These rely on the pulse channels, it was discovered that if the tone level is fixed at `1`, the volume level (which alters the amplitude) conditions the shape of the waveform.

smspower.org describes various designs that enable the playback of 1-bit, 4-bit and 8-bit PCM samples. Although, storage requirements skyrocket with higher sample resolutions and rates, so these techniques are best exploited in homebrew games.

[12] See "NES / Famicom Architecture" - Section 6.1.4 "Sample"

It is worth noting that streaming samples consumes a good amount of CPU cycles, and since there is only one processor in this system, the game may need to be halted for a short period.

3.7 I/O

Like other systems from its generation, the CPU is primarily responsible for handling I/O. In this case, the Z80 processor is unique for its specialised I/O addressing, but CPU cycles are still spent moving bits between components.

On the other side, the SMS uses a dedicated **I/O controller** chip to interface with the joypads and to enable or disable parts of the system, which alters the address map. Furthermore, this controller is essential for supporting the FM expansion, as the FM module exposes ports that conflict with the rest of the system.

3.7.1 Available interfaces

In addition to the two controller ports, the system contains one proprietary cartridge slot, one 'Sega Card' slot, and one expansion slot reserved for 'future accessories'. The latter was never utilised, except for the FM expansion in the Mark III. Even so, the SMS and Mark III featured different expansion port designs [66].

3.7.2 Top interruptors

Another speciality about this console is the inclusion of two buttons on the top of its case: `PAUSE` and `RESET`. You can already guess what they do!

Pressing the `PAUSE` button sends a non-maskable interrupt to the CPU [67]. The interrupt handler is stored within the game itself, meaning it is up to the game to honour the press.

In contrast, and for some strange reason, the `RESET` button is handled as a keypress on the controller.

Figure 3.18: *Top of the case [3].*

3.8 Operating System

There's a small **8 KB BIOS ROM** fitted on the motherboard that gets executed whenever the console is powered on. The program itself does not qualify as an 'Operating System'; it is more accurately described as a **Boot Manager**.

3.8.1 Medium selector

The main goal of the BIOS is to bootstrap a valid game (from either game slot) in the following order of priority: the Sega Card, the cartridge, and the expansion module.

The boot process works as follows:

1. The console is switched on.
2. The BIOS copies part of its code to main RAM.
    - This is a crucial step, since the program will start manipulating I/O ports, which will eventually disable access to the ROM!

3. Show the splash screen (only in USA/Europe models).
4. Check each slot for a valid game.
    - This is done by talking to the I/O controller chip to activate the required slot. Then, the boot program copies the game header (16 bytes) from each slot to check if the game content is valid (thus, properly inserted). The header must have `TMR SEGA` encoded.
5. Perform the region check.
6. Redirect execution to the game.

3.8.2 Surprise screen

If any of the checks fail, the console loops indefinitely while showing a screen that prompts the user to insert a valid game.

Figure 3.19: *USA/Europe error message (after the initial splash).*

I have to say, in terms of the design of the error screen, the creative differences between regions are quite significant. The first time I heard the colourful Japanese version, I thought

Figure 3.20: *Japanese 'error' message (enhanced by the FM chip!).*

it was based on *Electric Light Orchestra* (the band), but it is actually from *Space Harrier* (the game). Also, the perspective effect on the floor is accomplished by altering the colour palettes.

3.8.3 More regional differences

Because the Japanese variant was backwards compatible with the SG-1000, the header check is replaced with an 'integrity check' that instead reads data from the first 256 bytes multiple times to detect if it is garbage.

Furthermore, the Mark III doesn't have a BIOS, so the slots are activated with hardware switches. Furthermore, the cartridge is the medium with the most priority.

3.8.4 Updatability and later BIOS chips

The BIOS ROM, by its nature, is **not updatable**. Although, as new console revisions entered the market, it was discovered that Sega also updated the BIOS program.

Later ROMs even embedded entire games! As a consequence, the chip got bigger and was accompanied by a dedicated mapper.

3.9 Games

To make a long story short, games were written in plain Z80 assembly, that's it. There were no compilers or high-level tools back then, apart from the assembler.

3.9.1 Medium

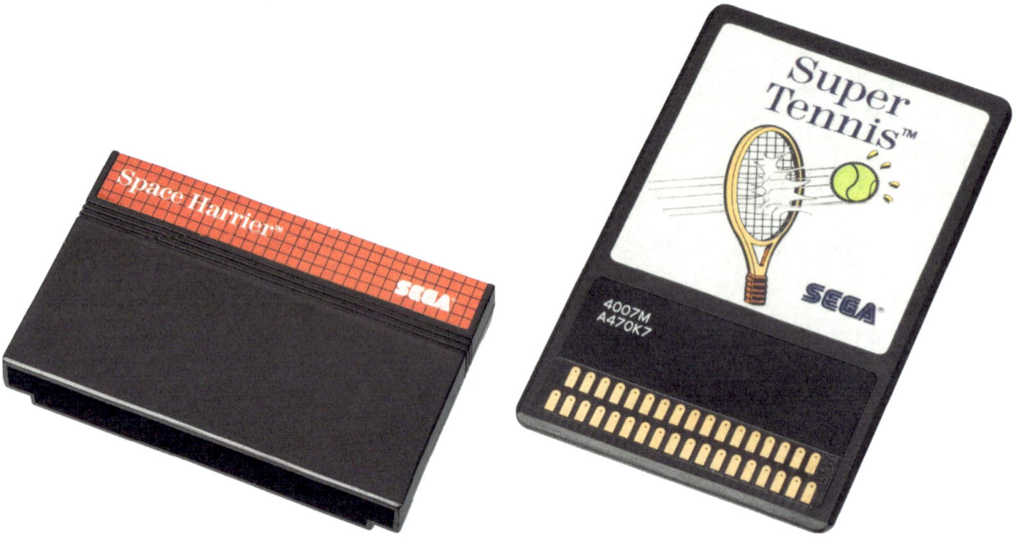

(a) *Example of game cartridge [3].*

(b) *Example of Sega Card [3].*

Figure 3.21: *The two channels of distribution.*

The Master System supports two different media for distributing games:

- The **Cartridge**: The most common one, capable of addressing up to 48 KB of memory. However, by including a mapper, the system could access a wider range and handle additional chips, such as battery-backed RAM for storing saves.

  - Sega offered to developers official mappers called 'Paging Chips'. The most powerful one could map up to 512 KB of memory.
- The **Sega Card**: Visibly thinner and cheaper to manufacture, but it could only access up to 32 KB of memory. Since SEGA never designed a mapper for this medium, the largest card found on the market contained a 32 KB ROM.

3.10 Anti-Piracy and Region locking

Unlike Nintendo, Sega did not employ aggressive methods to control the distribution of their games. They did, however, prevent American and European systems from running Japanese games by altering the shape of the cartridge slot and implementing a different ROM header check.

Furthermore, American and European systems were required to include the aforementioned `TMR SEGA` code in their header. I suppose this enabled them to prevent unauthorised distribution by leveraging trademark laws.

3.11 That's all folks

Having previously written the Nintendo DS article really puts into perspective how complicated technology has become. The Master System is very straightforward by comparison, even after some 'technical nitpicking' I may have expressed here and there.

Anyway, I hope this article provided you with a comprehensive overview of the state of technology of the early-to-mid-80s. I also want to thank the smspower.org community and the /r/Emulation discord for reading the first draft and pointing out *lots* of corrections and suggestions.

Until next time!
Rodrigo

Dedicated to the memory of Jacinto 'Pocho' Fornasier.

This article was originally published on October 12, 2020 and last updated on June 7, 2025. See the online repository[13] *for the complete changelog.*

[13] https://github.com/flipacholas/Architecture-of-consoles

4

PC Engine / TurboGrafx-16 Architecture

A small but quick leap

4.1 A quick introduction

In a bold move, Hudson and NEC joined forces to pioneer the 4th generation of consoles. Unfortunately, their efforts were gradually overshadowed as the competition emerged. Nonetheless, their console remains one of the most compact designs of that era.

4.2 Models and variants

Just like the Master System[1], NEC shipped numerous adaptations and unusual variations, which can initially be difficult to follow. So, for future reference, here are the most significant models:

- **PC Engine**: The first console featuring this architecture, but it was only released in Japan. It resembles a small white box with minimal ports.
- **TurboGrafx-16**: A redesigned version of the PC Engine for the American market. It retains the same features, but with a different external appearance. This reminds me of the NES/Famicom adaptation[2].
- **Supergrafx**: An enhanced version of the PC Engine with a completely different case and upgraded hardware. Its exclusive features are beyond the scope of this article.

[1] See "Sega Master System Architecture" - Section 2 "Models and variants"

[2] See "NES / Famicom Architecture" - Section 2 "Models and variants"

- **PC Engine Duo/TurboDuo**: A combination of the PC Engine/TurboGrafx and the aftermarket CD-ROM^2 expansion.

This article will focus on the PC Engine/TurboGrafx-16, but will also explore the expansions that culminated in the release of the PC Engine Duo/TurboDuo.

4.3 Supporting Imagery

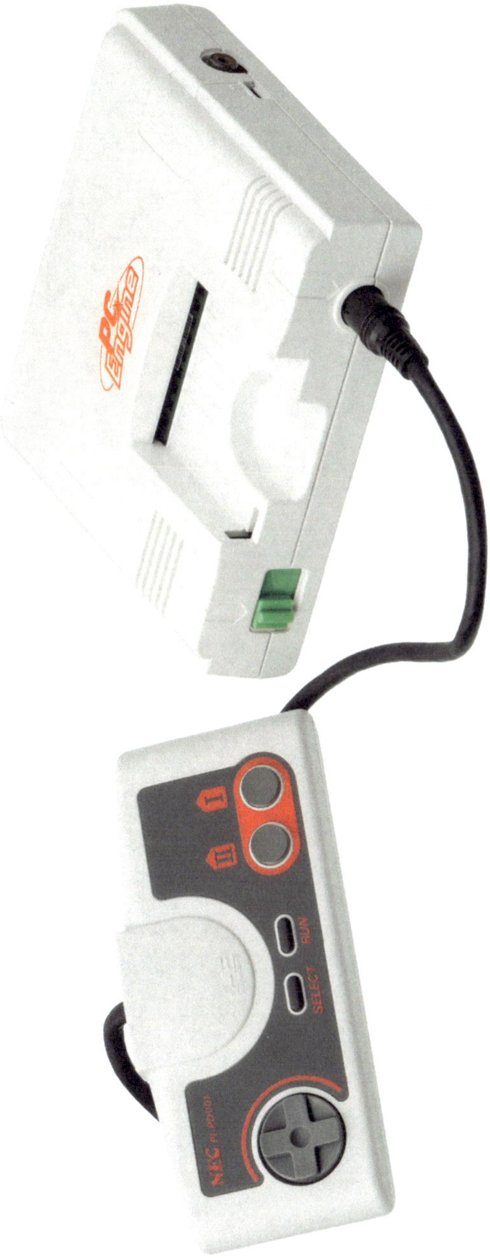

Figure 4.1: *The PC Engine. Released on 30/10/1987 in Japan. [3]*

Figure 4.2: *The TurboGrafx-16. Released on 29/08/1989 in America, 22/11/1989 in France and 1990 in the UK and Spain. [3]*

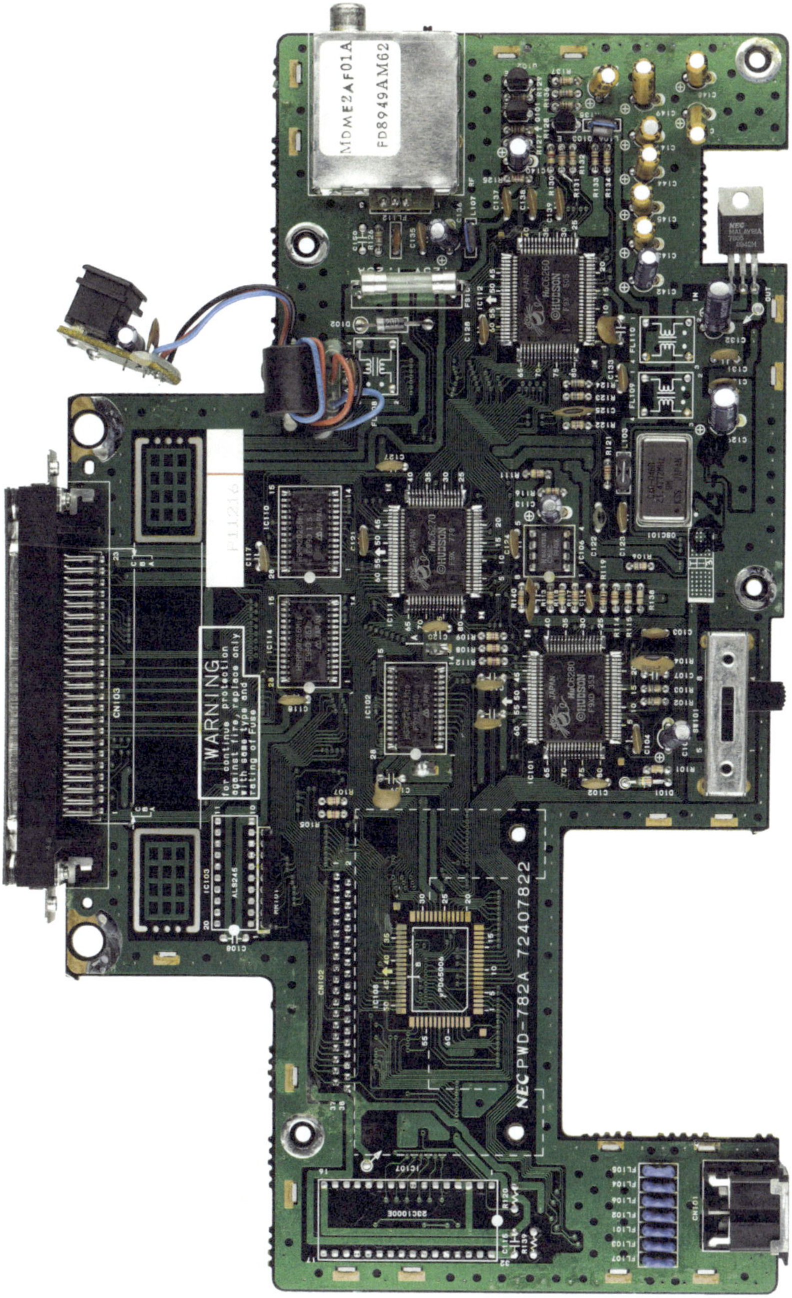

Figure 4.3: *Motherboard [3]. Showing the TurboGrafx's motherboard. The PC Engine one was considerably smaller and stacked.*

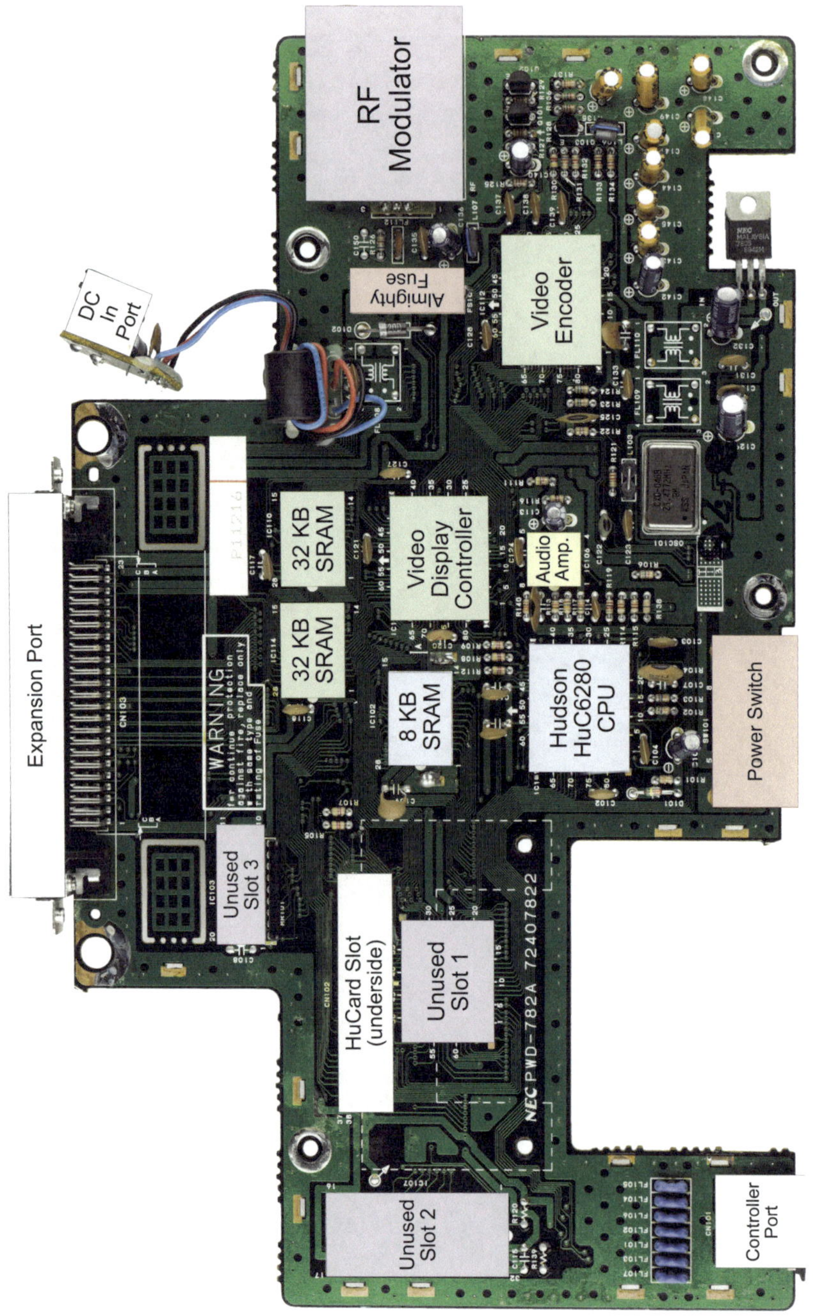

Figure 4.4: *Motherboard with important parts labelled.*

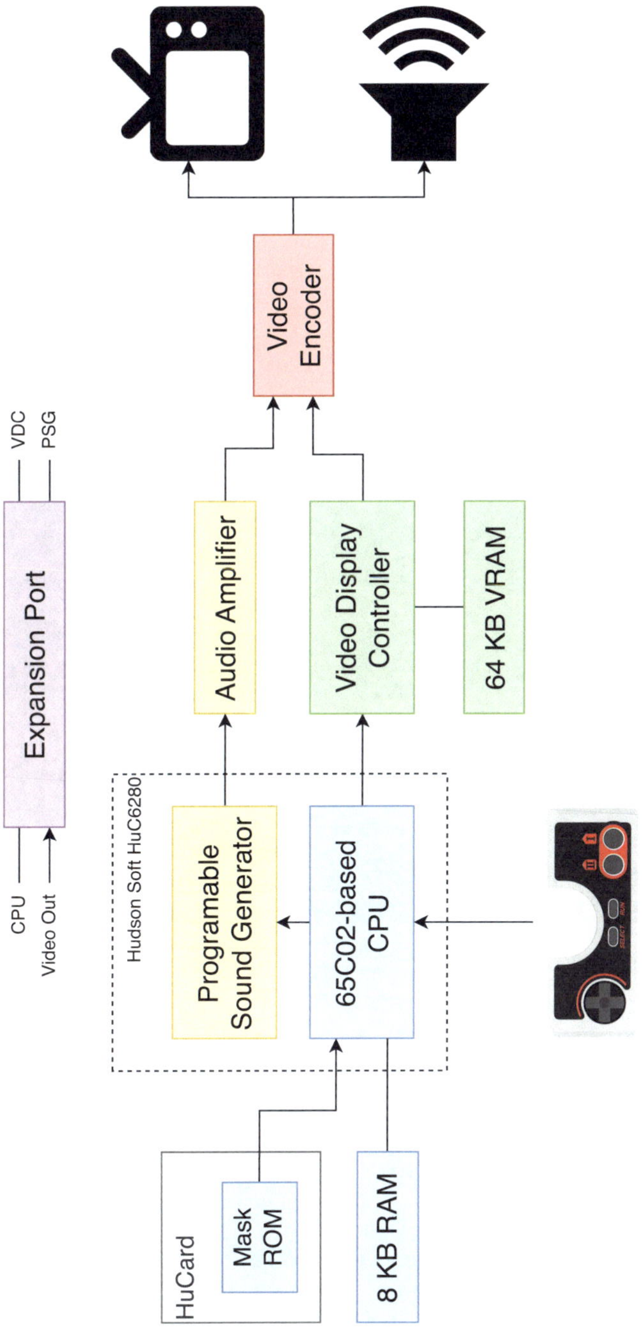

Figure 4.5: *Main architecture diagram. Looks pretty simple, huh?*

4.4 CPU

Inside this console, we find the **HuC6280**, a chip developed by **Hudson Soft** that integrates two components. One of them is the CPU, which can operate at two speeds: **~1.79 MHz** and **~7.16 MHz**.

Figure 4.6: *The HuC6280 chip on the PC Engine's motherboard*

The HuC6280 is not an off-the-shelf component, like the Z80[3]; it is instead a proprietary CPU designed by NEC. Its specification seems to replicate much of the behaviour of the famous **MOS 6502** and **WDC's 65C02**. That being said, what does this mean for the programmer?

Before we start, I have already covered the MOS 6502 CPU in the NES article[4] and described a 16-bit variant made by WDC and Ricoh in the SNES article[5], in case you wish to review them first.

The 65C02 is another modified version of the MOS 6502, made by Western Design Center

[3] See "Sega Master System Architecture" - Section 4 "CPU"
[4] See "NES / Famicom Architecture" - Section 4.2 "Core functionality"
[5] See "Super Nintendo / Famicom Architecture" - Section 3 "CPU"

(WDC). It is significantly more efficient due to its **CMOS** manufacturing approach. From the software perspective, the 65C02 introduces a handful of new instructions and modifies the behaviour of some existing ones [68].

While we could discuss more about the 65C02, I find it more relevant to focus on the features added by Hudson (which complement the 65C02), as they are critical to efficiently operate this console.

Compared to the 65C02, the HuC6280 includes [69]:

- **Additional opcodes**, some of which target the components surrounding the CPU.
- An **8-bit I/O port** for interfacing with external components.
- An **interrupt controller** to handle interrupts from other devices.
- A **timer**, which counts down from a specified value and, upon completion, dispatches an interrupt to the CPU.

Finally, there are **8 KB of RAM** available for general-purpose use.

4.4.1 Memory access

One aspect I have not yet mentioned is that NEC also added a **Memory Management Unit** (MMU) adjacent to the CPU, allowing it to handle **21-bit addresses** (remember the original 6502 only supports 16-bit addresses) [70]. Thus, the amount of memory that can be accessed raises from 64 KB to **2 MB**.

This MMU is very different from any modern-day MMU; I would say it is closer to a mapper[6]. Having said that, the MMU in the PC Engine consists of **eight 8-bit registers** (called **Mapping Register** or 'MPR') that combine with the CPU's 16 address lines to form a 21-bit address bus.

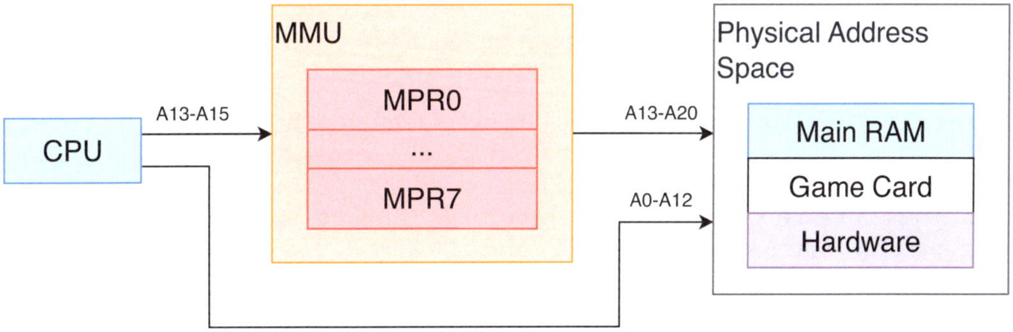

Figure 4.7: *Addressing approach of the MMU.*

[6]See "NES / Famicom Architecture" - Section 4.3.3 "Going beyond existing capabilities"

The process works as follows:

1. The CPU can read from or write to any MPR using the special `TAM` and `TMA` instructions, respectively.
2. When physical memory is accessed, the MMU reserves the address lines A13-A15 from the CPU to select one of the eight MPRs.
3. The final address is calculated by combining the CPU lines (placed at A0-A12) with the MMU lines (placed at A13-A20, where the output is the 8-bit value of the selected MPR), resulting in a 21-bit address.

Consequently, this MMU groups physical memory in 8 KB pages (13 CPU lines = 8 KB pages), which is the amount of memory the CPU can access without swapping or altering the MPR value.

Anyway, don't overwhelm yourself if this seems too complex (it is just an unconventional modus operandi some may find intriguing).

4.5 Graphics

Graphics are managed by the **Hudson Soft HuC6270**, a separate chip also referred to as the **Video Display Controller** or 'VDC'. The HuC6270 draws everything that the player sees on the screen, and its functionality is very similar to Sega's counterpart[7]. For this article, I will focus on the unique aspects of Hudson's offering.

4.5.1 Organising the content

First things first, the VDC is a **tile engine** (a standard feature until the 5th generation showed up) - but note that the PC Engine includes **64 KB of VRAM**, which is a significant amount compared to the competition. This may lead to new types of content, which we will explore later.

The arrangement of graphics data can be somewhat confusing: both the CPU and VDC use 16-bit addresses, but while the CPU can only handle 8-bit words, the HuC6270 stores 16-bit words in VRAM [71]. This means that a single address in RAM stores one byte, whereas an address in VRAM stores two bytes. Developers therefore needed to account for this discrepancy when transferring data to VRAM.

The reason for this lies in the way Hudson organised the circuitry: The VDC has a 16-bit address bus, but **only the first 15 lines are controlled** (the last one is always set to `0`), meaning odd addresses are fetched from the second byte. I am unsure why Hudson went down this path, but it would make more sense if the system had 128 KB of VRAM instead

[7] See "Sega Master System Architecture" - Section 5 "Graphics"

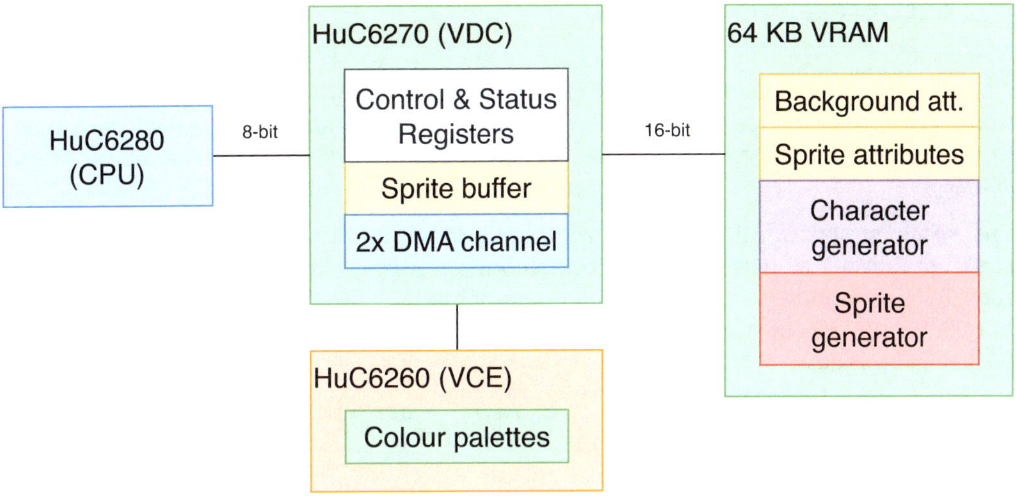

Figure 4.8: *Memory architecture of the VDC.*

(since a 16-bit address bus can only access up to 64 KB, doubling the data bus could allow up to 128 KB to be retrieved). Perhaps this was the original plan for Hudson/NEC?

4.5.2 Constructing the frame

Aside from the aforementioned granularity oddity, the VDC is functionally straightforward. The subsystem has three main components: The **VDC** and **VRAM**, which we already discussed, and the **Video Colour Encoder** (also called 'VCE'; we will examine it in due course).

The system supports **multiple resolutions**, this is because the game can modify a set of registers that act as parameters for controlling the display timings, which in turn alter the CRT's scan timings. The minimum resolution is **256 × 224 pixels** [72], while some homebrew projects have demonstrated that this system can achieve resolutions as high as **512 × 240 pixels**.

Now, let's see how a frame is drawn step by step. For this, I will borrow assets from *Bonk's Adventure*.

4.5.2.1 Tiles

As a quick reminder, tiles are simply **8x8 pixel bitmaps** that the renderer fetches to draw portions of the screen. With the VDC, the frame is composed of two planes: the background layer and the sprite layer.

Inside VRAM, there is an area called **Character generator**, where tiles exclusive to the background layer are defined. Each pixel of a tile occupies four bits, allowing to use up to 16 colours. In theory, up to 4096 background tiles can be defined, but this is reduced in practice due to VRAM being much smaller.

Sprites, on the other hand, are drawn using tiles from a separate memory location in VRAM. This is called **Sprite Generator** and differs from the previous Character generator, as tiles here are **16x16 pixels** wide.

The video encoder is a separate chip that stores **32 colour palettes** (16 for the background and 16 for sprites) [73]. Each palette stores 16 colours, and each colour is 9 bits wide (3 bits for Red, 3 bits for Green, and 3 bits for Blue).

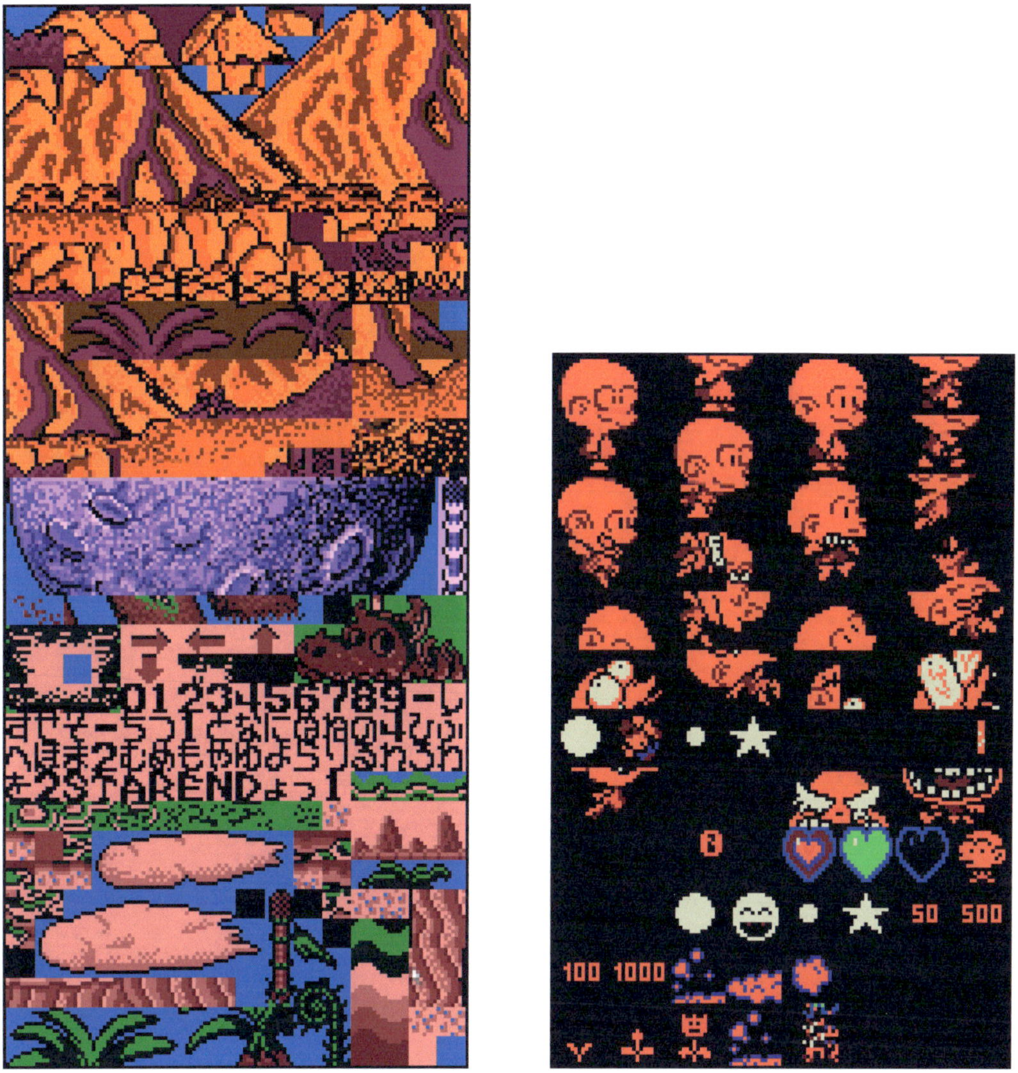

(a) *Background tiles.*

(b) *Sprite tiles.*

Figure 4.9: *The two types of tiles Found in VRAM.*

4.5.2.2 Storing tiles

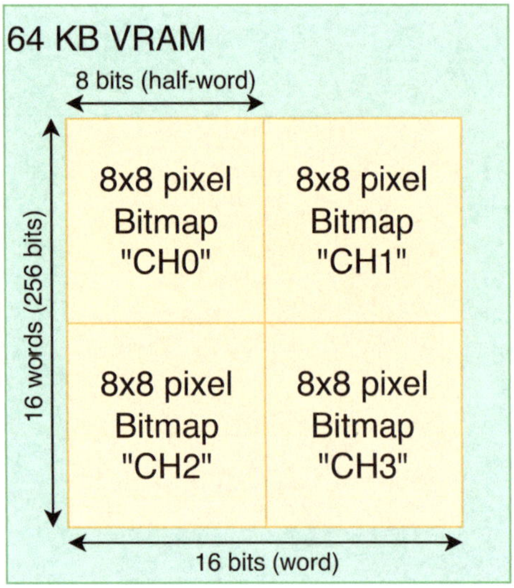

(a) *Structure of a single Background tile.*

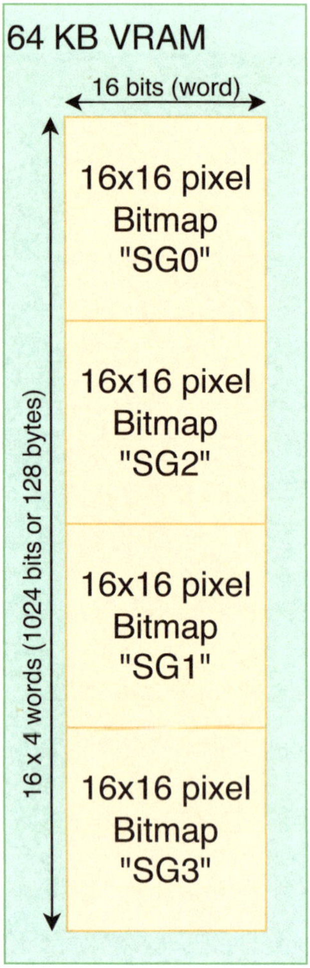

(b) *Structure of a single Sprite tile.*

Figure 4.10: *How tiles are structured in VRAM.*

(This section is written for those interested in how Hudson leveraged the 64 KB of VRAM with its 16-bit granularity, but you don't need to fully understand it to follow the rest of the article).

So far, we have discussed that each pixel of a tile is stored using 4 bits (or half a byte, also called a **nibble**). Now, Hudson dictates that **tiles are encoded as four 8x8 bitmaps** (called 'CH0', 'CH1', 'CH2', and 'CH3', respectively). Each map is 1-bit wide, but when the four are combined, they form the final tile with 4-bit pixels.

Due to the 16-bit alignment, **each 16-bit word stores a single row of two 1-bit bitmaps** (8 rows + 8 rows). So, writing eight entries results in two maps being stored (instead of just one). Please have a look at the diagrams for a clearer understanding.

The same applies to Sprite tiles, but since they are 16x16 bitmaps, each bitmap occupies 16 words. To put it another way, storing a single sprite tile requires 64 words (resulting in 8 bytes from VRAM).

4.5.2.3 Background Layer

Figure 4.11: *Rendered background layer.*

The background layer is constructed by filling the **Background Attribute Table** with entries in VRAM. The position of each entry defines the X/Y coordinates of the tile on the screen. Each entry contains the tile index from the Character Generator and the colour palette.

The maximum dimension of this layer is **1024 x 512 pixels** (128 x 64 tiles), but programmers can configure a 256 x 256 pixels (32 x 32 tiles) layer as the minimum.

As always, this layer is scrollable by changing particular registers in the VDC.

4.5.2.4 Sprite Layer

Figure 4.12: *Rendered Sprite layer.*

The VDC contains an internal memory called **Sprite Attribute Table Buffer**, where up to 64 sprites can be defined. Each entry in the table stores the independent X/Y position, colour palette, tile index, and horizontal/vertical flip. Furthermore, there is an attribute that allows to combine a sprite with another.

Each entry is 8 bytes long, although some space is wasted due to the 16-bit granularity.

To top it all off, **the CPU can't access this table**, so it must be completed in VRAM first and then transferred to the VDC via a DMA channel.

Regarding limitations, only be up to 16 sprites can appear per scan-line. On the other hand, interrupts can be configured to notify the game in case of sprite overflow or collision[8].

Figure 4.13: *Tada!*

4.5.2.5 Result

Until now, we have seen how the VDC performs most of the heavy work, but the final task is actually delegated to the **Video Colour Encoder** or 'VCE'. Found on the motherboard as the **HuC6260** chip, its primary function is to receive 9-bit data streams from the VDC, apply the colour palettes, and send the result to the TV as an analogue signal.

If you have read previous articles, you may be familiar with the importance of timing. This case is no exception: to avoid unwanted artefacts (such as 'snow'), the VCE can only be updated during a vertical interrupt.

4.5.3 Video Output

The video encoder outputs RGB (along with Sync) and YPbPr, which is ideal for use with a SCART cable or component cable, respectively. This looks promising so far...

[8] See "Sega Master System Architecture" - Section 5.3.1 "Collision detection"

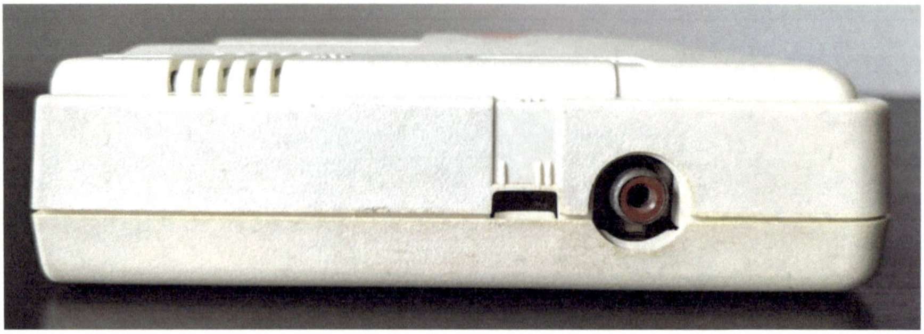

Figure 4.14: *RF port at the right side of the PC Engine.*

Figure 4.15: *The 'Turbo Booster' for the TurboGrafx-16 [3], connected to the Expansion port to supply video composite and power.*

... Unfortunately, Hudson decided to fit an RF modulator as the only way to get video out-of-the-box, so it's not that great after all. But then again, the PC Engine was designed in the 80s, so this approach guaranteed compatibility with most TVs of the same region.

On the bright side, the 'Expansion Port' exposes pins that carry RGB video and multiple sync types, but an external accessory is required to take advantage of them.

4.6 Audio

The PC Engine contains a Programmable Sound Generator[9] or 'PSG', like many other third-generation consoles analysed on this website. However, this PSG particularly relies on the **waveform memory** (also called 'waveform buffer') approach to synthesise sound, rather than using a predefined set of waveforms (e.g., pulse, triangle, etc.). Waveform memory enables programmers to define their own waveforms, which gives greater flexibility for soundtrack arrangements.

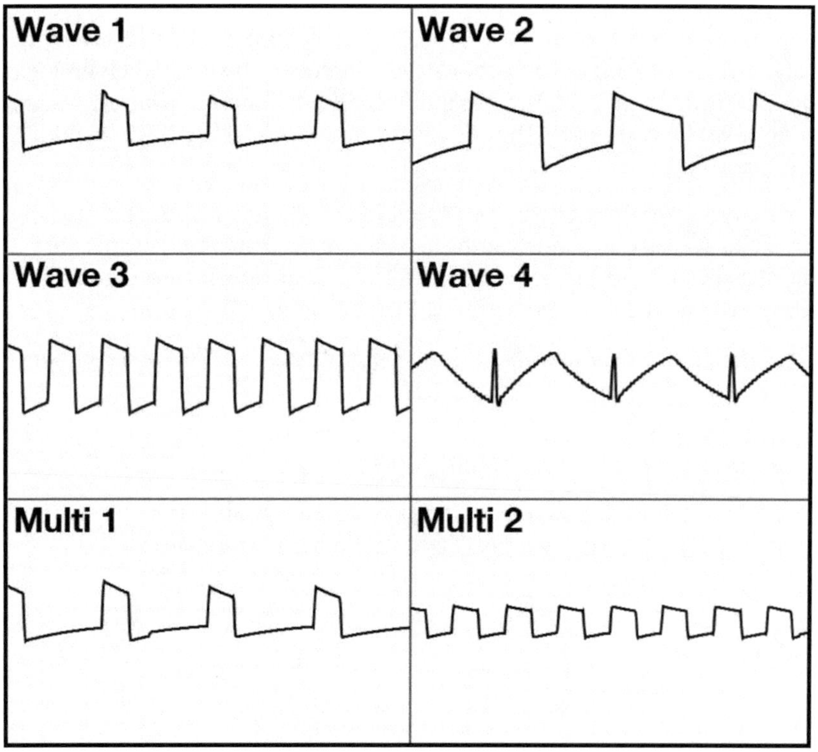

Figure 4.16: *Oscilloscope display during a game of R-Type (1987).*

The system features **six audio channels** [74], each of which is configured by writing to a set of registers. These store the attributes of the channels, including:

- **Waveform shape**: The waveform cycle is generated using thirty-two 5-bit values, each corresponding to the amplitude of the wave at a specific time.
  - Some games, such as *Fire Pro Wrestling 2* and *Bloody Wolf*, even altered these

[9] See "Sega Master System Architecture" - Section 6 "Audio"

values during playback to obtain unique sounds (at the expense of audible clicks during transfers).

- **Frequency control**: Two 8-bit registers adjust the frequency of the channel to produce different musical notes using the same waveform.
- **Amplitude level**: A single 8-bit register stores two 4-bits values that determine the volume of the channel. These values correspond to the 'Left' and 'Right' **panning control**, a pioneering feature compared to what the competition offered.

4.6.1 Extra functions

Some groups of channels have additional modes of operation. For instance, the last two channels are connected to a **noise generator**. Moreover, the second channel can act as a **Low-Frequency Oscillator** (LFO) to modulate the first channel. I initially assumed this to be a synonym for FM synthesis[10], but LFOs are more of a 'subset' that produce a **vibrato effect**.

Speaking of modes, there's another one available called **Direct D/A** (DDA), which enables the CPU to write directly to the audio buffer (bypassing the PSG). Consequently, the PC Engine can play **PCM samples**, which are still 5-bit and tightly dependent on CPU cycles. Nevertheless, two channels can be combined to reproduce 10-bit samples! [75].

All in all, this makes the PC Engine's PSG an exceptionally flexible piece of hardware.

4.6.2 Final sound

The PSG mixes all audio channels and outputs a stereo signal. But again, unless you find a way to bypass the RF port, you will only hear mono audio from your telly.

4.7 I/O

This console supported a wide range of accessories, some of which completely revamped its internal capabilities (by providing more RAM, for instance) and external functionality (e.g., by adding more ports or additional storage media).

This was largely due to the inclusion of the **Expansion Port** at the back of the console, which gave access to the following components [76]:

- A **+5 Volts line** to power the accessory.
- A **Voltage input line** to bypass the original PSU and power the console through the accessory.

[10] See "Mega Drive / Genesis Architecture" - Section 5 "Audio"

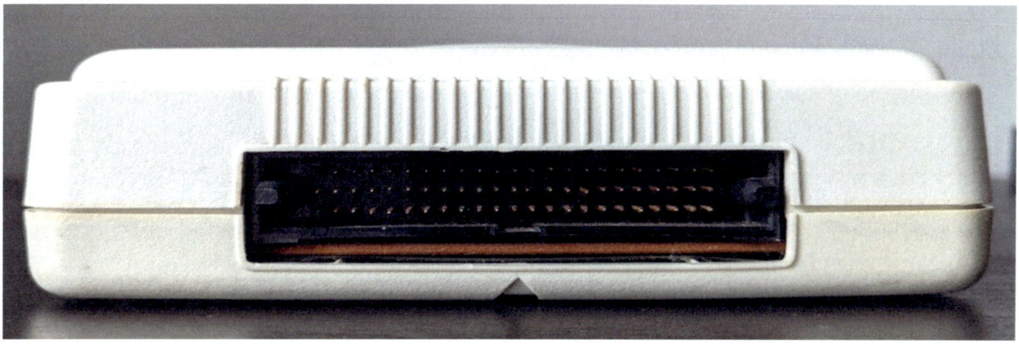

Figure 4.17: *The Expansion Port at the back of the PC Engine.*

- The **Audio Input and Output buses**, allowing to send and/or receive stereo audio.
- The **CPU data and address lines**, enabling the CPU to access the accessory and vice versa.
- The **VDC data lines**, allowing the accessory to tap into the video encoder's input. I'm not sure what for though.
- The **CPU control lines**. These expose miscellaneous information, such as the HuCard, a CD detection flag, the speed mode used, and various interrupt lines.
- The **Analogue video out**, including RGB + Vertical Sync and Horizontal Sync + Composite sync.

I'm curious to know the extent to which NEC or Hudson envisioned this console. Were they attempting to build some sort of 'modular console' that could be upgraded to seamlessly transition into the next generation?

4.7.1 The rest

I have yet to mention the controller (or Joypad, as some sources call it). It is very similar to other offerings. The console provides only one controller port, and games check a single address in memory to retrieve key presses. That address returns a 4-bit value [77].

4.8 Operating System

There is no internal ROM, 'BIOS' or any other software that runs before the game, meaning the console does not have an Operating System. The reset vector is located at addresses `$FFFE` and `$FFFF` (remember that the internal registers are 8-bit, but memory addresses are 16-bit, requiring two words to initialise the program counter). These addresses point to the game card [78].

This also means that it is the programmer's responsibility to handle 'housekeeping' (e.g., initialising memory, setting up the MMU, and so on).

4.9 Games

Programs are written in 6502 assembly, spiced with extra 65C02 opcodes and the custom instructions introduced by Hudson.

4.9.1 Standard Medium

Instead of relying on those *chunky and boring* cartridges everyone else seems to like, NEC and Hudson devised a new medium, this time with the size of a credit card, called **HuCard**. It was derived from an older medium called 'Bee Card', used in some MSX games.

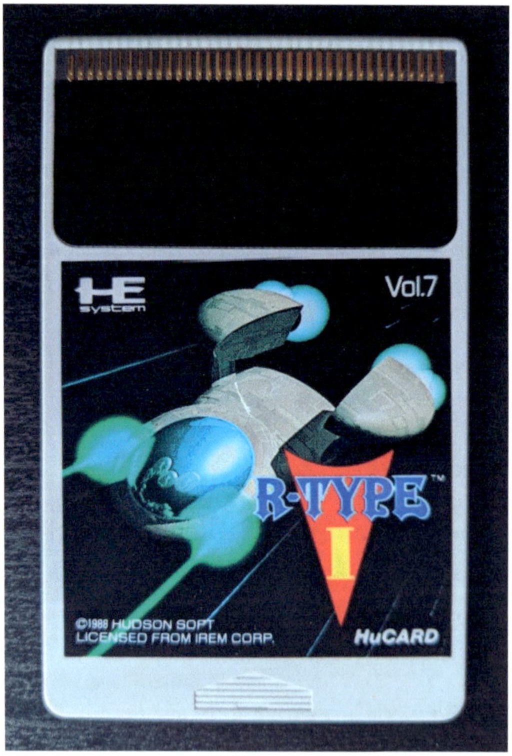

Figure 4.18: *Typical retail game.*

Interestingly, they are very similar to the Sega Card[11], featuring 38 pins instead of 35 [79]. Internally, however, the differences are more significant:

- The CPU memory map can access up to **1 MB of HuCard memory without a mapper**, which is why the majority of games were limited to 1 MB ROMs. Even so, games like 'Street Fighter II' resided in a 2.5 MB ROM! [80]
- There is an **Audio In** pin, which apparently allows the card to supply an extra audio channel.

4.9.2 CD-ROM Expansion

That expansion port opened the door to a wide range of accessories and expansion units, eventually transforming the simple PC Engine into something entirely different. As if that wasn't enough, the HuCard slot also complemented the possibilities of expansion. For this article, I will focus on the most notable upgrades, some of which were incorporated into later revisions of the console.

Figure 4.19: *CD-ROM² Reader (TurboGrafx-16 version) [3]. Were they in the Discman business back then?*

Let's take a look at the **CD-ROM²** expansion, which consists of a CD-ROM reader and a special HuCard called the **System Card**. The latter acts as a **BIOS** to bootstrap the game

[11] See "Sega Master System Architecture" - Section 9.1 "Medium"

Figure 4.20: *Base required to connect the console to the reader [3]. It also supplies power and composite video out.*

and provide routines to interface with the reader. Internally, the CD-ROM reader included **64 KB of RAM** for general-purpose use, another **64 KB of RAM** for streaming ADPCM samples, and **2 KB** for save data. As you can guess, this enabled game developers to take the advantage of extra storage and CD audio, while providing publishers with the economic benefit of distributing games on a popular medium.

Years later, NEC released another CD module called the **Super CD-ROM²**. While the reader's hardware remained mostly unchanged, its general-purpose RAM was increased to 256 KB. Customers that already owned a CD-ROM² unit could 'upgrade' it by purchasing the **Super System Card**, which included the additional RAM (and one more I/O routine!). On top of all that, NEC later shipped BIOS updates in the form of the **Arcade Card**, which now housed **2 MB of RAM**.

CD-based games relied strictly on the BIOS card they were developed for, although newer cards were backwards compatible (with some exceptions). Thus, the Arcade Card became

Figure 4.21: *How it looked with everything fitted [3].*

the preferred choice for users who wanted to play *almost* all CD-ROM-based games. I say 'almost' because third-party companies also released their own BIOS cards (e.g., the 'Games Express CD Card'), which were required to play games specifically from those studios.

With the Super CD-ROM², NEC and Hudson also shipped a new variant of the PC-Engine/TurboGrafx-16 called the **Turbo Duo**, which bundled the console, reader and BIOS card into a single package.

4.9.3 More expansions

If you are curious about other expansions, I recommend checking out the online catalogue [81].

4.10 Anti-Piracy and Homebrew

HuCards are region-locked, meaning that a PC-Engine game will not work on a TurboGrafx-16 (or vice versa) without modification. This is because the order of the data lines is inverted on the American version. However, as you can guess, this isn't something a cheap adapter can't tackle. That said, games may include routines to verify the system's region.

In contrast, CD-ROM games are neither region-locked nor copy-protected, but they still require a System Card to bootstrap, and the card itself is region-locked.

4.11 That's all folks

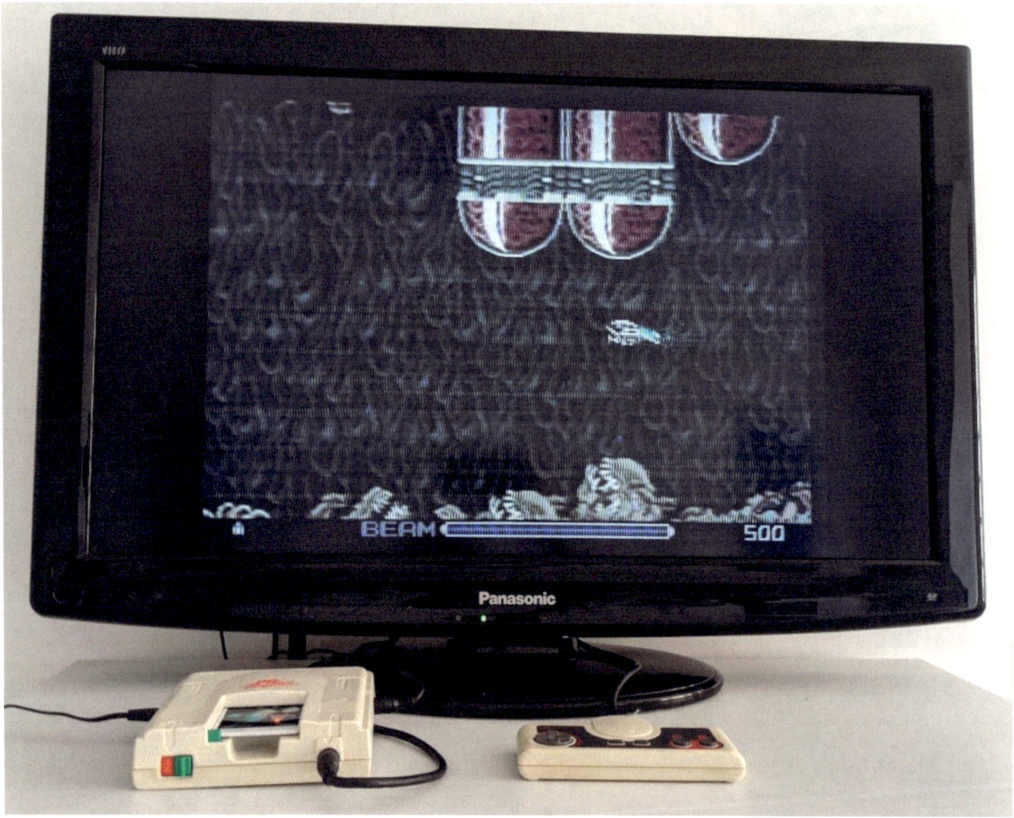

Figure 4.22: *My PC Engine connected with the RF cable (*nostalgic purposes… I think*). Big thanks to Matt for donating it!*

You have reached the final article of the year!

2020 has been an 'eventful' year for the website (setting aside the many challenges that have affected all of us). The year began with the Wii article[12] and carried on with the PS2[13], Xbox[14], Nintendo DS[15], Master System[16], and finally, this one.

The number of visitors has grown significantly too. It had a slow start at first, but during the summer, there was a remarkable increase in traffic. I would like to thank Hacker News users, OSNews, Reddit, Gigazine, YouTubers, Twitter users and many other forums and individuals for sharing the articles. And of course, a big shout-out goes to the donors whose generosity has helped keep the site afloat!

Have a nice Christmas, a Happy New Year 2021, and until next time!
Rodrigo

This article was originally published on December 18, 2020 and last updated on June 7, 2025. See the online repository[17] for the complete changelog.

[12] See "Wii Architecture"
[13] See "PlayStation 2 Architecture"
[14] See "Xbox Architecture"
[15] See "Nintendo DS Architecture"
[16] See "Sega Master System Architecture"
[17] https://github.com/flipacholas/Architecture-of-consoles

5

Mega Drive / Genesis Architecture

New techniques of composition

5.1 A quick introduction

Sega (and their TV ads) want you to know: Developers can't come up with decent games unless the console provides faster graphics and richer sounds.

Their new system includes lots of *already familiar* components ready to be programmed. This means that, in theory, developers would only need to learn about Sega's new GPU… right?

5.2 Supporting Imagery

Figure 5.1: *The Mega Drive. Released on 29/10/1988 in Japan. [3]*

Figure 5.2: *The Genesis. Released on 14/08/1989 in America. [3]*

Figure 5.3: *The Mega Drive. Released on 09/1990 in Europe. [3]*

Figure 5.4: *Motherboard [82]. Showing the Japanese 'VA0' revision. Notice the unusual daughterboard on top of the VDP used to fix post-manufacturing glitches (properly corrected in later revisions).*

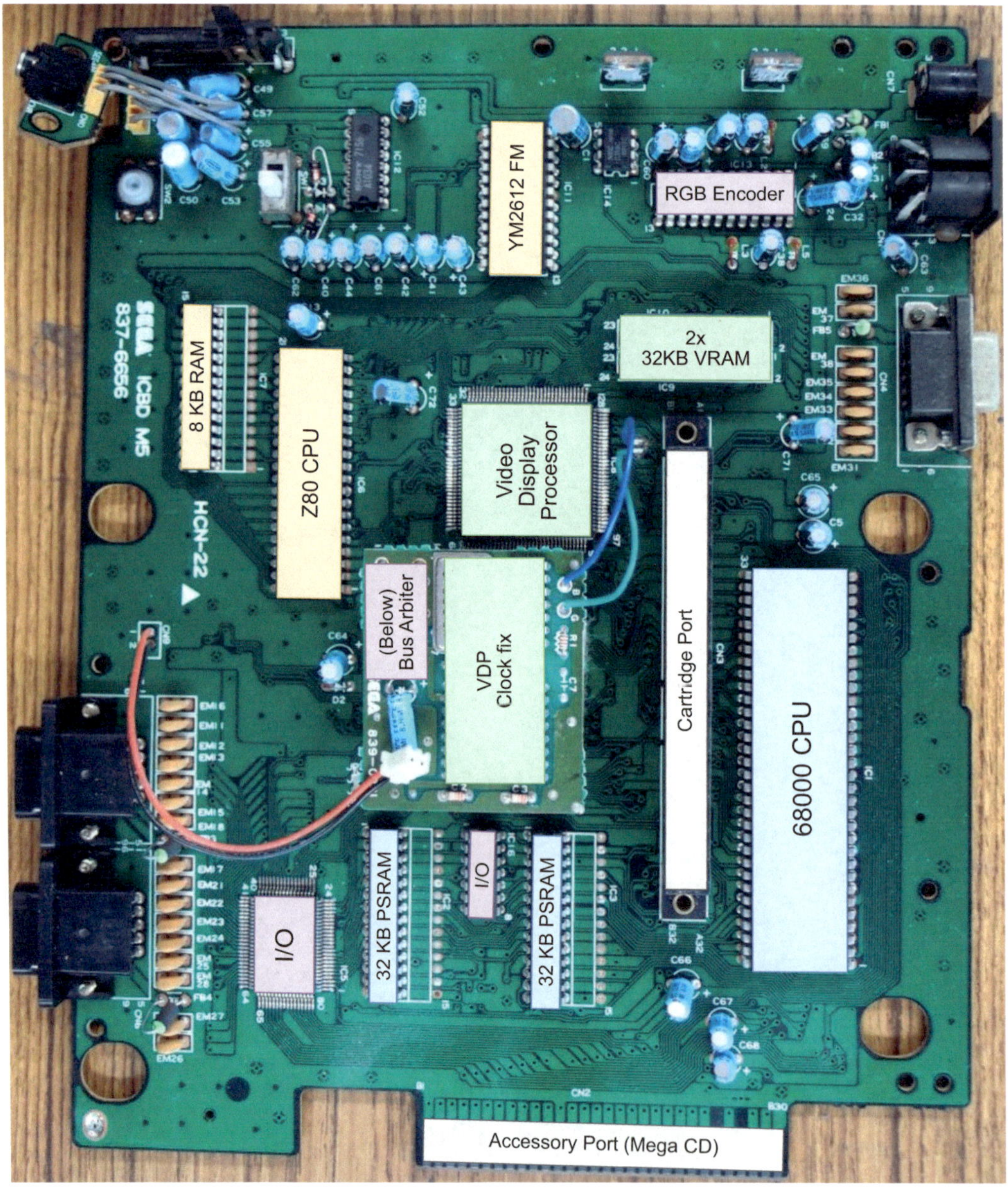

Figure 5.5: *Motherboard with important parts labelled.*

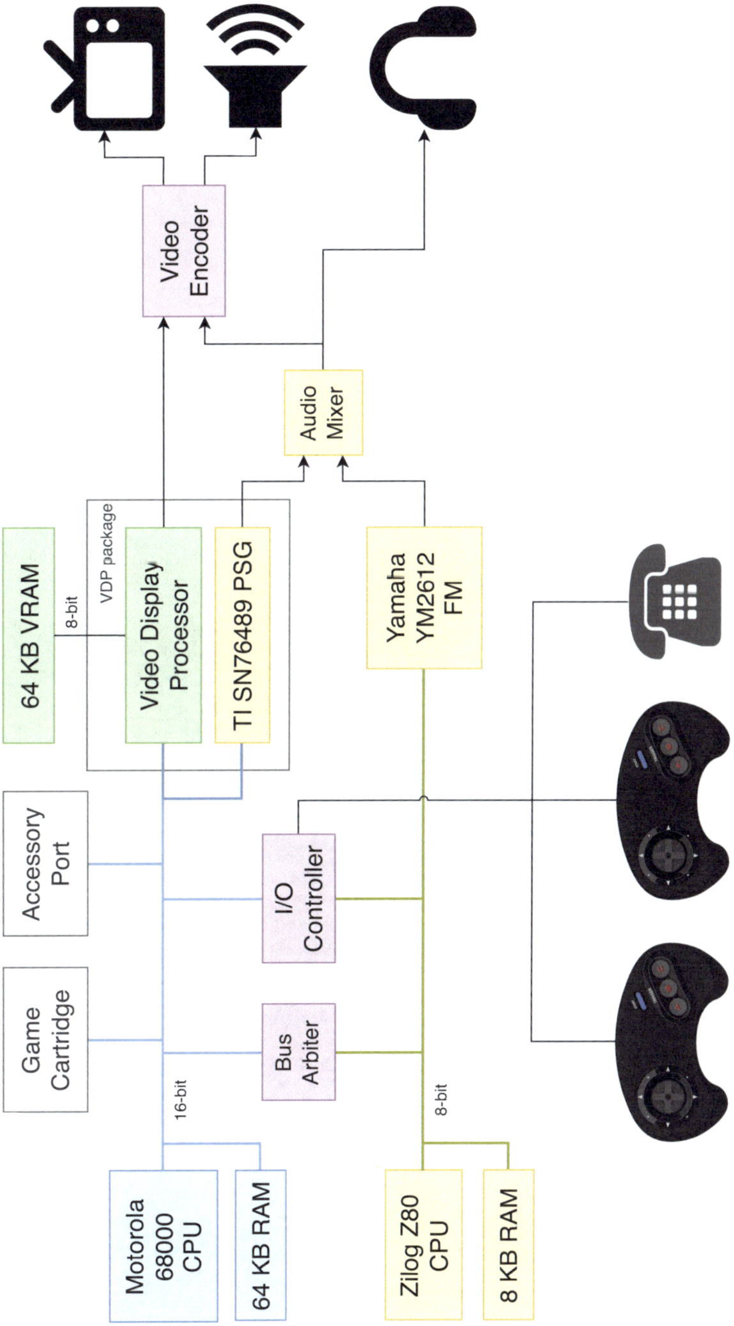

Figure 5.6: *Main architecture diagram.*

5.3 CPU

This console features two general-purpose processors from two distinct generations.

5.3.1 The leader

Firstly, we've got a **Motorola 68000** running at **~7.6MHz**. This is a new class of CPU which deserves a bit of story-telling...

5.3.1.1 Powering a decade

The Motorola 68000 or '68k' served as a generational leap in the history of microprocessors. Having learnt from the mistakes of the 6800[1], the company started over with a new team that could offer an affordable door to the 32-bit space. In there, much larger chunks of data could be processed, enabling programmers to provide new capabilities previously unknown to the consumer.

Figure 5.7: *Apple's Macintosh (1984) and Lisa (1983). While at very different price points, both relied on the Motorola 68000 to display their innovative user interface.*

Released in 1979, the 68k arrived in time to power the next decade of microcomputers. While initially struggling after loosing IBM's contract to Intel, it didn't take long until other companies and start-ups adopted this chip to power their new inventions. Some

[1] See "NES / Famicom Architecture" - Section 4.1 "A bit of context"

implemented incremental improvements over their predecessors, while others achieved unthinkable capabilities, to name a few:

- A **Graphical User Interface** (GUI). New 68k-based products from Amiga, Apple, Atari and Sinclair debuted a novel form of user interaction. This time, founded on iconography, shapes and colours - and controlled with a 'Mouse'.
- **Workstation applications**: These cost-effective machines were now capable of processing huge workloads, with some degree of specialisation. This led to the rise of networking infrastructure, graphics design and research equipment - among others.
  - This also coincided with the arrival of UNIX-based operating systems to the masses, leading to an uneasy proliferation of 'standards' and subsequent lawsuits.

It's worth pointing out that much of this functionality wasn't new - it had simply been reserved for the costly minicomputers or prohibitive mainframes. The milestone lies in the fact all of this could now be accessed from the typical office or household.

Figure 5.8: *The Motorola 68000 chip on the Mega Drive, this one is second-sourced from Hitachi.*

By the end of the 80s, however, interest in the 68000 faded in favour of a new wave of RISC CPUs[2]. Yet, prices had come down enough for companies like Sega to take an interest in bringing in it to the console market.

5.3.1.2 Features

Having set the scene, let me tell you what the 68000 provides [83]:

[2]See "PlayStation Architecture" - Section 3.1.1 "A bit of history"

- The **68000 ISA**: A new instruction set with plenty of features, including a set of multiplication and division opcodes. Some instructions are 8-bit long (called 'byte'), others are 16-bit long (called 'word') and the rest are 32-bit long (called 'long-word').
- **Sixteen general-purpose 32-bit registers**. Bear in mind, this CPU splits the set into eight 'data registers' (where arithmetic computations may be performed) and eight 'address registers' (exclusively used for storing memory addresses).
  - Nevertheless, this is a big step, considering the 6502 and Z80 only provide 8-bit registers.
- A **16-bit Arithmetic Logic Unit** (ALU): Meaning it needs extra cycles to compute arithmetic operations on 32-bit numbers, but it's fine on 16-bit/8-bit ones.
- An external **16-bit data bus**: As you can see, while this CPU has some '32-bit capabilities', it hasn't been designed to be a complete 32-bit machine. The width of this bus implies better performance when moving 16-bit data around.
  - Interestingly enough, Motorola debuted a complete 32-bit CPU, the **68020**, four years before this console's release. But I imagine costs would've skyrocketed had Sega chosen the latter chip.
- A **24-bit address bus**: This means that **up to 16 MB of memory can be accessed**. Memory addresses are still encoded with 32-bit values inside the CPU (the upper byte is just discarded).

If you wonder the reason behind using 24-bit addresses in a CPU that can handle 32-bit words: the equipment of that era was hardly asking to manage 4 GB of memory. Given that implementing unused lines is costly in terms of both performance and money, Motorola reached a sensible compromise with 32-bit registers and 24 address lines, preparing developers for the arrival of the full 32-bit CPU (the 68020) five years later.

5.3.1.3 A peculiar instruction set

Before the RISC revolution[3], there was a prior school of thought that attempted to consolidate how instruction sets were designed. In essence, consumer CPUs of the 70s (like the 6502 or the 8080) provide instructions that have already predefined how memory will be accessed (this is called the 'addressing mode'). A choice of multiple addressing modes enables the CPU to handle different use cases. However, the number of addressing modes tends to proportionally increment the complexity of the instruction set.

To remedy this, with the 68000, Motorola detached the instruction function (the 'opcode') from the addressing mode, making the latter just another parameter (or 'operand'). In doing so, developers could now use the same opcodes with their addressing mode of choice (based on their needs).

This principle is called **instruction set orthogonality**, and it greatly influenced the new generation of CPUs in the late 70s, but quickly dissipated as RISC designs[4] took over, effectively shifting the burden onto compilers. In any case, the Motorola 68k series enjoyed

[3] See "PlayStation Architecture" - Section 3.1.1 "A bit of history"

[4] See "Game Boy Advance Architecture" - Section 3.1.1 "The rise of Acorn Computers"

great popularity during the 80s decade, and it wasn't until the early '90s that companies started the switch to another vendor.

5.3.1.4 The Mega Drive's role

Within this console, the 68k serves as the 'main' CPU and it's tasked with managing game logic, handling I/O and performing graphics calculations.

Consequently, the external bus is physically connected to [84]:

- 64 KB of general-purpose RAM.
- Cartridge ROM (up to 4 MB).
- Two Controllers.
- The Video Display Processor's registers, ports and DMA.
- Motherboard's registers (identifies the console).
- Expansion ports (used for 'future' accessories).
- The second CPU's RAM, intermediated by a *bus arbiter*.
- The Texas Instruments SN76489 (a PSG, acting as the second sound chip).

5.3.2 The second banana

There's another CPU fitted in this console: a **Zilog Z80** running at **~3.5 MHz**. This is the same processor previously analysed in the Master System article[5].

With the Mega Drive, however, the Z80 was mainly designated for **sound control**. Thus, its **16-bit address space** comprises the following [85]:

- 8 KB of RAM.
- The two sound chips available.
- A dynamic chunk of 32 KB mapped to the 68000's address space, selectable via a 'bus arbiter'.
  - In practice, however, the only reliable area to access here is the cartridge ROM [86].

Finally, it's important to note that **both CPUs can run in parallel**… under certain constraints, the next paragraphs explain more.

5.3.3 Memory available

The main CPU contains **64 KB** of dedicated RAM to store general-purpose data and the Z80 contains **8 KB** of RAM for sound-related operations.

[5]See "Sega Master System Architecture" - Section 4 "CPU"

5.3.3.1 Intercommunication

Sega chose two independent processors that have **no awareness of each other**, so how can games manage both at the same time? Well, the main program is executed on the 68000, and this CPU can subsequently write to the Z80's RAM. So, the 68000 can send a program to the Z80's RAM and instruct the Z80 to load it (by sending a reset signal to the Z80) [87]. Once the Z80 is under control, it can then be used to manage the sound subsystem and move memory around using the previously described method - all while the 68000 handles other operations.

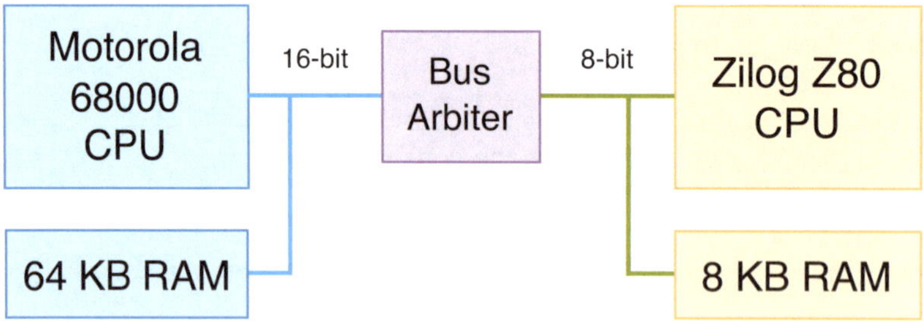

Figure 5.9: *Memory architecture of the Mega Drive/Genesis.*

There is one caveat, however: because one CPU must step into the other's bus, **both CPUs cannot access the same bus at the same time**. To address this, an extra component called **Bus Arbiter** is operated to stall either processor, enabling memory manipulation without any hazards.

It's worth noting that this design can underperform if not managed properly, so games have to take special care of the bus arbiter to ensure that neither CPU is stalled for longer than necessary.

5.4 Graphics

The answer is *Blast Processing!* What else do you need to know?

Okay, if you want to know the *real* answer: graphics data is processed by the 68000 and rendered on a proprietary chip called **Video Display Processor** (or 'VDP' for short), which then sends the resulting frame (in the form of scan lines) for display.

The VDP runs at **~13 MHz** and supports multiple resolution modes depending on the region: up to **320x224 pixels** in NTSC and up to **320x240 pixels** in PAL.

5.4.1 Behind the multiple display resolutions

Technically speaking, the VDP can fit either 40 or 32 columns of tiles[6] per scan-line, and the number of tile rows depends on the region (28 in NTSC or 30 in PAL) [88]. Although, most PAL games do not bother with the extra tiles allowed in PAL systems (as they probably need to keep consistency between the two regions, and NTSC is the common denominator) so they instruct the VDP to render with 28 rows (as in NTSC systems). Thus, the VDP has no option but to fill the unused area with a backdrop colour (also used during overscan).

You can identify which PAL games render in NTSC mode by checking the `Mode Set Register #2` in an emulator with debugging capabilities (e.g., Exodus). If the fourth bit from the right is `0`, the VDP is running in NTSC mode [89].

Figure 5.10: *To provide a quick multiplayer mode in Sonic 2 (1992), the game activates 'interlaced mode' to render a single-player level using 8x16 pixel tiles instead (along with other changes).*

Furthermore, there's an additional parameter that can be set on the VDP to stack two tiles to

[6] See "Sega Master System Architecture" - Section 5.2.1 "Tiles"

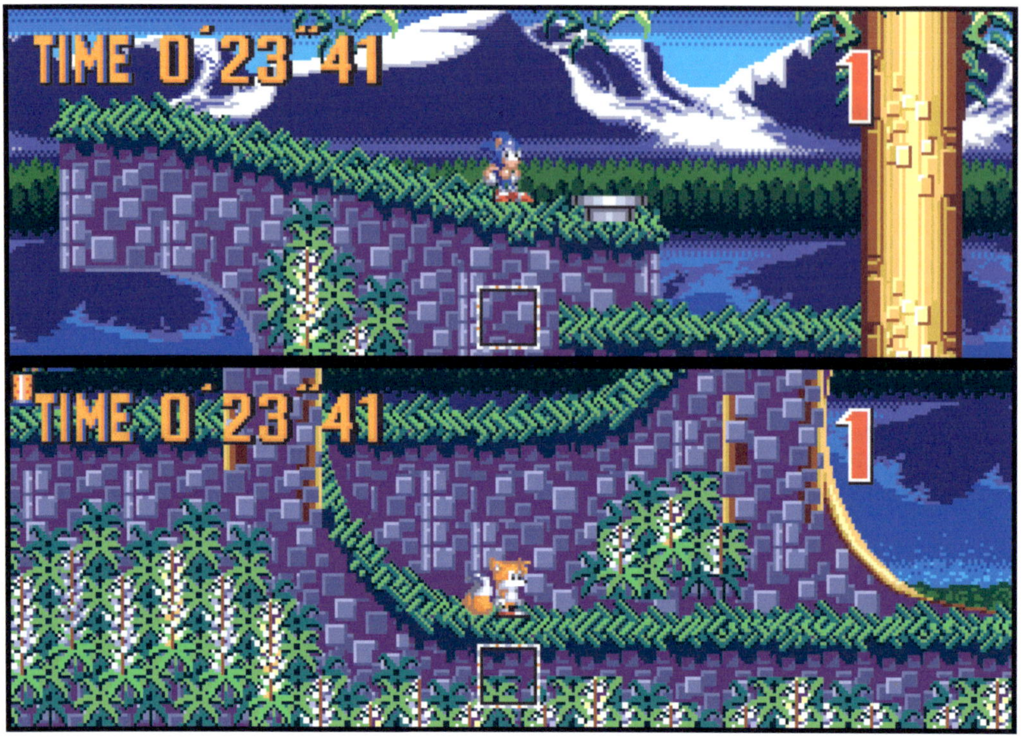

Figure 5.11: *By contrast, the more sophisticated multiplayer mode of Sonic 3 (1994) relies on dedicated 8x8 pixel tiles that are separate from single-player levels.*

form **8x16 maps** and then treat them as a single tile. Hence, doubling the vertical resolution. However, this halves the refresh rate as frames are now rendered with interlacing (one frame renders even scan-lines, the next beams odd ones, and so forth) so it's more limited in terms of functionality. The multiplayer mode of Sonic 2 is a good representation of this mode [90].

Finally, it's worth pointing out that the VDP automatically takes care of adding padding for the overscan area, so games don't have to worry about which areas are safe to draw graphics into (as it happened with the NES' 'danger zones'[7]).

5.4.2 Organising the content

In terms of processing the graphics data, this chip has two modes of operations:

[7] See "NES / Famicom Architecture" - Section 5.2 "Constructing the frame"

- **Mode IV**: The legacy mode that behaves like its predecessor[8].
  - This doesn't mean this console will play Master System games right away, as an additional accessory, the *Power Base Converter*, is required to fit previous cartridges into this console. The converter also instructs the I/O chip to place the Z80 in control.
- **Mode V**: The native mode of operation. We'll focus on this one.

What about Modes 0 to III? Well, these belong to the even older *SG-1000* and the Mega Drive does not support them.

As an interesting note, a former developer of this system told me that the command structure of Mode V (used to control the VDP) inherits the design from the TMS9918, the well-known video chip used in the SG-1000 [91]. This made it easier for third-party developers to operate Mode V without relying on official documentation (and subsequent licensing costs).

5.4.2.1 Memory available

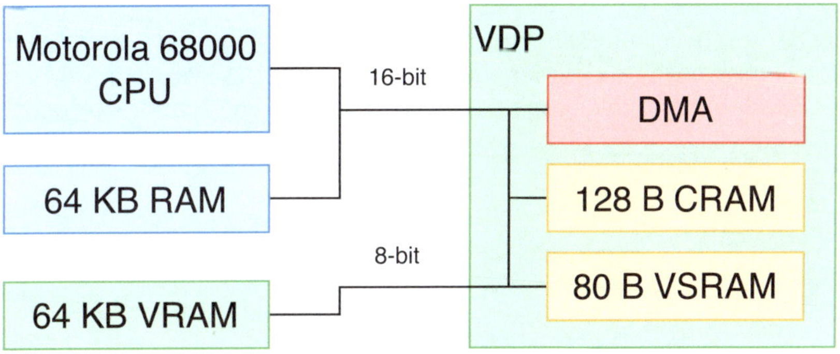

Figure 5.12: *Memory architecture of the VDP.*

The graphics content is distributed across three regions of memory [88]:

- 64 KB **VRAM** (Video RAM): Contains most of the graphics data.
- 80 B **VSRAM** (Vertical Scroll RAM): The VDP supports vertical and horizontal scrolling; and V-scroll values are stored in this separate space, for some reason.
- 128 B **CRAM** (Colour RAM): Stores four palette entries with 16 colours each (including `transparent`), the system provides 512 colours to choose from. Additionally, *Highlight* and *Shadow* effects can be applied to each palette to achieve a wider range of colours per palette.

[8] See "Sega Master System Architecture" - Section 5 "Graphics"

5.4.3 Constructing the frame

The following section explains how the VDP draws each frame. For demonstration purposes, *Sonic The Hedgehog* is used as an example. Before proceeding, I recommend checking out the *modus operandi* of its predecessor[9] since a lot will be revisited here.

5.4.3.1 Tiles

Just like Nintendo's PPU, The VDP is a tile-based engine, and as such, it uses **tiles** (basic 8x8 bitmaps) to compose graphic planes. In the case of the VDP, each tile is encoded with a 4-byte-long array, where each 4-bit entry corresponds to a pixel and its value corresponds to a colour entry (pointing to a colour palette).

Game cartridges store tiles in their **ROM** (found in their cartridge) but these must be copied to **VRAM** for the VDP to read them [92]. Traditionally, this was only possible during specific time frames and handled by the CPU, fortunately, this console added special circuitry to offload this task to the VDP (we'll get into details later on).

Tiles are used to construct a total of **four planes**, which, when merged, form the frame seen on the screen. Additionally, the tiles in these planes can overlap with each other, so the VDP determines which tile is visible based on the type of plane and the tile's **priority value**.

[9]See "Sega Master System Architecture" - Section 5 "Graphics"

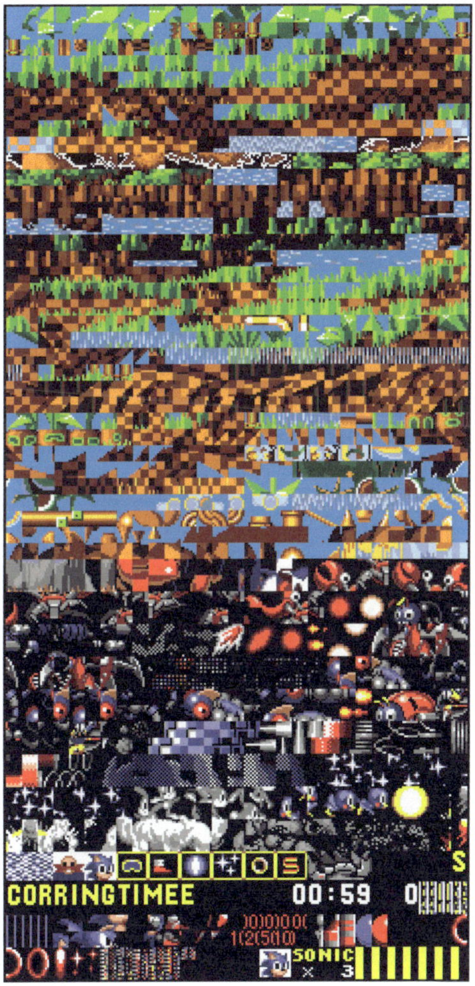

(a) *Multiple tiles squashed together. For demonstration purposes, a default palette is being used.*

(b) *A single 8x8 pixel tile.*

Figure 5.13: *Some tiles found in VRAM.*

5.4.3.2 Background

The Background plane, also known as **Plane B**, is a scrollable tilemap (set of tiles) containing **static tiles** [62].

This plane supports six different dimensions: 256x256, 256x512, 256x1024, 512x256, 512x512, and 1024x256. Programmers may select the dimension that best suits the requiring scrolling type.

Each tile can be **flipped horizontally and/or vertically** and have a **priority** set.

In the example shown (Figure 5.14), you will notice that the selected area for display is not a square... *It doesn't have to be!*. The VDP allows to set up horizontal scrolling values for the whole frame, each individual scan-line or every eight pixels. This means that developers can shape the selected area like a rhomboid and alter its angles as the player moves to simulate **perspective effects**. Tricks like this do not corrupt the plane; the VDP fetches each selected horizontal line and constructs a regular frame from it.

(a) *Allocated Background map.*

(b) *Allocated Background map with selected area marked.*

Figure 5.14: *Example of Background plane*

5.4.3.3 Foreground

The Foreground plane, also known as **Plane A** [62], shares the same properties as the Background Plane except this plane has a **higher priority**, meaning tiles rendered here will always be on top of the Background Plane.

Additionally, this plane can divide itself to form a new *sub-plane*: The **Window Plane**. The only difference is that the latter doesn't scroll.

All in all, you can see the new priority values and separate planes enable game designers to bring new types of scenery. Furthermore, by using different scroll speeds on each plane, a **parallax effect** can be achieved.

(a) *Allocated Foreground plane.*

(b) *Allocated Foreground plane with selected area marked.*

Figure 5.15: *Example of Foreground plane, the Window Plane is not used.*

5.4.3.4 Sprites

Figure 5.16: *Allocated Sprite layer.*

In this plane, tiles are treated as **sprites**. They are positioned on a **512x512 pixel** map and only a portion of it (the VDP's output resolution) is selected for display. This is convenient for hiding unwanted sprites or preparing others that will be shown in the future. The VDP also provides an old collision detection[10] function.

Sprites are formed by combining up to 4x4 tiles (32x32 pixel map) and selecting up to 16 colours (including *transparent*). If a bigger sprite is needed, multiple sprites can be combined into one.

There can only be a maximum of 20 sprites per scan-line and 80 per screen. Overflowing these limits will corrupt the entire layer.

The region in VRAM where sprites are defined is called **Sprite Attribute Table** [62] and each

[10]See "Sega Master System Architecture" - Section 5.3.1 "Collision detection"

Figure 5.17: *Allocated Sprite layer with selected area marked.*

entry contains the tile index, layer coordinates (x and y), `link` value (manages which sprites are drawn first), priority (the sprite with the highest priority is the one to be displayed during overlaps), colour palette index, and vertical and horizontal flip.

5.4.3.5 Result

While the frame is being drawn, the system sequentially calls different interrupt routines based on the position of the CRT's beam. As you have probably seen in previous consoles, this allows the CPU to prepare the next frame (or alter the current one).

Conventionally, two types of interrupts are called: **H-Blank** (at every horizontal line) and **V-Blank** (at the end of each frame).

H-Blank is called numerous times per frame, but is limited to executing short routines. V-Blank, on the other hand, allows for longer routines, with the drawback of only being

(a) *Resulting frame.*

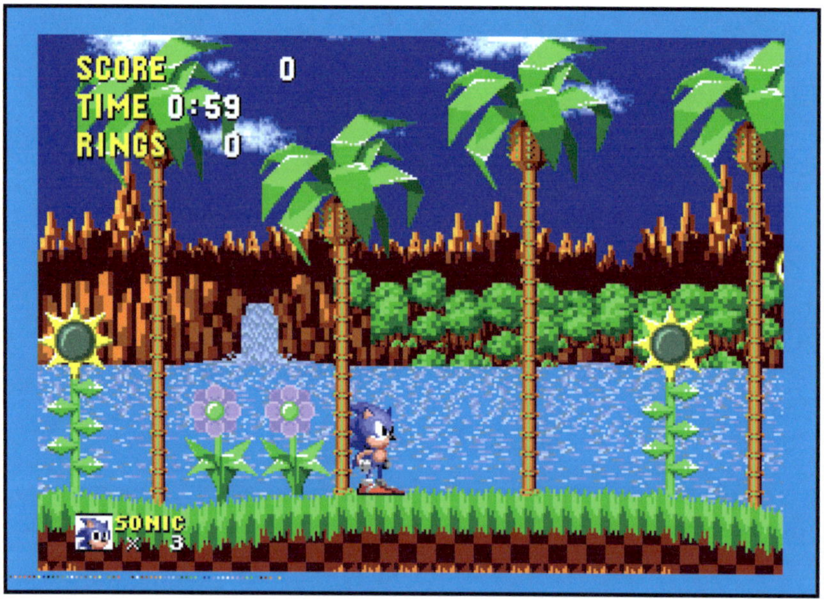

(b) *Frame broadcasted to the TV (in NTSC format). The VDP automatically adds an overscan area, which most CRT TVs will hide.*

Figure 5.18: *Tada!*

Figure 5.18: *CRAM dots in the bottom-left corner of the overscan area. Tada!*

called 50 or 60 times per second (depending on the console's region).

Notice that the overscan area in the example (Figure 5.18) exhibits some random coloured dots in the bottom-left corner. This phenomenon, known as **CRAM dots**, occurs when the CPU updates the palettes in CRAM while the VDP is beaming the remaining scan-lines (in the example, this happens during overscan). This conflict causes the VDP to fetch whatever value the CPU is writing at that moment, rather than the required location in CRAM. So, the image gets corrupted. In this particular case, the game updates CRAM only during overscan, so this anomaly goes unnoticed on traditional CRTs. At another level in the game, however, the game changes the palette mid-frame to simulate water effects. Hence, programmers tried to mask it by drawing a flickering water ripple in-between [93]. As you can see, it's all about balancing the extra colours with the CRAM side-effect.

5.4.4 A dedicated transfer unit

So far we've discussed what the CPU can do to update frames, but what about the VDP? Does it provide something more specialised? Well yes, this chip features a **Direct Memory Access** ('DMA' for short) that allows moving data between memory locations at a **faster rate** and **without the intervention of the CPU**.

The DMA can be activated during H-Blank, V-Blank, or active state (outside any interrupt) and can be used to write over VRAM, CRAM, and/or VSRAM [62]. However, during CPU RAM transfers using DMA, the CPU bus is blocked, so careful planning is critical for achieving performance.

Effective use of these features may enable high-resolution graphics, smooth parallax scrolling, and high frame rates. In the best cases, your game might even be featured in TV ads with lots of *Blast Processing!* signs over it.

5.4.5 Video Output

The first design of this console (commonly referred to as the 'Model 1') includes the same video out port as the Master System[11]. The subsequent 'Model 2' and 'Model 3' revisions switched to a mini-DIN port.

5.5 Audio

The audio capabilities of this console are somewhat unorthodox, to say the least. On one side, the Mega Drive incorporates audio technology from the previous generation. On the other hand, it introduces a novel (yet complex) synthesis technique. So, in some ways, you get two generations in a single console.

That being said, the Mega Drive is equipped with two sound chips: A **Yamaha YM2612** and a **Texas Instruments SN76489**.

5.5.1 Functionality

Let's now see what each chip offers, as they are *very* different.

5.5.1.1 Yamaha YM2612

The **Yamaha YM2612** is an **FM synthesiser** [94] that provides **six FM channels**, one of which can play **PCM samples** instead. It operates at one-sixth of the 68000's clock speed and outputs one channel at a time, but it alternates between each channel every four cycles to create the illusion of generating all six channels at once [95]. For this reason, the Yamaha YM2612's sampling rate is **~53 kHz**. Furthermore, it accepts PCM samples with a resolution of **nine bits** [96]. Yet, the ninth bit was never officially documented so commercial games only sent 8-bit samples. Apart from that, its bus is connected exclusively to the Z80.

Frequency Modulation (FM) synthesis is one of many professional techniques used for producing sound. It significantly rose in popularity during the 80s and made way to completely new sounds, many of which you can find by listening to the pop hits from that era (I would give you a list but my music taste[12] is a bit *experimental*).

In an *incredibly simplified* nutshell, the FM algorithm takes a single waveform (**carrier**) and alters its frequency using another waveform (**modulator**). The result is a new waveform

[11] See "Sega Master System Architecture" - Section 5.4 "Video Output"

[12] https://www.copetti.org/about#super-curated-repertoire

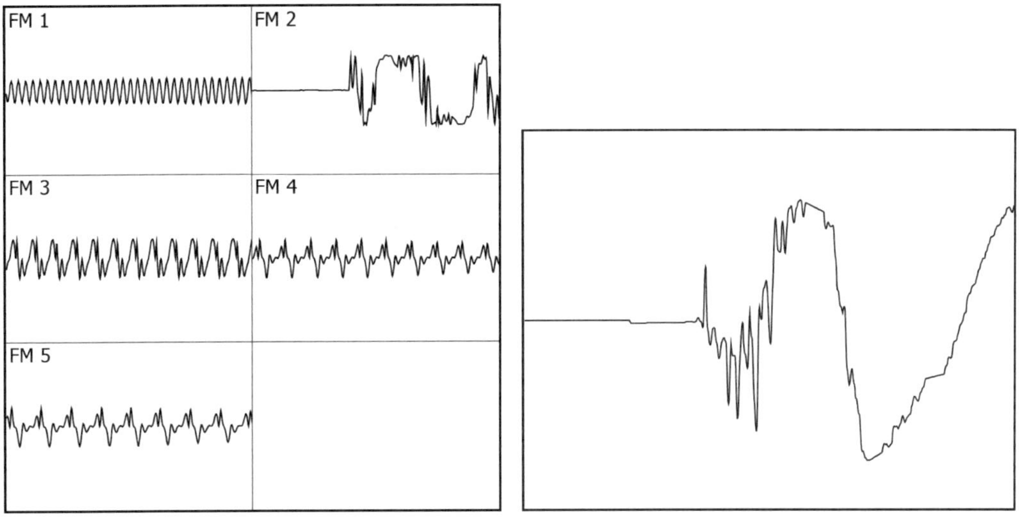

(a) *FM channels.* **(b)** *PCM channel.*

Figure 5.19: *Sonic The Hedgehog (1991).*

with a different sound. The carrier-modulator combination is called **operator** and multiple operators can be chained together to form the final waveform. Different combinations achieve different results. The YM2612 allows **four operators per channel**.

Compared to traditional PSG synthesisers, this was a drastic improvement: You were no longer stuck with predefined waveforms.

5.5.1.2 Texas Instruments SN76489

The **Texas Instruments SN76489** is a **Programmable Sound Generator** (PSG) capable of producing three pulse waves and one noise channel.

This is actually the original sound chip[13] from the Master System, now embedded within the VDP. It runs at the speed of the Z80.

Programming the PSG involves writing to a single 8-bit location (called `PSG port` [97]), which both CPUs can do so. Behind the scenes, its bus is connected only to the 68000, but the Bus Arbiter seamlessly manages access when the Z80 writes to it.

Notice in this example (Figure 5.20), the 'Pulse 3' channel remains muted. This is because the game activates a mode that reserves the third pulse for modulating the noise channel [98], a function featured on the Master System as well.

[13] See "Sega Master System Architecture" - Section 6 "Audio"

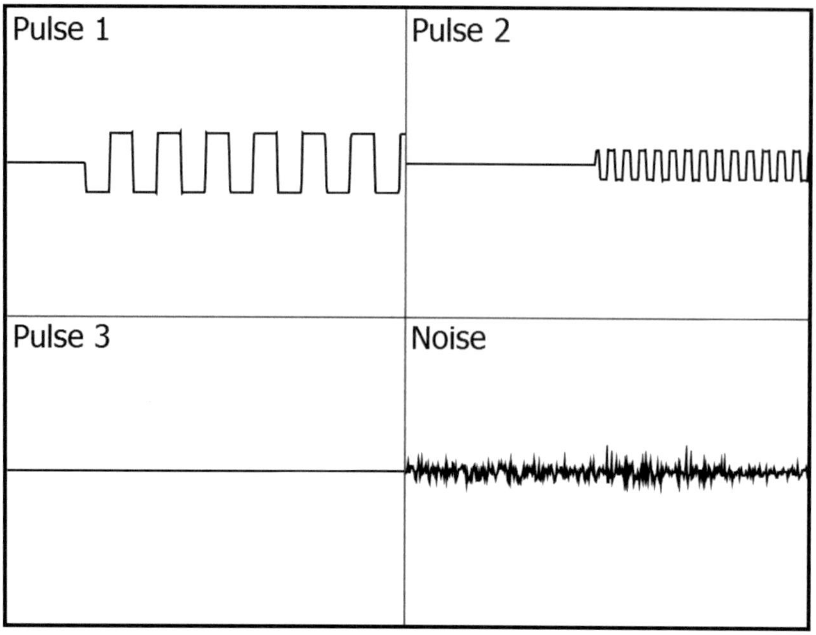

Figure 5.20: *PSG Channels. Sonic The Hedgehog (1991).*

5.5.1.3 Mixed

Both chips can output sound at the same time, then an extra component called **Audio Mixer** is responsible for receiving and combining both signals.

Finally, the resulting analogue signal is transmitted through the audio output line.

5.5.2 The conductor

The Z80 is an independent processor by itself, so it needs its own program (stored in the 8 KB of available RAM) to interpret the music data received from the 68000 or the cartridge ROM and effectively manipulate the two sound chips accordingly. This program is referred to as a **sequencer** or **driver**.

Nevertheless, the design of a sound driver is not completely dependent on the Z80 CPU. While the Z80's memory map suggests that this is the only processor capable of commanding the two audio chips in unison (which may be a relief for the 68000, as it is already fed up with other tasks), the Bus Arbiter can still shut down the Z80 to grant the 68000 access to the YM2612 [99]. This is not as efficient but it's still another option for programmers to consider. For instance, the first *Sonic The Hedgehog* implemented its sound driver on the 68000, whereas later entries offloaded this task to the Z80 [86].

5.5.3 Cracking sampling

Rather than sticking with ordinary drum kits, there have been occasions where music composers pushed the PCM channel to produce more natural sounds. Since this could only be implemented through software, games had to continuously sequence and stream their music without exceeding the Z80's limits. The main constraint was that, to fill its RAM during sequencing, the main bus had to be **blocked** first (preventing commands or samples from being sent to the audio chips during that timeframe). Otherwise, sound anomalies such as muting, frozen notes, or low sample rates could appear.

While an unaffordable challenge at first, certain games overcame this with the help of creative techniques. For instance, Traveller's Tales' *Toy Story* (1995) allocated the 68000 for sequencing the music [100]. This was a highly intensive task, meaning it could only executed at very particular points of the game, such as the main menu.

While one can argue it's still miles ahead from achieving CD-quality (16-bit at 44.1 kHz), the advancements made compared to it predecessors certainly deserve recognition. And it is always this type of skill what pushes the boundaries of music in the next generation of consoles.

5.5.4 Assisted FM Composition

Programming an FM synthesiser was already considered complicated using the Yamaha DX7's dashboard - now imagine the headaches of composing music with only 68k/Z80 assembly...

Fortunately, Sega later distributed a piece of software for MS-DOS PCs called **GEMS** to simplify the composition (and debugging) of Mega Drive music [101]. This comprehensive tool included numerous *patches* (pre-configured operators) to choose from, which may explain why some games have *very* similar sounds.

Moreover, their audio driver enabled games to instantiate more channels than the hardware allowed. With the use of **priority values**, the console played the music by dynamically dispatching channels to the available slots. Additionally, channels with high priority but no music were automatically skipped.

Channels also incorporated some **logic** by embedding conditionals within their data, allowing music to 'evolve' based on the player's progress in the game.

5.5.5 (Bonus) Mega CD Sound

Here is an interesting fact, the Mega CD add-on provided two extra channels for Audio CD (among other things). One of its most famous games, Sonic CD, featured very impressive compositions but, like all games, it had to loop. The problem was that looping tracks on a 1x

CD reader exposed noticeable gaps. So, the game included loop fillers that were executed from another PCM chip while the CD header was returning to the start.

For some reason, these fillers are only found on early betas of the game and they didn't make it for the release. However, the 2011 remake finally included them.

5.6 Games

Games are primarily written in **68000 assembly**, while the sound driver is implemented in **Z80 assembly**. Both reside in the cartridge ROM and can be to 4 MB in size without the need for a mapper[14].

5.6.1 Extra functions

In terms of expandability, this design wasn't as modular as the NES[15] or the SNES[16]. Hence, later add-ons like the 32x (which included a new chipset that took over the 68k) had to bypass the VDP, necessitating the use of a 'Connector Cable'.

Only one custom chip was produced for cartridges: the **Sega Virtua Processor** (SVP) [102], a rebranded Samsung SSP1601 (itself a 16-bit Digital Signal Processor). The new chip produced polygons that were subsequently encoded as tiles for the VDP to read. In any case, only one game shipped with it, as the SVP proved too expensive to manufacture.

5.6.2 Early network attempts

Before online services became widely adopted and standardised, Sega tried its luck with **Sega Meganet**, a dial-up service for games to use. Meganet required users to purchase a separate accessory called the *Sega Mega Modem*, plug it to the back of the console (where the DE-9 connector is), and finally connect it to the phone line. Games treated the modem unit as another controller, with the addition of communicating with it serially [103] (as opposed to the parallel encoding used for controllers).

Be as it may, this feature only lasted a couple of years before Sega removed the DE-9 connector in later revisions and discontinued the service entirely.

[14] See "NES / Famicom Architecture" - Section 4.3.3 "Going beyond existing capabilities"
[15] See "NES / Famicom Architecture"
[16] See "Super Nintendo / Famicom Architecture"

5.7 Anti-piracy / Region Lock

To block imported games, Sega slightly altered the shape of the cartridge slot between regions, although it kept the same pinouts. Games could also perform 'region locking' by checking the value of the `Version` register, which outputs the console's region code.

There were two simple ways to bypass this: purchasing a third-party cartridge converter or disassembling the console and bridging the pins on the motherboard to alter the value of the `Version` register.

When it comes to software anti-piracy measures, the easiest check involved verifying the SRAM size. Bootleg cartridges often bundled more space than needed to fit any title, so games checked for the expected size during startup. Programmers could also implement extra checksum checks at random points in the game to counteract attempts to bypass the initial SRAM checks. The only way to defeat this was to painstakingly find all the checks and remove them one by one…

5.8 That's all folks

This article was originally published on May 18, 2019 and last updated on June 7, 2025. See the online repository[17] for the complete changelog.

[17] https://github.com/flipacholas/Architecture-of-consoles

6

Super Nintendo / Famicom Architecture

Old hardware with mind-blowing features

6.1 A quick introduction

It seems Nintendo managed to deliver the next generation of graphics and sound without using expensive off-the-shelf components. But there's a catch: the new console was also **designed with expandability in mind**. In a world where CPUs are evolving faster than the speed of light, Nintendo ultimately relied on game cartridges to make its console shine.

6.1.1 Models and revisions

Kids across the globe saw this console in various shapes, colours, and names. Nevertheless, the internal differences were less noticeable. As you may already know, due to the spread of analogue standards, models from different regions exhibit variations in their analogue signals (e.g., video output) to accommodate these differing standards. Compared to its predecessor[1], however, the architectural differences are less pronounced. For instance, on this occasion, Nintendo did not include exclusive circuitry for audio expansion[2], which significantly impacted the quality of games across regions.

The company did ship hardware revisions during its lifespan, but their main purpose was to reduce the number of dedicated components on the motherboard, thereby lowering manufacturing cost.

[1]See "NES / Famicom Architecture"

[2]See "NES / Famicom Architecture" - Section 6.2.1 "Extra Channels"

6.2 Supporting Imagery

Figure 6.1: *The Super Nintendo (in Europe) or Super Famicom (in Japan). Released on 21/11/1990 in Japan and 11/04/1992 in Europe. [3]*

Figure 6.2: *The Super Nintendo. Released on 13/08/1991 in America. [3]*

Figure 6.3: *Motherboard [104]. Showing revision 'SNS-RGB-CPU-01'. Earlier revisions had the Sound Subsystem connected as a daughterboard, later ones unified both PPUs.*

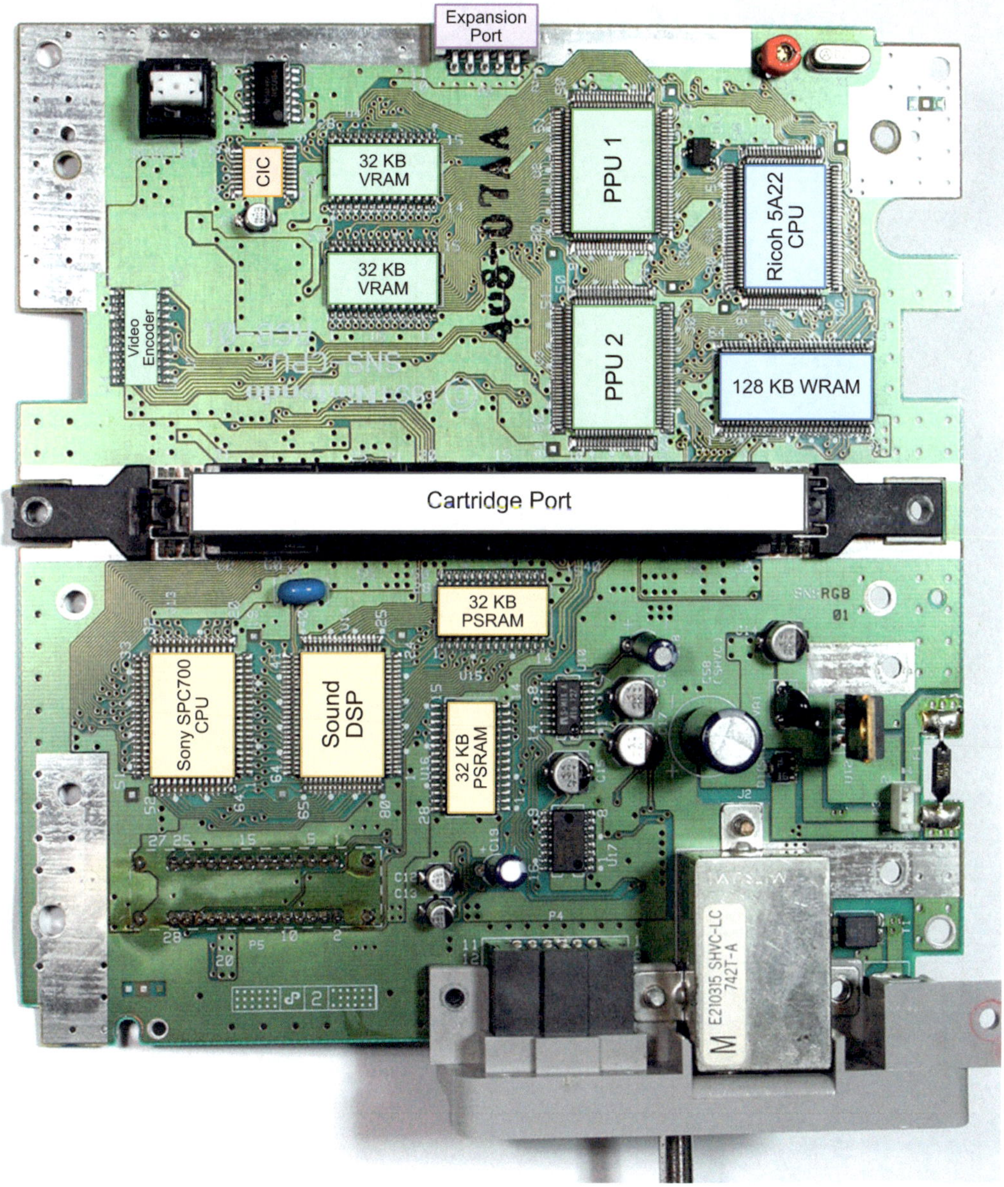

Figure 6.4: *Motherboard with important parts labelled.*

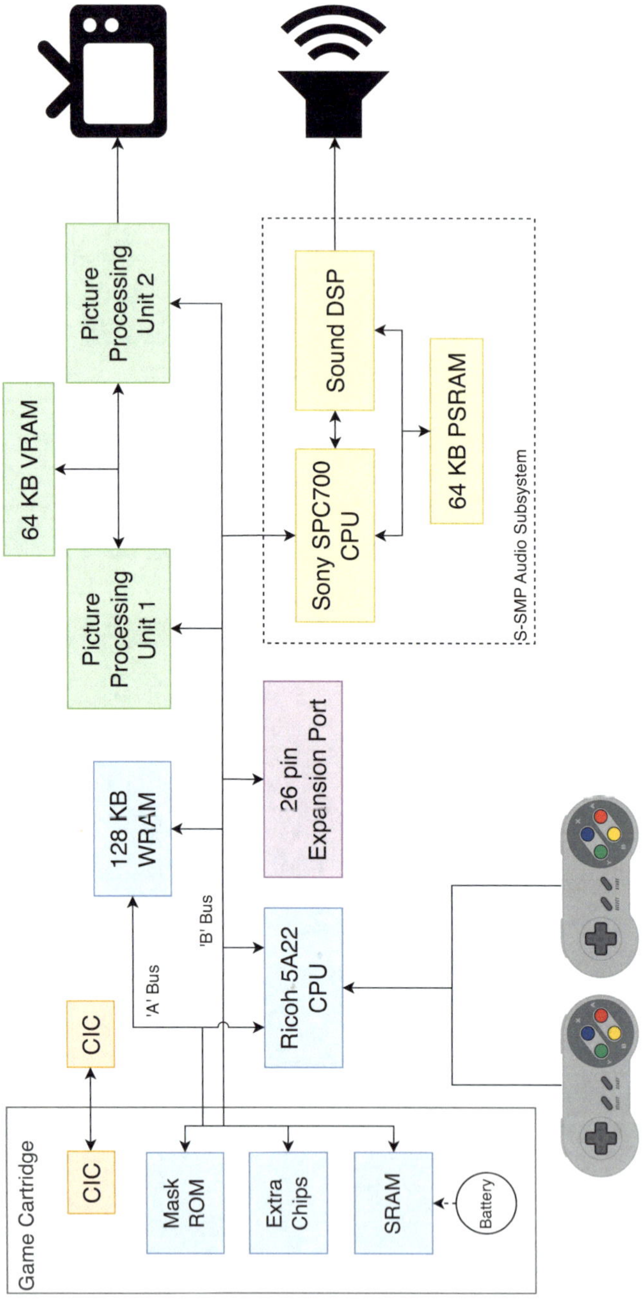

Figure 6.5: *Main architecture diagram. Bus 'A' and 'B' are address buses, the data bus follows the trail of bus 'B' and it's 8 bits wide.*

6.3 CPU

The Super Nintendo's choice of processor is a peculiar one. Unlike its competition[3] bundling a fully-fledged 68000, the SNES' chip is not a radical departure from its predecessor. To recap, the NES employed a modified 6502[4] CPU, an admired ingredient of late-70s and early-80s computers. Now, to pave the way for the new decade (the 90s), Nintendo opted for a more conservative (and cheaper) solution: the **WDC 65C816**, a 16-bit extension of the 6502.

6.3.1 Modernising the 6502

The 65C816 CPU originates from Western Design Center (WDC), particularly from Bill Mensch, a former member of the 6502 team (at MOS) and the 6800 team (at Motorola). In 1978, one year after leaving MOS, Mensch founded Western Design Center, a semiconductor company that produces clones of the MOS 6502 with attractive enhancements (e.g., CMOS design, extra opcodes, circuitry fixes, new addressing modes, etc.).

Figure 6.6: *The WDC 65C816 chip found on the Apple IIGS.*

One day, Apple approached WDC to design a backwards-compatible variant of the 6502 that could process larger amounts of data. This resulted in the WDC 65C816 CPU, released in 1983. Curiously enough, Apple encountered many setbacks during the development of a

[3]See "Mega Drive / Genesis Architecture" - Section 3 "CPU"

[4]See "NES / Famicom Architecture" - Section 4.2 "Core functionality"

computer that would use the new CPU, until three years later, with the release of the Apple IIGS.

Figure 6.7: *In the end, the Apple IIGS and the Super Nintendo became the only major adopters of the 65C816 CPU.*

Meanwhile, Nintendo was enjoying a good relationship with Ricoh and their set of bespoke chips for the NES. I haven't found the exact document outlining what connected Ricoh to WDC, but what I can confirm is that at some point in time, WDC agreed to license their 65C816 designs to Ricoh [105]. Consequently, the latter tailored it to meet the new requirements of the Super Nintendo, it became the **Ricoh 5A22** and was exclusively supplied to Nintendo.

6.3.2 The new CPU

As you've seen before, the main processor of this console is the **Ricoh 5A22**, a superset of the 65C816.

Figure 6.8: *The Ricoh 5A22 chip, labelled 'S-CPU' by Nintendo.*

Unlike the Apple IIGS, which enjoyed backward compatibility with Apple II software, the Super Nintendo is **not compatible with NES games**. To be fair, based on the choice of processor, there's a slight possibility that the SNES was originally planned to be compatible with NES games, who knows.

Moving on, the CPU employs a **variable clock speed**, reaching up to **3.58 MHz** for register operations and dropping to **1.79 MHz** when accessing the slowest buses (i.e. the serial/controller port).

Now, to properly understand the functionality of the 5A22, we must first look at what the 65C816 provides:

- The **65816 ISA**: The debut 16-bit instruction set of the 65C816. It is based on the 6502 ISA but does not implement undocumented instructions that some NES games resorted to [106].
  - The size of instructions can vary between 1 byte (8 bits) and 4 bytes (32 bits), depending on how memory addresses are referenced (a.k.a. the 'addressing

mode' used) [107].
  - The broken BCD mode[5] is **functional** again (I'm guessing as a consequence of *appropriate* licensing).
- **10 different modes of operation**: Due to a combination of backwards compatibility with the 6502, the return of the BCD mode (missing on the NES), and the ability to switch between groups of 16-bit and 8-bit registers [68], developers can utilise this CPU using different combinations of these.
  - Unlike later MIPS CPUs[6], there isn't a mixed instruction set with dedicated opcodes for 8-bit and 16-bit words. Instead, the same instruction set is interpreted differently depending on the mode activated.
  - For compatibility reasons, the CPU always starts in 'emulation' mode (pure 6502), and it is up to the program to switch to a particular 'native' mode to enable 16-bit functionality. On a side note, it is amusing how Intel's x86 still follows the same modus operandi[7] in their modern CPUs.
- **Three 16-bit general-purpose registers**. This set matches the 6502's (`X`, `Y` and `A`). However, due to the different modes of operation, these registers can now switch between 16-bit and 8-bit.
  - Compare this number to the sixteen 32-bit registers[8] the competition offered - quite a contrast!
- **16-bit internal data bus** and an **8-bit external data bus**: This results in performance penalties when moving values larger than 8 bits across memory (as the CPU requires additional cycles), a common occurrence considering most instructions are 16-bit long. However, the overall impact is alleviated thanks to Ricoh's DMA units (explained later on) and the variable clock speed.
- **24-bit address space**: Allows the CPU to access **up to 16 MB worth of memory**. This is similar to the Motorola 68000[9], except the 65C816 obtains its 24-bit addresses by combining extra 8-bit registers (`DBR` and `PBR`) with the original 16-bit addressing lines of the 6502 [108]. Overall, this methodology is similar to housing an internal mapper[10].

Looking at this, I have to confess that the 65C816 feels excessively cumbersome for little gain. Compared to other offerings such as the Motorola 68000[11], it is not difficult to conclude why the Apple IIGS remained the only personal computer to adopt the 65C816. Nonetheless, throughout this article, you will see how Nintendo and Ricoh managed to turn the limitations of this CPU into opportunities to revamp its game library.

---

[5] See "NES / Famicom Architecture" - Section 4.2.2 "Scrapped functions"
[6] See "Nintendo 64 Architecture" - Section 3 "CPU"
[7] See "Xbox Architecture" - Section 7.1 "Boot Process"
[8] See "Mega Drive / Genesis Architecture" - Section 3.1 "The leader"
[9] See "Mega Drive / Genesis Architecture" - Section 3 "CPU"
[10] See "PC Engine / TurboGrafx-16 Architecture" - Section 4.1 "Memory access"
[11] See "Mega Drive / Genesis Architecture" - Section 3.1 "The leader"

6.3.3 Ricoh's additions

In 1983, the 65C816 CPU was conceived as a general-purpose successor of its 1975 ancestor, with all the associated requirements and constraints. Yet, Nintendo planned its console to last throughout the 90s, meaning Ricoh had to step up its game (if you'll pardon the pun).

First on the list was tackling its arithmetic limitations - the 65C816 lacks dedicated instructions for multiplication or division. As a result, Ricoh incorporated **multiplication** and **division units**, enabling the CPU to perform these types of operations via hardware (rather of software). Instead of conventional instructions, they are operated through registers.

The multiplier receives 8-bit numbers and outputs 16-bit ones [109]. Conversely, the divider takes a 16-bit dividend and an 8-bit divisor; and returns a 16-bit quotient along with a 16-bit remainder [110]. Both units only support positive numbers (called 'unsigned').

Now, you may be wondering 'why is this relevant?'. The significance of these additions will become clear when we explore the novelties of the Super Nintendo's graphics chips (in the 'Graphics' section).

6.3.3.1 Speedy memory access

The second challenge was to increase its data bandwidth. Hence, **two exclusive DMAs** (Direct Memory Access) were added to move data around without the intervention of the CPU, resulting in faster speeds. For this design to work, regions of memory are referenced using two distinct address buses [111]:

- A **24-bit 'A Bus'** controlled by the CPU: Connects the cartridge, CPU, and WRAM.
- A **8-bit 'B Bus'** controlled by the S-PPU: Connects the cartridge, CPU, WRAM, S-PPU, and the Audio CPU.

When setting up a DMA transfer, the *origin* bus must differ from the *destination* bus.

Furthermore, the two DMAs are not identical and serve very distinct functions [112]:

- The **General-Purpose DMA** performs transfers at any time, temporarily halting the CPU until the transfer is finished.
- The **Horizontal DMA** (HDMA) performs a small transfer after each horizontal scan (while the CRT beam is preparing to draw the next row). This prevents prolonged CPU interruption, but transfers are limited to 4 bytes per scanline.

Finally, the system provides **eight channels** for DMA transfers, enabling to dispatch up to eight independent transfers at once.

6.3.3.2 The 16-bit Segmentation Fault

The primitive Open Bus behaviour[12] is also present in this console. Furthermore, there has been speculation about the existence of an internal register called **Memory Data Register** (MDR), which is believed to store such values [113].

For comparison, the 68000 employs a vector table to handle exceptions, ensuring execution is redirected whenever a fault is detected.

6.3.4 (Lots of) more memory

It's fascinating to realise how much content the NES managed to display with only 2 KB of RAM[13]. Well, the Super Nintendo now features **128 KB of SRAM** (still referred to as 'Work RAM' or WRAM) - a staggering 6400% increase in general-purpose memory compared to its predecessor.

So, what can developers do with this? Anything they desire, really. WRAM is used to store variable data for the game. The more space available, the greater the amount of information that can be stored and processed (thus, reducing reliance on cartridge hardware[14]).

However, as the following sections will demonstrate, the Super Nintendo is a fairly complex machine (albeit its 'simplistic' CPU). I tend to call this console a 'collection of mini-computers/subsystems'. Each subsystem may need data from the CPU, meaning programmers may reserve portions of WRAM to process that information - thus justifying the need for 128 KB of memory.

6.4 Graphics

After everything discussed so far, let me tell you that the graphical subsystem of this console is a true feat of engineering. Given its constrained CPU, one might assume the SNES could never cast a shadow on its competitor[15], which boasts a '32-bit' Motorola 68000. Yet, Nintendo and Ricoh engineers devised clever tricks that exploit the behaviour of CRT displays, effectively expanding the console's capabilities without the need for expensive, state-of-the-art components.

Before diving deeper into this topic, I strongly recommend reading the NES article[16] first, as it introduces key concepts that will be revisited here.

[12] See "NES / Famicom Architecture" - Section 4.3.1 "Segmentation Fault"
[13] See "NES / Famicom Architecture" - Section 4.3 "Memory"
[14] See "NES / Famicom Architecture" - Section 4.3.2 "Cartridge/game data"
[15] See "Mega Drive / Genesis Architecture"
[16] See "NES / Famicom Architecture" - Section 5 "Graphics"

6.4.1 Design

As with any other console of its generation, the Super Nintendo draws graphics using 2D tiles (8 x 8 pixels). The NES initially achieved this through it signature **Picture Processing Unit** (PPU), which beams the image in sync with a CRT screen. The Super Nintendo follows suit but incorporates more sophisticated techniques to obtain richer results.

6.4.1.1 The chipset

The Super Nintendo houses two different PPU chips that constitute the graphics subsystem, collectively known as the **Super PPU** or 'S-PPU'.

Figure 6.9: *The two PPU chips.*

Each PPU package serves specific functionality [111]:

- **PPU 1**: Renders graphics (tiles) and applies transformations such as rotation and scaling.
- **PPU 2**: Provides visual effects, including windowing, mosaic, and fading, over the rendered graphics.

This separation, from a programming perspective, is redundant, as both chips are effectively treated as a single unit.

6.4.1.2 Display modalities

The NTSC system outputs a standard resolution of **256 x 224 pixels** at **~60 Hz** [114]. The European variant, adhering to the PAL specification, outputs **256 × 240 pixels** at **~50 Hz**.

Be as it may, most games do not utilise the additional pixels and instead display a *letterbox* (black lines).

Now, here's the tricky part: traditional TVs have an aspect ratio of 4:3. Yet, if you do the math, the Super Nintendo's output resolution has an **aspect ratio of 8:7**. Consequently, once the image is beamed on the TV, it looks **horizontally stretched**, resembling a **292 x 224 pixels** frame instead (in the case of the NTSC variant) [115]. Put simply, pixels on the Super Nintendo have an aspect ratio of 8:7, rather than being 'perfectly square'.

The reasoning behind Nintendo's deviation from the standard aspect ratio boils down to **cost**. You will soon see that the S-PPU is very rich in functionality, but not fast enough to render everything at the pace of the CRT beam [116]. Rather than adding more circuitry to the board, Nintendo opted to short the width of the visible image, allocating extra space for the horizontal blanking period instead.

Nevertheless, some games like 'Chrono Trigger' account for this factor by intentionally using squashed shapes, which then look correct after being stretched by the TV. This, however, remains an exception, since the majority of games take no extra measures to compensate for this effect.

(a) *Rendered frame with a resolution of 256 x 224 pixels. This is what the console sends to the TV.*

(b) *Stretched frame as seen from the TV (with an apparent resolution of 292 x 224 pixels).*

Figure 6.10: *Kirby's Dream Land 3 (1997).*

6.4.2 Organising the content

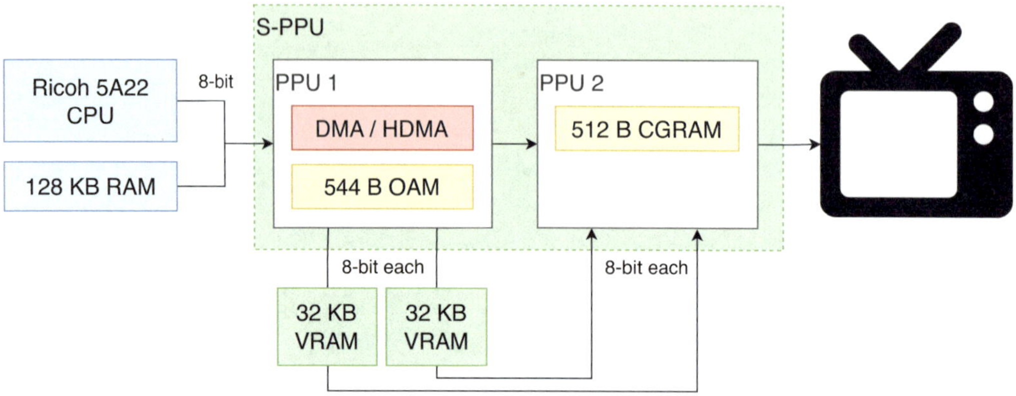

Figure 6.11: *Memory architecture of the S-PPU.*

Due to cost and performance reasons, graphics data is distributed across three memory regions:

- 64 KB **VRAM** (Video RAM): Stores tiles and maps (tables) used to build background layers.
- 512 B **CGRAM** (Colour Graphics RAM): Fits 512 colour palette entries, with each entry occupying a *word* (16 bits).
- 544 B **OAM** (Object Attribute Memory): Contains tables referencing 128 tiles that will be used as *sprites*, along with their attributes.

VRAM is implemented using **two 32 KB chips**, each accessed simultaneously via a separate 8-bit bus. This allows the PPU 1 to fetch 16-bit values per cycle, making it particularly efficient for retrieving multiple consecutive pixels in real time [117]. Additionally, each VRAM chip is connected to a dedicated 16-bit address bus, rather than a shared one. This will prove useful when the PPU 1 needs to switch to alternative memory arrangements - something we'll explore in more detail when we talk about 'Mode 7'.

6.4.3 Constructing the frame

Let's now see how a frame is rendered on the console and subsequently displayed on TV. For demonstration purposes, *Super Mario World* will serve as example.

6.4.3.1 Tiles

Just like its predecessor, the S-PPU uses tiles to build sophisticated graphics. Although, there are significant improvements compared to the original PPU:

Figure 6.12: *Some 16x16 Tiles found in VRAM.*

- **Game cartridges are no longer wired to the PPU**, meaning tiles must first be copied to VRAM (similar to Sega's Mega Drive[17]). This is where the DMA unit becomes very handy.
- **Tiles are no longer restricted to their traditional dimension** (8x8 pixels) - they can now be up to **16x16 pixels** wide.
- When tiles are stored in memory, these are **compressed based on colour depth** (in other words, the number of colours per pixel). The unit of measurement for this is **bpp** (bits per pixel). The minimum value is **2 bpp**, meaning each pixel occupies two bits and has only 4 colours available. The maximum is **8 bpp**, allowing for 256 colours per pixel (at the expense of consuming a full byte of memory).

(a) *Background Layer 1 (BG1).*

(b) *Background Layer 2 (BG2).*

Figure 6.13: *Background maps in VRAM.*

Figure 6.13: *Background Layer 3 (BG3).*
Background maps in VRAM.

6.4.3.2 Background

The Super Nintendo can generate up to four different background planes. Using either 8x8 or 16x16 tiles, blocks[18] are made of 32x32 pixels (2x2 tiles). That being said, each background layer can extend up to 1024x1024 pixels in size (32x32 tiles). The region in VRAM where these layers are configured is called **Tilemap**, and is structured as a table (continuous values in memory).

Each Tilemap entry contains the following attributes:

- Vertical and horizontal flip values.
- Priority (either `0` or `1`).
- Palette reference from CGRAM.
- Tile reference.

As always, these planes are scrollable. However, the number of features available - such as colour depth, number of layers, independent scrolling regions, and size of selection - depends on the **Background Mode** activated on the S-PPU, which brings us to the next section...

[17] See "Mega Drive / Genesis Architecture" - Section 4 "Graphics"

[18] See "NES / Famicom Architecture" - Section 5.2.2 "Background Layer"

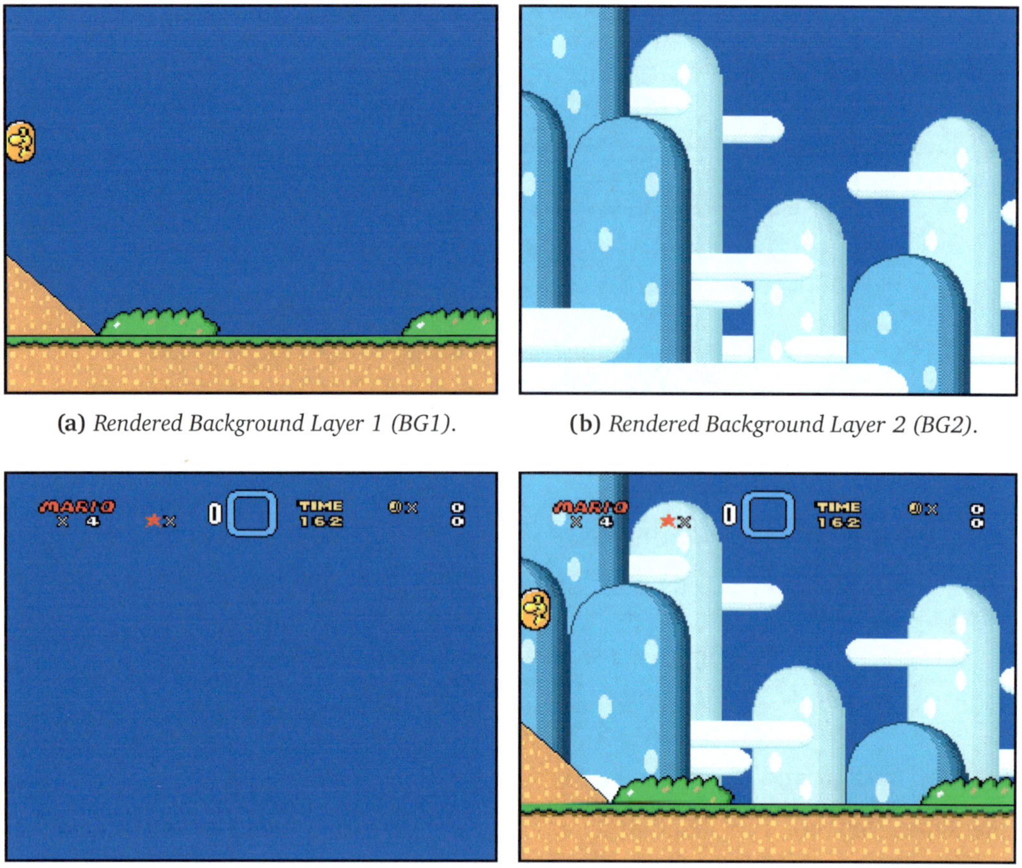

(a) *Rendered Background Layer 1 (BG1).*

(b) *Rendered Background Layer 2 (BG2).*

(c) *Rendered Background Layer 3 (BG3).*

(d) *Rendered Background Layers combined.*

Figure 6.14: *Rendered Background layers after selection and transparency are applied.*

6.4.3.3 Modes

The S-PPU provides many operations for backgrounds, but these cannot be chosen arbitrarily. Instead, programmers must choose from **eight background modes**, each offering a distinct set of features [118]:

- **Mode 0**: 4 layers with 4 colours each.
  - The colour palette is particularly bland, as this mode prioritises the highest number of layers.
- **Mode 1**: 2 layers with 16 colours each + 1 layer with 4 colours.
  - One layer can be split into foreground and background.
  - This is the most commonly used mode.

- **Mode 2**: 2 layers with 16 colours each.
  - There is an extra effect available: layers can have each of their columns scrolled independently (similarly to the Game Boy wobble effect[19] but applied vertically).
- **Mode 3**: 1 layer with 256 colours + 1 layer with 16 colours.
  - Colours can be defined using RGB values instead of referencing CGRAM.
- **Mode 4**: Mode 2 and 3 combined (Column scroll + RGB colour mapping).
  - The first layer supports 256 colours, while the second is limited to just 4 colours.
- **Mode 5**: 1 layer with 16 colours + 1 layer with 4 colours.
  - The selected area features an outstanding resolution of **512 x 224 pixels**, which will be horizontally squashed to fit on the screen (the final output remains 256 x 224 pixels!). This comes at the cost of rendering 16 x 8 pixels tiles as 8 x 8 ones, and 16 x 16 pixels tiles as 8 x 16 ones.
  - Furthermore, the vertical resolution can be extended by activating **interlacing**, reaching **512 x 448 pixels**, which now maintains correct proportions with the output frame. In exchange, interlacing applies the same squashing effect to tiles - this time vertically. This is useful when displaying larger amounts of information (e.g. multiplayer or split-screen).
- **Mode 6**: A combination of Mode 2 and 5 (high resolution + column scrolling), though it is restricted to a single layer with 32 colours.

As you can see, programmers can now decide whether to prioritise colour depth, number of layers, special effects, or resolution.

6.4.3.4 Sprites

A dedicated memory region called **Object Attribute Memory** (OAM) stores a table with references of up to 128 sprites, each with the following properties [119]:

- **Size**: The S-PPU can combine up to 16 tiles into a 4x4 tile quadrant to build a sprite.
- **Tile references**: Specifies the tiles used to draw the sprite.
- **Screen position**: Only sprites within the visible area will be rendered.
- **Priority**: Since multiple layers overlap, the graphic with the highest priority will be shown. Priority is also determined by the background mode in use.
- **Colour palette slot**: Allows selection from 9 palette slots in CGRAM.
- **X/Y Flip**: Enables horizontal and vertical flipping.

The S-PPU can render **up to 32 sprites per scanline**; overflowing this will only make the S-PPU discard the ones with the lowest priority.

[19] See "Game Boy / Color Architecture" - Section 4.3.1 "Wobble effect"

Figure 6.15: *Rendered Sprite layer.*

6.4.3.5 Result

The S-PPU renders each scanline on-the-fly, first processing the relevant portion of each layer and then mixing them.

One of the key constraints of NES games was that graphical updates could only occur during **V-Blank** - the brief interval when the CRT beam was returning to the starting point provided a reasonable time frame to reshuffle some tiles without breaking the image.

Well, now thanks to the enhanced capabilities of the SNES, this limitation now takes on a different meaning.

You see, because the new DMA/HDMA units enable programmers to perform memory transfers without waiting for V-Blank [120], games can now update tiles, colours, and registers without waiting for the entire frame to be drawn. In fact, the possibilities extend even further: since games can now **modify S-PPU settings mid-frame**, it becomes possible to **activate different background modes at different stages within the same frame**, unlocking new and original game designs!

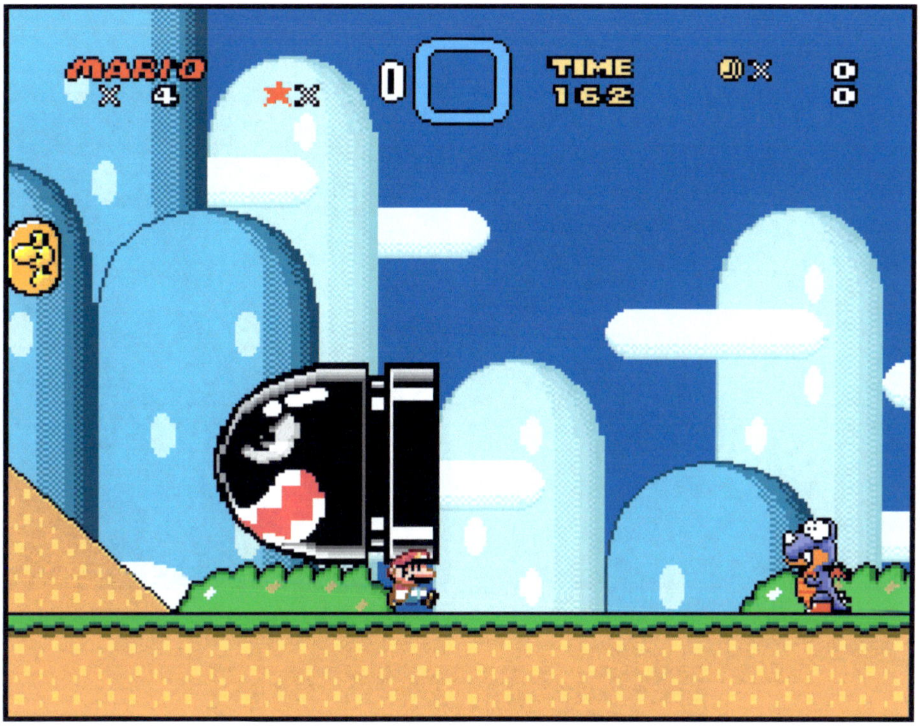

Figure 6.16: *Tada!*

6.4.4 *That* feature

Truth to be told, I still haven't mentioned the most important characteristic of this console...

Introducing **Mode 7**, *yet another* background mode - but this time, with a completely different way of working. While it can only render a single 8 bpp background layer, it provides the exclusive ability to apply the following **affine transformations** on that plane [118]:

- Translation.
- Scaling.
- Rotation.
- Reflection.
- Shearing.

Mode 7 is controlled via a **rotation matrix**, which alters its parameters. Without delving into linear algebra, depending on the desired effect, the CPU must perform some trigonometric functions (sine and cosine) to populate the entries of this table accordingly. This

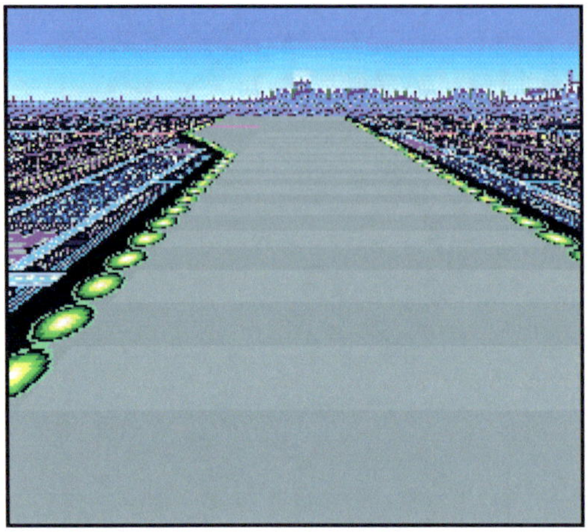

(a) *Rendered Background layer.*

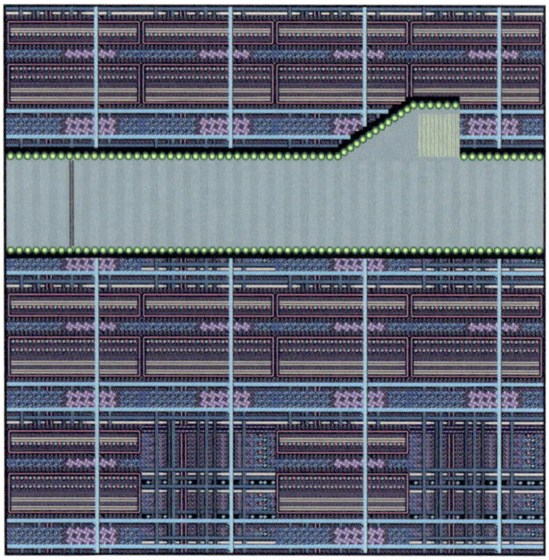

(b) *Allocated Background map.*

(c) *Rendered frame on the screen. The first quarter of scan-lines uses another mode to simulate distance, Mode 7 starts at the second quarter (this is possible thanks to HDMA).*

Figure 6.17: *Deconstruction of F-Zero (1990).*

is computationally expensive for the 65C816, even when using fixed-point precision. For this reason, with the 5A22, Ricoh integrated multiplication and division registers to offload some cycles.

By the way, you may notice that the list of transformations does not mention **perspective**, despite its presence in the example game, F-Zero (Figure 6.17). This effect is achieved by adjusting the rotation matrix at each HDMA call, creating a pseudo-3D effect in the process. This should give you an idea of just how versatile the S-PPU truly is!

Finally, due to the use of affine transformations, it is no longer useful to fetch adjacent pixels from VRAM. So, to maintain acceptable bandwidth, the memory map is restructured in a way that benefits the new pipeline. Thus, the first VRAM chip stores the **Tilemap** (where tiles are referenced), while the second stores the **Tileset** (where tiles are stored). Considering entries in both tables are 8 bits long, this setup allows the PPU 1 to retrieve references and tiles in a single cycle.

6.4.4.1 Generous circuits

Since Mode 7 requires additional computations, the PPU 1 incorporates dedicated circuitry to process the rotation matrix. Now, here is the interesting part: **it also exposes the registers for developers to access** when idle (in other words, when using Mode 0 to 6, or during V-Blank) [109].

The PPU 1's multiplier is both faster and more capable than the CPU's, as it accepts 16-bit numbers, both positive and negative (signed).

Reflecting on this 30 years later, I must say this concept is an earlier precursor to computer shaders[20].

6.4.5 More colour magic

Behind every rich frame is a flexible rendering pipeline. Well, if all the previous advancements weren't impressive enough, the S-PPU features a **versatile colour blender** that enables to customise how layers are merged. Unlike other sprite engines with fixed rendering steps, Nintendo's engineers exposed multiple parameters within the S-PPU's pipeline, enabling developers to alter how certain pixels of different layers interact to form the final frame.

This functionality is collectively known as **Color Math** [121], but it is also called 'Screen Addition/Subtraction' - despite also supporting division by two. In any case, this pave the way for **realistic transparency, dynamic lighting, and other creative effects**.

In essence, the process works as follows [122]:

1. Internally, the S-PPU houses two rendering pipelines: **Main Screen** and **Sub Screen**, where programmers can assign backgrounds layers and the sprite layer to each.

[20] See "Xbox 360 Architecture" - Section 4.5 "The impact on the industry"

(a) *The lamp sways along with the light, such daunting effect is accomplished by altering the S-PPU's masking options.*

(b) *The parrot follows you around with a torchlight, which can point to either direction and bounce. This plays very well with the overall atmosphere.*

Figure 6.18: *Donkey Kong Country (1994) exploited the capabilities of the S-PPU's blender to astonishing levels.*

    - The Sub Screen can also be filled with a solid colour instead of receiving layers.
    - High-resolution modes (Mode 5 and 6) consume the Sub Screen's resources, preventing Color Math from working in those modes.
2. The pixels of both screens can be masked using individual window parameters.
3. The S-PPU separately merges the background layers within Main and Sub Screen, respecting the priority of each layer and window settings.
4. Finally, the S-PPU lets programmers decide how to merge the content of Main Screen and Sub Screen. It can **add** or **subtract** the two screens, and then **divide** the result by two (achieving transparency effects).
    - Division by two is computationally cheap in digital circuits, as it only requires to shift the value one position to the right.

In the second *Donkey Kong Country* example (Figure 6.18), Main Screen consists of a single white layer, while Sub Screen contains the rest of the scenery. However, the latter is encoded with **inverted colours**. At the last stage of the pipeline, the S-PPU applies subtraction and division, producing a correctly coloured frame with transparency effects and enhanced brightness - effectively simulating the torchlight.

6.4.6 Cause of frame drops

On a different topic - what causes games to lag? When the V-Blank interrupt is triggered to allow graphics updates, the game may still be executing heavy code, causing it to miss the V-Blank window. As a result, graphics cannot be updated until the next V-Blank call, and since the frame remains unchanged, this manifests as a drop in frame-rate [123].

Conversely, extensive processing during a V-Blank can block the S-PPU from outputting the video signal, as the bus remains occupied. This can lead to black lines appearing during a scan, though this effect is barely noticeable since the frames refresh 50 or 60 times per second.

6.4.7 A convenient video out

All of the aforementioned advancements would be meaningless unless the console could transmit its picture to the TV through a medium both can understand. With the Super Nintendo, the company debuted some sort of *universal-but-proprietary* connection called **Multi Out**, capable of carrying many types of signals at the same time, including **Composite**, **S-Video** and **RGB** [124].

Nintendo bundled a 'Multi Out-to-Composite' cable with the console, as composite video was pretty much the common denominator of TVs at the time.

In Europe, however, the **SCART** port was widely popular, particularly among set-top boxes and VCRs. A major advantage of SCART is its ability to support multiple signal types, allowing AV equipment to select the most optimal format without compatibility issues.

As far as I know, only French consumers were offered an official SCART cable that took advantage of the RGB pins exposed on the Super Nintendo [125].

Consequently, Nintendo altered the pinout of its PAL consoles to comply with the SCART protocol, replacing the 'composite sync' pin with a 12-volt signal - which instructs the TV to use a 4:3 aspect ratio. Thus, while Multi Out is theoretically universal, RGB cables, if any, are region-specific.

I think the practical benefits of Multi Out have become more apparent in recent years, as it allows users to leverage the RGB output on their modern tellies without tampering with the console's internals. However, unlike Composite and S-Video, RGB requires an extra 'sync' signal. For this, cables can be wired up to capture the sync signal from Composite or S-Video - or for best results, use a dedicated sync line called 'composite sync'. Unfortunately, as noted earlier, the latter signal is exclusive to NTSC consoles.

6.5 Audio

Just like its graphical abilities, the audio department of this console has undergone a significant overhaul. I would argue it even offers the most advanced synthesising techniques of its generation.

6.5.1 Architecture

Some companies partnered with Yamaha[21], while others devised an in-house solution[22]. Well, Nintendo partnered with **Sony** - the electronics conglomerate behind the *Walkman* - to supply a sophisticated synthesiser.

And so, Sony delivered quite an audio subsystem, consisting of the following components:

- **The S-DSP**: Plays **ADPCM samples** across **eight channels**, they are mixed and sent through the audio output. The S-DSP processes samples with **16-bit resolution** at a **32 kHz** sampling rate, and offers various sound manipulation techniques:
  - **Stereo Panning**: Distributes audio channels to create a stereo soundscape.
  - **ADSR Envelope Control**: Adjusts how the volume changes over time.
  - **Delay**: Simulates echo effects. It also includes a frequency filter to cut out selected frequencies during the feedback (not to be confused with *Reverb*!).
  - **Noise generator**: Generates pseudo-random waveforms resembling white static.
  - **Pitch modulation**: Allows some channels to influence each other's pitch, similar to FM synthesis (used by its competitor[23]).

[21] See "Mega Drive / Genesis Architecture" - Section 5 "Audio"
[22] See "PC Engine / TurboGrafx-16 Architecture" - Section 6 "Audio"
[23] See "Mega Drive / Genesis Architecture" - Section 5 "Audio"

- **The SPC700 CPU** (also known as 'S-SMP'): An independent 8-bit CPU that drives the S-DSP and receives commands from the main CPU [126].
- **64 KB of PSRAM**: Stores audio data and programs, with the main CPU responsible for loading content into it.
  - If 'Delay' is enabled, some memory is reserved for feedback data. This is can be dangerous - if not managed carefully, feedback storage could override existing data!

The audio subsystem operates in parallel with the main CPU. When the console powers on, the SPC700 boots a 64-byte internal ROM that sets it up to receive commands from the main CPU [127]. After this setup, it remains idle until instructed.

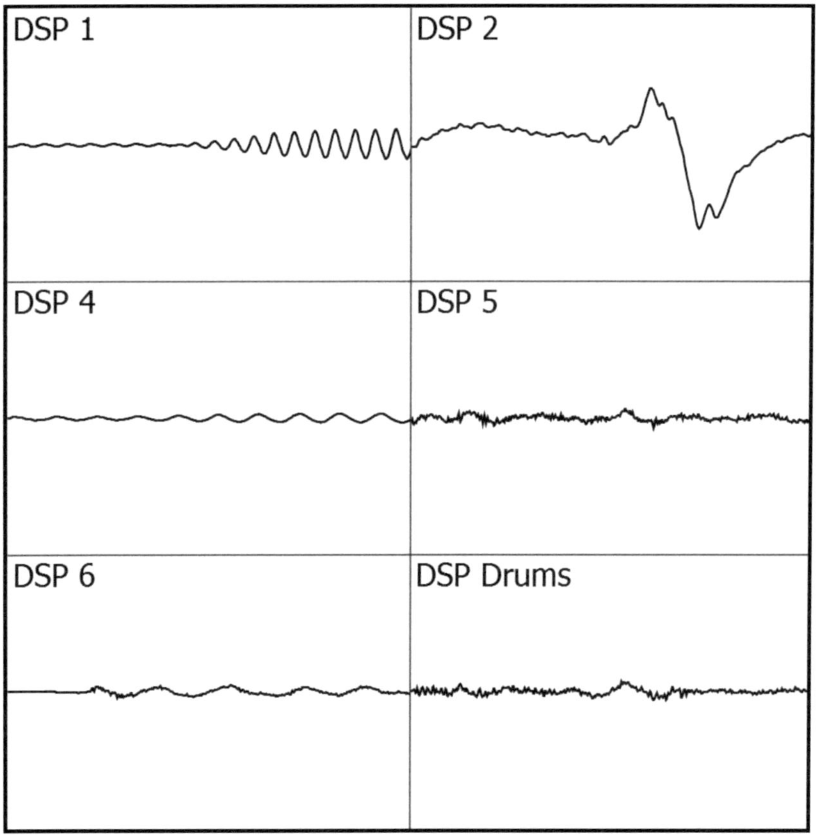

Figure 6.19: *All audio channels.*
Oscilloscope display of Star Fox (1993).

For the S-SMP to do independent work, it needs to load a type of program known as **Sound Driver**. This software instructs the chip on how to manipulate raw audio data sent by the main CPU to PSRAM, as well as how to control the S-DSP.

As evident, the sound subsystem was a major leap forward compared to previous generations, but it also posed significant programming challenges. The documentation provided by Nintendo was infamous for its vague explanations and omission of critical features, forcing developers to conduct their own research.

As a result, a wide variety of sound drivers emerged in the market [128], with some uncovering impressive capabilities.

6.5.2 Evolution from the NES

To visualise the evolution of sound from the NES to the Super Nintendo, here is an excerpt from two music scores - one from an NES game and another from its Super Nintendo sequel. Both feature the same composition.

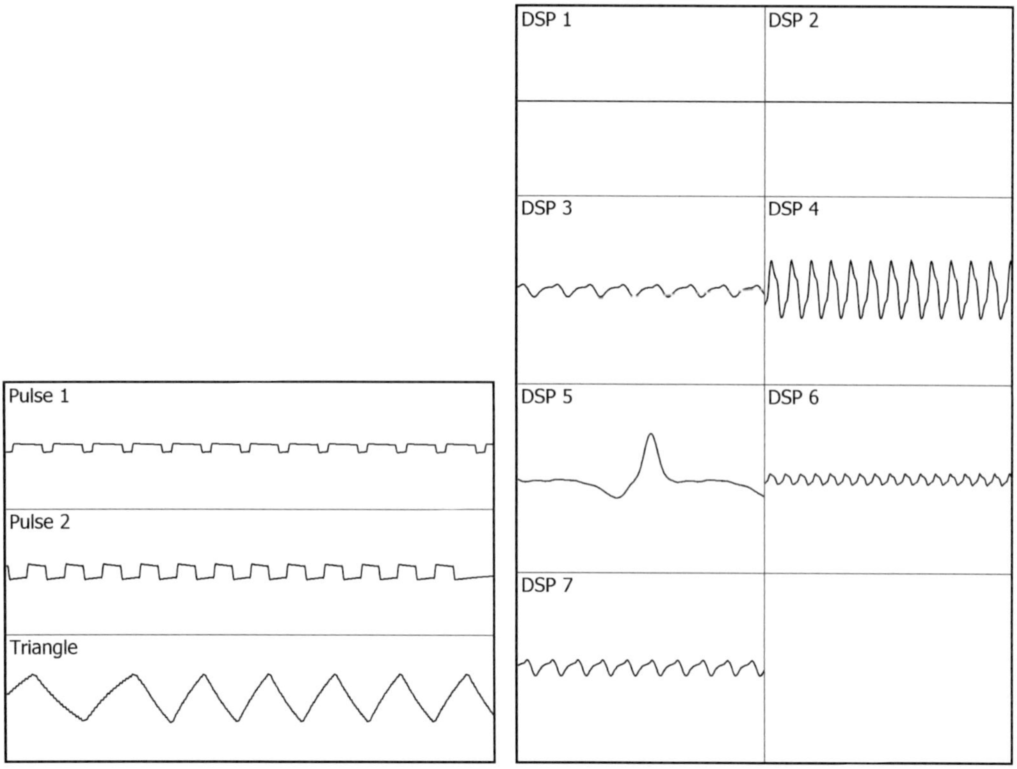

(a) *Mother (1989).* (b) *Mother 2/Earthbound (1994).*

Figure 6.20: *Oscilloscope display of the same score across the two different games.*

6.5.3 Stereo confusion

The S-DSP's volume controls are organised into signed 8-bits values [101], meaning that volume levels can be set to **negative values**. *But hang on*, if '0' represents mute, what happens when the volume is set to '-1'? Well, it **inverts the signal**.

This technique is particularly useful for creating a **surround effect**, accomplished by setting the stereo channels **out of phase** - where one channel outputs the normal signal while the other outputs the same signal but inverted.

Unfortunately, abusing this feature results in very unpleasant results, such as the feeling that the music is playing inside your head. For this reason, most SNES emulators bypass this setting altogether.

Additionally, out-of-phase stereo is cancelled out on mono devices, so those games needed to provide a stereo/mono selector to avoid muting their own soundtrack.

6.6 Games

To be blunt, the main program is written in plain **65816 assembly** and the music driver is written in **SPC700 assembly**. Needless to say, you won't find any of the commodities available on 21st-century equipment.

There were, however, some tools distributed by Nintendo, Intelligent Systems and Ricoh to make life easier for programmers, these included [129]:

- Different types of **development units**, capable of being controlled by a **debugger** from a host machine (typically running MS-DOS).
- **Flashable cartridges** (a.k.a. *Flashcarts*) - not for *piracy*, but to enable developers test their code on retail units.
- 65816 and SPC700 **assemblers**.
- **Development Manuals** explaining from a low-level perspective how this console works. These often included guidelines and norms that developers had to follow to get their game approved by Nintendo (necessary for distribution).

Curiously enough, several game studios - including Argonaut Software, Accolade, and SN Systems - developed custom in-house equipment, often providing more capabilities than the official offerings (e.g. memory editors, floppy disk readers, ISA-based devkits, etc.) [130].

6.6.1 Cartridge configuration

When it comes to accessing the cartridge, things get a lot more confusing compared to the relatively simpler mapping model of the NES. I find it interesting nonetheless, especially for understanding how it could be expanded.

The 65C816 features a 24-bit address bus, enabling to access up to 16 MB worth of data. However, due to the console's architecture, a portion of the address space is reserved for memory-mapped components[24]. Moreover, the 65C816 only comes with 16 address lines, which are then combined with internal registers to construct a 24-bit address. This is analogous to housing an internal mapper[25] and requiring bank switching[26] to access extra data beyond the boundaries of the address bus. If you explore other systems of the same generation, you'll find this methodology somewhat familiar.

Figure 6.21: *Example cartridge boards designed with different configurations [3]. From top to bottom: LoROM (dual ROM with battery-backed SRAM), LoROM (single ROM with battery-backed SRAM) and LoROM (single ROM)*

That being said, when it comes to designing a cartridge, there are many ways to electrically connect the address pins between the ROM and CPU, each utilising bank switching in a different way.

There are two fundamental models that enables accessing up to **4 MB of ROM** and **64 KB of SRAM** [131], and they work as follows:

[24]See "NES / Famicom Architecture" - Section 4.3 "Memory"
[25]See "PC Engine / TurboGrafx-16 Architecture" - Section 4.1 "Memory access"
[26]See "NES / Famicom Architecture" - Section 4.3.2 "Cartridge/game data"

- With the **LoROM Model**, ROM Data is arranged in 32 KB chunks with 128 banks available to choose from [132]. SRAM, though fitting within two banks, is accessible across 15 banks, where ROM data is also present.
  - This setup requires frequent bank switching during execution. On the other side, half of the banks are also mapped to WRAM, meaning ROM, SRAM, and WRAM can be accessed without switching banks.
- With the **HiROM Model**, ROM space is structured into full banks, meaning data is stored in 64 KB chunks across 64 banks. This configuration reduces the need for bank switching, but at the cost of not being able to read ROM, WRAM and SRAM within the same bank.

In both cases, a significant portion of ROM space is mirrored across the leftover area of the CPU's address space. However, here's the interesting part: one half of the space operates at ~2.68 MHz while the other can reach **3.58 MHz** - but only if the ROM chip supports the higher speed and the CPU's `FastROM` flag is enabled [133].

Additionally, cartridges that bundle SRAM must house a **MAD-1** (or similar) chip, which performs address decoding. This component is particularly crucial for correctly latching the pins that select between ROM and SRAM chips [134].

6.6.1.1 Beyond convention

Now, when programmers require more space, derivative models of LoROM and HiROM come into place. Two common variations, known as **ExHiROM** and **ExLoROM**, extend the ROM's addressing space by reducing the mirrored area. Both can access **~7.9 MB of ROM**.

Alternatively, and most importantly, LoRom and HiROM can also be adapted to accommodate **enhancement chips** within the cartridge. These are additional processors that expand the capabilities of the console. To name a few examples of new configurations:

- The **MMC** model enables bank switching via the local enhancement chip. This was used by components like the **S-DD1** or the **SPC7110**, both function as hardware tile decompressors.
- The **Super Accelerator System** model was designed for the highly regarded **SA-1**, a secondary **65C816-based CPU** operating at **10.74 MHz** with extra functionality. It builds upon the MMC model, incorporating new circuitry for the additional memory-mapped components.
- Two extra configurations - one based on LoROM and the other on HiROM - make way for the **DSP series**. These chips are derivatives of the NEC µPD77C25 CPU, but running a different program. They provide vector and matrix computations [135]. Various games have used them for affine transformations, graphics decompressing and shortest path calculations.
- The **SFX** model targets the popular **Super FX GSU** chip. This configuration maps up to 8 MB of ROM, with 2 MB shared between the main CPU and the Super FX. The rest of the address space includes additional backup RAM and SRAM. Developed by Argonaut,

Figure 6.22: *Star Fox (1993) uses the Super FX GSU chip to render 3D surfaces. Behind the scenes, the S-PPU only sees a background layer made of* erratic *tiles.*

the Super FX is a proprietary processor specialising in **3D surface rendering** and **2D affine transformations**. The processed graphics are then streamed as tiles for the S-PPU to display. Several notable games leveraged this technology to render 3D models and extend Mode 7 for sprites (as Mode 7 can only transform backgrounds).

It's difficult to overlook the impact this engineering had on 90s gaming, with many titles surpassing the console's expectations - and without requiring expansion modules and whatnot. You could say this complicated Nintendo's plans for a successor console, which may explain the cancellation of advanced games like Star Fox 2.

6.7 Anti-piracy / Region Lock

With the Super Nintendo, Nintendo assumed again the sole authority over game distribution. To enforce its policies, the company devised three layers of protection to prevent unauthorised cartridge distribution and circumvention of royalties.

Firstly, the external shape of cartridges **is different between regions**, so they won't fit on consoles from different areas. Be as it may, this could be easily bypassed using a third-party adapter.

Secondly, like the NES, this console still incorporates the **10NES** protection system[27] to lock out unauthorised distributors. However, the CIC chip was eventually cloned.

As a final layer - specifically designed to combat bootlegging - games included a chain of piracy checks within their program, such as:

1. **SRAM size verifications**: Bootleg cartridges often contain large SRAM blocks to accommodate various games.
2. **Code integrity checks**: A series of checksums embedded throughout the game's code verify whether the previous SRAM size verification routines have been removed. These checks are dispersed at different stages of the game, making them difficult to locate and remove.

While these measures could be nullified by manually stripping out the routines, this was a time-consuming task. After all, they would be scattered around the game only to upset the player (and eventually make them buy a legitimate copy). Truth to be told, you'll notice that most ROMs available online have had all their piracy checks removed.

6.8 That's all folks

This article was originally published on June 28, 2019 and last updated on June 14, 2025. See the online repository[28] *for the complete changelog.*

[27] See "NES / Famicom Architecture" - Section 8 "Anti-piracy and region lock"
[28] https://github.com/flipacholas/Architecture-of-consoles

Figure 6.23: *My modded SNES with an American cartridge. That game was only released in the states. Luckily, a lad was selling it in Glasgow!*

7

Neo Geo Architecture

The arcade at home

7.1 A quick introduction

Straight from the arcade world, the Neo Geo was, without a doubt, the most expensive hardware of the 4th generation. This begs the question: how capable was it and how did it compare to the rest?

In this entry, we'll take a look at the result of one company (SNK) setting aside budget restrictions and shipping a product meant to please both arcade owners and rich households.

7.1.1 Models and variants

The Neo Geo is exceptional in the sense it was designed for two markets at the same time: the arcade and the home. Consequently, SNK produced a single architecture which was sold in the form of **two variants**, each catering to a particular market:

- The **Multi Video System** or 'MVS' is the form tailored for arcade centres. Its I/O follows the 'JAMMA' specification (with some deviations [136]), facilitating integration with arcade cabinets. Alongside, its specialised motherboard provides extra circuitry for handling coin-based payments. Be as it may, throughout its lifetime, SNK ended up shipping tons of revisions, some of which could accommodate up to six game cartridges at once [137].
- The **Advanced Entertainment System** or 'AES' is the simplified design for homes. While smaller and with reduced I/O, it doesn't compromise its fundamental capabilities.

I suppose I should also mention the **Neo Geo CD**, which is the successor to the AES variant and embraced the CD-ROM for game distribution. Just like its previous forms, there were multiple revisions of this model.

In any case, for this analysis, I'll be focusing on the AES variant, as that's the one I've got with me. I will, nevertheless, make deserved references to the MVS when it comes to bonus functionality.

7.2 Supporting Imagery

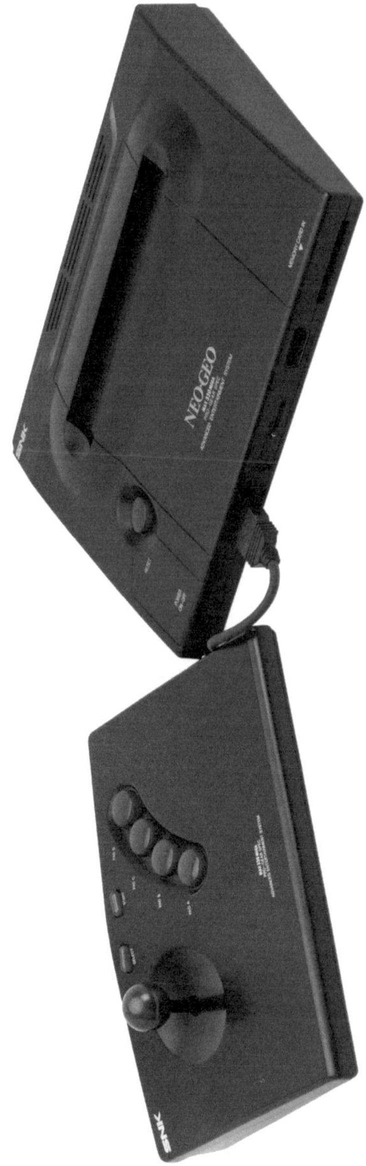

Figure 7.1: *The Neo Geo 'AES'. Released on 26/04/1990 in Japan and on 01/07/1991 America and Europe [3]*

Figure 7.2: *Motherboard [3]. Showing revision 'NEO-AES3-6'. I took this photo using the model I bought. Also, the previous owner re-arranged some capacitors to improve the video signal.*

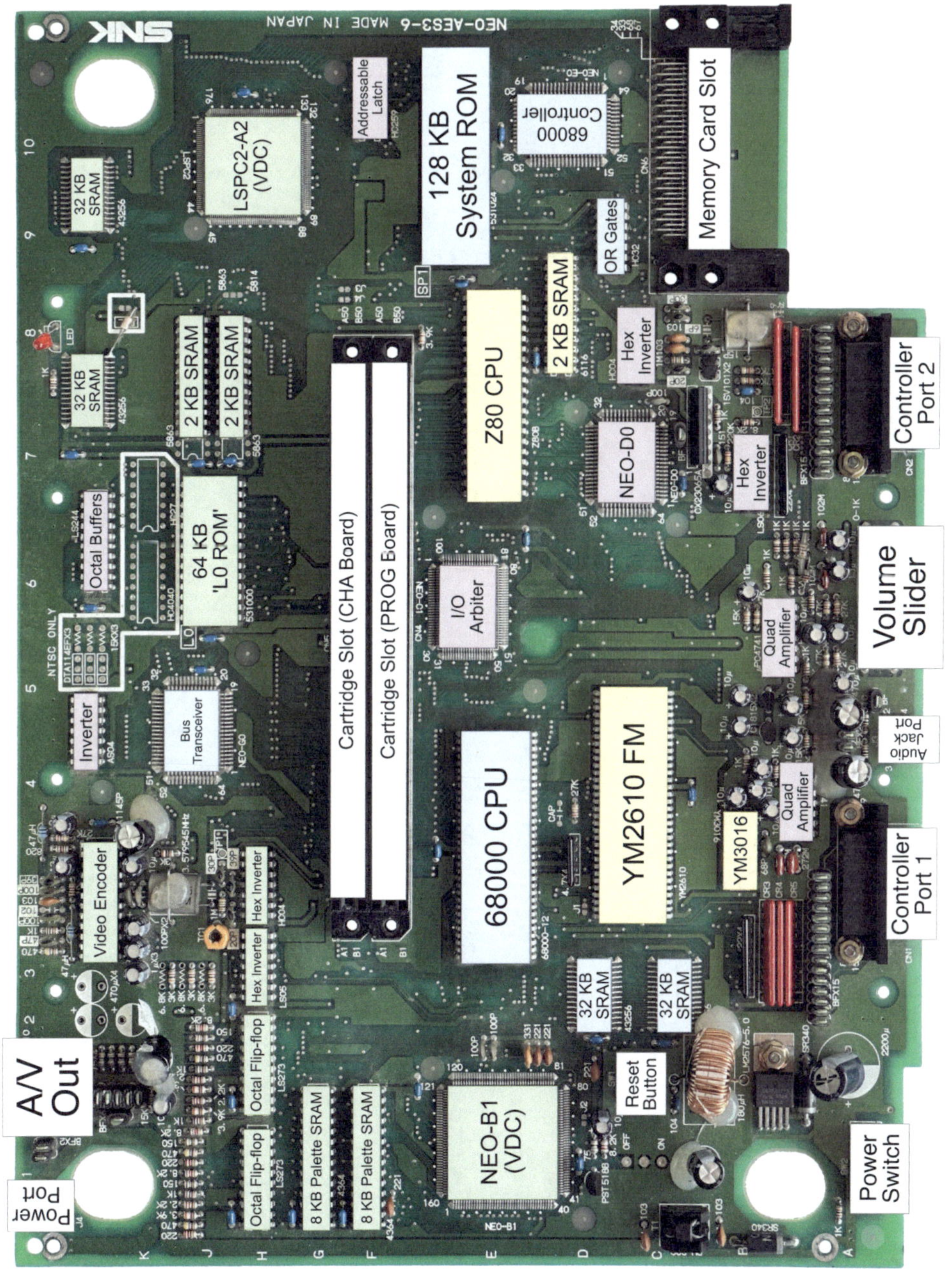

Figure 7.3: *Motherboard with important parts labelled.*

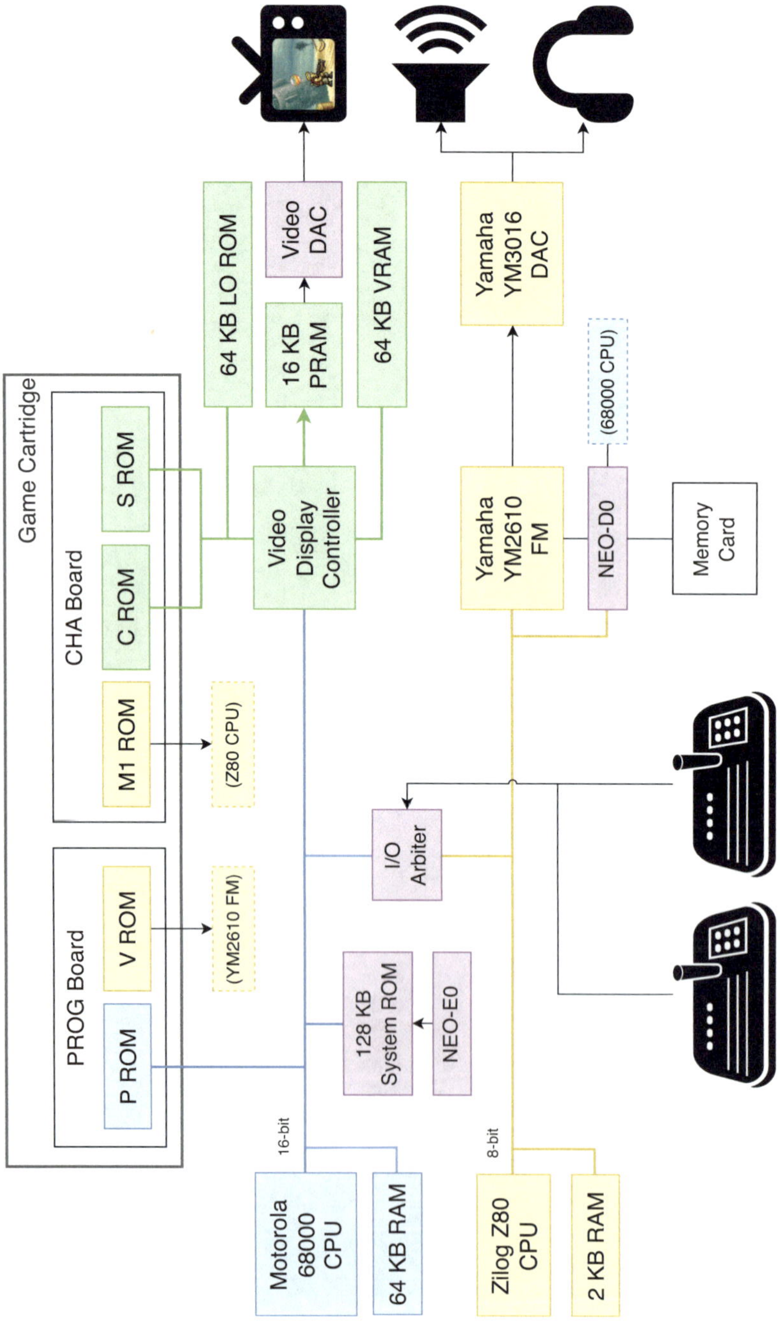

Figure 7.4: *Main architecture diagram.*

7.3 CPU

The system features a **dual-processor** configuration consisting of a **Motorola 68000** and a **Zilog Z80** CPU, two major icons of 80s electronics. The 68000 is tasked with executing the **main program** (also known as *the game*) while the Z80 is relegated to **sound management** [138]. You may recall identical roles in the Mega Drive/Genesis[1], but that's where similarities end, as the chip variants and layouts are somewhat divergent.

Figure 7.5: *The Motorola 68HC000 chip inside the Neo Geo, this one is second-sourced from Toshiba.*

To give you an example, the Neo Geo's 68000 runs at **12 MHz** (4 MHz faster than the Mega Drive's). Additionally, the specific chip fitted is the **68HC000**, a variant distinguished by its use of CMOS gates (as opposed to the previous and less-efficient NMOS process).

If you want to know what's inside the 68000 and the Z80, I have done previous analyses in the Mega Drive/Genesis[2] and the Master System[3] articles, respectively. Thus, for the Neo Geo study, I will focus on their new uses.

[1] See "Mega Drive / Genesis Architecture"
[2] See "Mega Drive / Genesis Architecture" - Section 3 "CPU"
[3] See "Sega Master System Architecture" - Section 4 "CPU"

7.3.1 A multitude of support chips

The most notable difference between the Neo Geo and any home console of the same generation is that, during the design of the former, SNK wasn't constrained by the budget limitations of the average household. In doing so, the motherboard features an extraordinary number of integrated controllers that not only remove many bottlenecks from the CPUs but also expand their capabilities.

The list of chips is lengthy, but the most confusing aspect is that, throughout revisions, SNK redesigned the chipset, either by unifying multiple chips or splitting them. So, for now, let me tell you that the motherboard contains the following groups of 'accelerators':

- **68k Controllers**: To seamlessly switch between vector tables. I explain this area in the next paragraphs.
- **Z80 Controllers**: To alleviate the memory addressing limitations.
- **I/O Arbiters**: To delegate all I/O operations, saving cycles along the way.
- **Video Display Controller**: To carry out all graphics operations. This will be discussed in a dedicated section called 'Graphics'.
- **Cabinet controllers**: For the arcade variant only (the 'MVS'). These handle the coin slot, provide a scoreboard, and perform system diagnostics.
- **Home controllers**: Likewise but only found on the home variant (the 'AES'). In this group, we find a video encoder that generates TV-compliant video signals.

From now on, I will use these titles to refer to any group throughout the article. In some cases, I will also name specific chips within the groups to denote special importance.

7.3.2 Sophisticated I/O handling

Let me introduce you to a noble capability of the 68000 which I have not covered until now: the **vectorised interrupt table**. Earlier CPUs like the 6502[4] and the Z80[5] had a constrained design for handling I/O communication. Whenever an external device wanted the attention of the CPU, the former had to send an interrupt request which, in turn, required the CPU to run a software routine to process it. The amount of information provided during the request was very limited, meaning the CPU needed to spend extra cycles to investigate 'who' triggered the interrupt and 'why' the CPU was interrupted.

To be fair, CPUs like the Z80 provided extra circuitry to allow the peripheral to tell the CPU which instruction to execute next. Nevertheless, this wasn't widely adopted.

The 68000 improved this technique by treating interrupts as **exceptions**. Peripherals are required to identify themselves when they interrupt the CPU [139]. the latter then uses the identifier to compose a memory address, which in turn points to a tailored software routine.

[4]See "NES / Famicom Architecture" - Section 4.2 "Core functionality"

[5]See "Sega Master System Architecture" - Section 4 "CPU"

All in all, this enables programmers to handle I/O communication efficiently, as they can now catalogue their dedicated interrupt handlers in a memory area called **autovector table**, and the CPU will execute each automatically.

The Neo Geo takes advantage of this design with the addition of a controller chip called the **NEO-E0**. Essentially, both the Neo Geo's Operating System and the game implement a dedicated exception table; this is because the OS table focuses on hardware interfacing and the game table is used during normal execution. However, the 68000 is only aware of one at a time. So, the NEO-E0 provides automatic bank switching[6] that ensures the 68000 reads from the right table at all times.

7.3.3 Inter-process communication

Whenever a system features a dual-processor layout, there must be a way for both CPUs to communicate. In this console, SNK implemented inter-process communication (IPC) through the use of an **I/O arbiter** chip. The latter exposes a single 8-bit register, which the 68000 can write to [140].

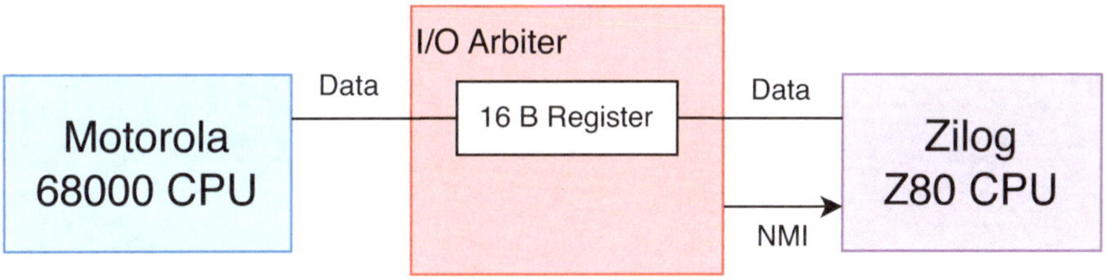

Figure 7.6: *Representation of the IPC channel between the 68000 and the Z80.*

Once the register is updated, the arbiter will send a non-maskable interrupt to the Z80. From then on, the Z80 may read the value (mapped to a port[7]) and react accordingly. This includes writing back to that register, so the 68000 receives new data. However, for some reason, the 68000 is not interrupted (so it needs to perform some sort of polling).

The specific I/O arbiter chip has changed across different motherboard revisions. It was first implemented with the 'PRO-B0' chip and later replaced with the 'NEO-C1'.

7.3.4 Anti-unpleasantries

Speaking of interruptions, something that arcade cabinets cannot afford is requiring constant maintenance.

[6]See "NES / Famicom Architecture" - Section 4.3.3 "Going beyond existing capabilities"
[7]See "Sega Master System Architecture" - Section 4.3 "Accessing the rest of the components"

We are no strangers to games suddenly freezing due to a software bug. The fix is no mystery either: just power cycle and start the game again. Now, imagine if this were to happen to an arcade cabinet. Unless the owner happened to be nearby, the broken cabinet would only be losing money.

The Neo Geo - having inherited the requirements of coin-slot machines - provides an 'auto-repair' process by bundling a **Watchdog program**. This is found in the I/O arbiter chip [141].

Figure 7.7: *Arcade cabinets can't afford to be continuously serviced. They're already busy trying to lure players.*

The system works as follows: games are required to periodically notify the watchdog of their presence (by writing to a particular register). In the unfortunate event that the watchdog does not receive a ping after a certain period, it will assume the program has frozen and proceed to reset the system.

Thanks to this, MVS owners did not need to keep an eye on their cabinets. Meanwhile, those lucky kids who could afford an AES system did not even have to move from their luxury sofas whenever their games crashed.

If that weren't enough, MVS motherboards complement this system by fitting an extra microcontroller, the **NEO-F0**. This drives the **coin lockout** mechanism, preventing users from wasting coins on failed systems [142], among other things.

7.3.5 Memory available

Memory is scattered across the motherboard and the game cartridge (which, by the way, is massive in size). Remember this is an expensive system, so memory bandwidth and capacity were top priorities.

In the case of general-purpose memory, there are **64 KB of RAM** available to the 68000. Meanwhile, the Z80 is provided with **2 KB**.

MVS models additionally include another **64 KB**. This is battery-backed and intended to store game scores, so it is not available for general purposes, however.

Curiously enough, this system does not feature any form of **Direct Memory Access** (DMA) to speed up memory transfers. I presume it is not a requirement, considering the number of dedicated buses.

7.4 Graphics

The Neo Geo is the pinnacle of tile-based graphics, its richness of colours is comparable to frame-buffer-based systems[8] (which only became affordable four years later). Be as it may, when it comes to effects, the Super Nintendo[9] has managed to do more with less.

7.4.1 Design

The graphics subsystem revolves around the typical **Video Display Controller** (VDC) model, but this time it is surrounded by a considerable number of components. The result is a console that can display tons of sprites - so many, in fact, that the iconic background layers[10] are no longer relevant. This makes sense, as backgrounds were originally devised to tackle the limited number of sprites.

That being said, the console broadcasts a frame compliant with NTSC and PAL signals (the choice depends on the region). In this case, they carry a dimension of **320 x 224 pixels** (for NTSC) or **320 x 256 pixels** (for PAL) [143].

---

[8]See "Sega Saturn Architecture" - Section 4 "Graphics"

[9]See "Super Nintendo / Famicom Architecture" - Section 4 "Graphics"

[10]See "NES / Famicom Architecture" - Section 5.2.2 "Background Layer"

(a) *Metal Slug 3 (2000).*

(b) *Neo Turf Masters (1996).*

Figure 7.8: *Example of Neo Geo games.*

(c) *Neo Drift Out (1996).*

(d) *Art of Fighting 3: The Path of the Warrior (1996).*

Figure 7.8: *Example of Neo Geo games.*

Figure 7.8: *Windjammers (1993).*
Example of Neo Geo games.

7.4.1.1 The chipset

The group of chips in charge of drawing to the TV has evolved as new revisions were released. Over the years, SNK alternated between NEC and Fujitsu to manufacture their integrated circuits.

For explanatory purposes, let us start by describing the most notable chips in the set:

- The **Motorola 68000**. You already know it as the main CPU. Its main role is to fill the VRAM and Palette RAM; and set up the VDC (using a set of exposed registers).
- The **Video Display Processor** (VDC): Based on the information stored in multiple memory chips, it generates scan lines and sends them to 'Palette RAM', which will, in turn, generate the required colour pixels.
  - The physical appearance of the VDC will vary depending on the motherboard model. For instance, the first revision housed three chips (the 'LSPC-A0', 'NEO-B0' and 'NEO-C0'), whereas later ones use a combination of the 'LSPC-A2' and the 'NEO-B1'.
- The **Video DAC**: Converts the colour stream received from 'Palette RAM' into a video signal.

Don't worry if the previous explanation is too dense. All of this will be explained more calmly in the following sections. Now, let's move on to analysing the information these chips

(a) *The 'LSPC-A2' chip.*

(b) *The 'NEO-B1' chip.*

Figure 7.9: *In my motherboard revision, these two components make up the Video Display Processor (VDC). Both were produced by Fujitsu.*

operate on.

7.4.2 Organising the content

Graphics data is distributed across **two separate boards**. The first is the **console's motherboard**, and the other is found in the **game cartridge**. You may recall a similar arrangement implemented in the NES/Famicom[11].

On the motherboard, we find:

- **68 KB of VRAM**: Stores sprite attributes and tile references.
  - Physically, VRAM is divided into **4 KB of 'Fast' VRAM** and **64 KB of 'Slow' VRAM**. Each is connected via a dedicated bus and exhibits drastically different latency. This conditions the number of cycles the CPU must wait after updating its content.
- **Four line buffers**: Store the scan lines rendered by the VDC. They only encode tile data that must be combined with other data in Palette RAM.
- **16 KB of Palette RAM**: Stores the palettes of colours used by the graphics. This block is also tasked with sending pixel colours to the Video DAC.
- **64 KB of 'L0 ROM'**: It so happens the VDC can **shrink sprites**. To achieve this, the 'L0 ROM' stores lookup tables that tell the VDC which scan lines to render based on the zoom value requested. [144].

The corresponding board in the game cartridge is referred to as **CHA Board** and fits the following:

- Multiple **C ROM** chips: Store tiles for the Sprite Layer.
- An **S ROM**: Stores tiles for the 'Fix' Layer (I explain this layer in the next section).

[11] See "NES / Famicom Architecture" - Section 4.3.2 "Cartridge/game data"

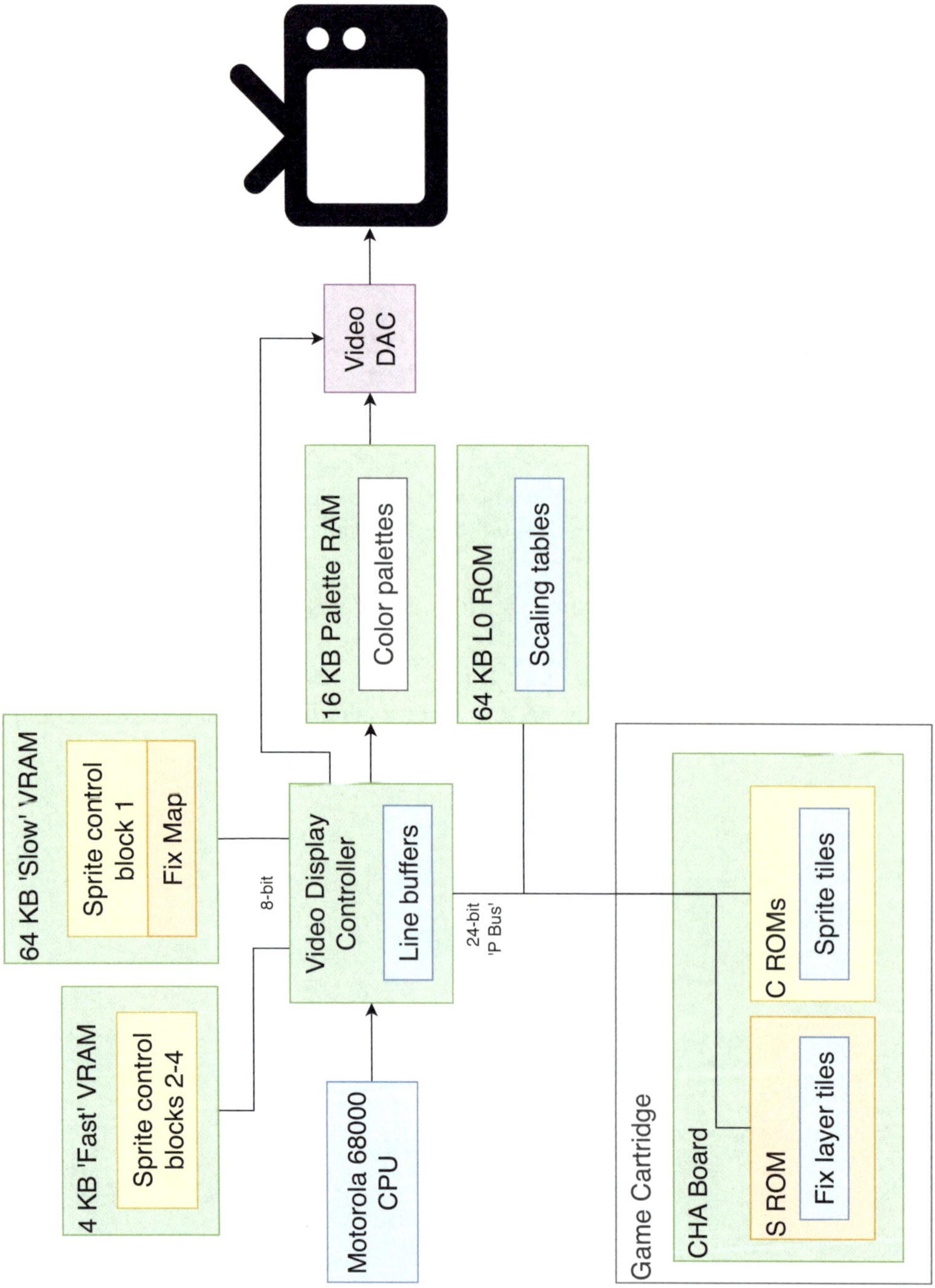

Figure 7.10: *Memory architecture of the graphics subsystem*

7.4.3 Constructing the frame

Now that you've had a glance at the most important components, let me give you a quick summary of how the graphics subsystem turns data into an image - in other words, how it renders a frame:

1. The CPU fills VRAM with the required references for the sprite layer and Fix layer.
2. Based on the information in VRAM, the VDC fetches graphics from C ROMs and the S ROM, and stores them in the line buffers.
3. While fetching occurs, the VDC uses the information in the line buffers to latch Palette RAM. This causes the latter to send colour pixel data to the Video DAC.
4. The Video DAC outputs a video signal to the TV.

Based on these steps, let me provide a thorough explanation using *Art of Fighting 3* as an example.

7.4.3.1 Tiles

Traditionally known as 8 x 8 pixel bitmaps, tiles are the primary ingredient to build the graphics of the 4th generation. Due to its unique attributes, the Neo Geo only draws two types of graphics: **fix tiles** and **sprites**. Thus, tiles are encoded and stored separately depending on the graphic type. In both cases, each pixel is encoded using **4 bits** (in other words, 4 bpp), meaning it can select up to **15 colours plus transparency**.

In terms of colour composition, Palette RAM allows storing **256 colour palettes** [25]. Each palette is made of sixteen colours referencing **16-bit RGB** values. Among all the available slots, there are two reserved entries: the 'Reference colour', which must be hardcoded to `$8000` (pure black); and the 'Backdrop colour' which encodes an arbitrary colour that is displayed in the absence of tiles.

The CPU may update Palette RAM at any moment, but it should only do so during blanking periods. Otherwise, a snowing effect will appear.

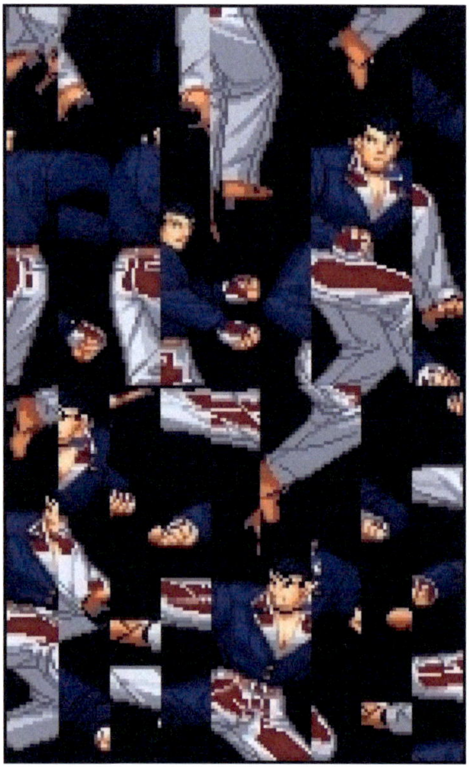

(a) *Various tiles.*

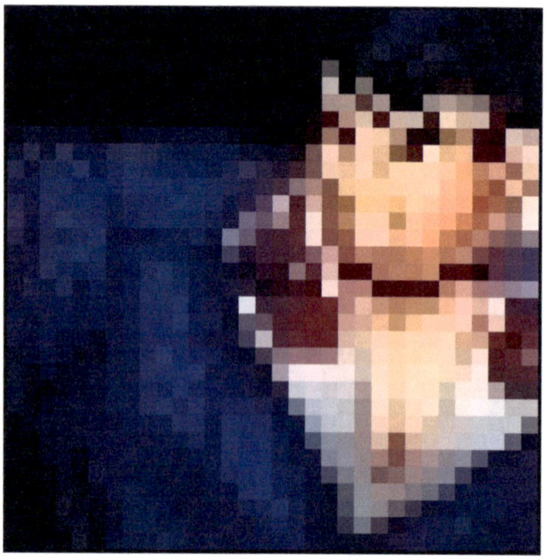

(b) *A group of four tiles.*

Figure 7.11: *Some tiles found in C ROM.*

7.4.3.2 Fixed plane

The Fixed plane is a layer **320 x 256 pixels** (40 x 32 tiles) wide [145], pretty much the entire screen. Its tiles displayed are completely static and only have access to 16 colour palettes. In practice, this is used to display 'always-on' information, similar to the window layer[12] of the Game Boy.

When broadcasted to a CRT screen, the displayed area will be smaller. Thus, its safe area[13] is 38 x 28 tiles wide.

Fixed tiles are declared in a region of VRAM called **Fix map**. It takes the form of a 40 x 32 table, and each entry corresponds to a position on the screen.

The S ROM stores the exclusive tiles for the fixed plane in the cartridge. The VDC can only

[12] See "Game Boy / Color Architecture" - Section 4.2.3 "Window"

[13] See "NES / Famicom Architecture" - Section 5.2 "Constructing the frame"

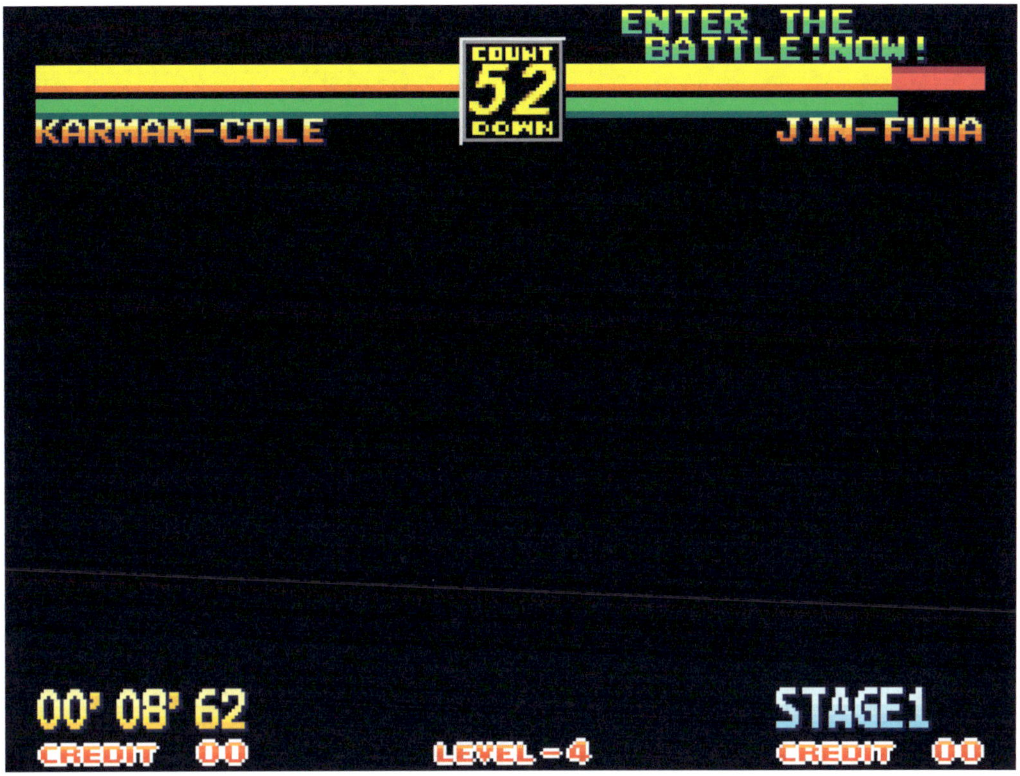

Figure 7.12: *The Fixed plane with a black backdrop.*

address up to 128 KB, but this limitation can be extended by bundling a mapper[14] [146].

[14]See "NES / Famicom Architecture" - Section 4.3.3 "Going beyond existing capabilities"

7.4.3.3 Sprites

Figure 7.13: *The Sprite layer, notice how it's used for all the areas of the scene (not just the two characters).*

As you may know, sprites are **freely moving tiles**. Yet, in the case of the Neo Geo, the tiles used for sprites are exceptionally **16 x 16 pixels** wide. With that in mind, the VDC can compose sprites ranging from **16 x 16 pixels** (1 x 1 tiles) to **16 x 512 pixels** (1 x 32 tiles). The reason for providing such tall compositions is that any sprite can also be **combined horizontally** by 'attaching' them to the previous one (though they still count as separate sprites). Overall, there is a limit of **96 sprites per scan line** and **381 per frame** [147], a large number compared to its competitors.

In terms of effects, sprites can be **flipped** and/or **shrunk**. These attributes are stored in the 'fast' block of VRAM, allowing the CPU to update them without considerable latency.

Due to their complexity, sprites are encoded in four areas in VRAM called **Sprite Control Blocks** (SCB), each of which stores the following attributes [148]:

- **SCB1**: Tile reference, colour palette reference, and X/Y flip.

- **SCB2**: Horizontal and vertical shrink.
- **SCB3**: Y position, vertical size (in terms of tiles) and whether the sprite is attached to the previous one.
  - Sprite attachment causes the second sprite to inherit the predecessor's attributes, except for the horizontal shrink.
- **SCB4**: X position.

As you can see, for practical reasons, the last three blocks are stored in fast VRAM, while the first is stored in slow VRAM [149].

7.4.3.4 Result

Figure 7.14: *Resulting frame shown on the screen.*

While competitors[15] are known for rendering at the pace of the CRT beam, the Neo Geo implements a **line buffer rendering** system. With this approach, the console stores the rendered scan lines in the aforementioned buffer, rather than beaming them directly to

[15] See "NES / Famicom Architecture" - Section 5.2 "Constructing the frame"

the screen. Since the VDC incorporates enough memory for two scan lines, this allows the VDC to render one scan line while displaying the other, thereby enabling games to update graphics during **active display** (aside from H-Blank[16] and V-Blank[17]).

Truth be told, the VDC will still be accessing VRAM at the same time, so the CPU must wait between 12 and 16 cycles [149] (depending on the operation) before accessing VRAM again; otherwise, the next operation will be ignored (hence the use of two VRAM variants).

7.4.3.5 Broadcasting the frame

To broadcast the rendered scan lines, the process varies depending on the console variant (AES or MVS).

The home model adds a video encoder to generate the composite and RGB signals. The A/V connector is somewhat similar to that of the Master System[18] and MegaDrive[19], but is not interchangeable.

There is nothing of the sort in the MVS model, as the JAMMA protocol leaves that task to the cabinet's monitor. Thus, the motherboard sends a raw RGB plus sync signal.

7.5 Audio

Remember the Z80 CPU I mentioned at the start of the article? It is still the typical **4 MHz** CPU you have seen in many other consoles and microcomputers, but now it's got the privilege of driving a very versatile sound chip: the **Yamaha YM2610**.

The YM2610 is another FM synthesiser[20] from the popular Japanese manufacturer. It is closely related to the YM2612[21] featured in the Mega Drive[22], but do not let its name fool you, as the Neo Geo version is a bit more premium (albeit with some compromises).

Both the YM2610 and YM2612 are part of the high-end 'OPN' series, meaning Yamaha enables four operators per FM channel. Now, the Neo Geo's chip features **four FM channels**, which, to be fair, is two fewer than the YM2612. That is as far as the weaknesses go.

The FM channels are provided with a **Low-Frequency Oscillator** (LFO) to modulate either the amplitude or frequency of the operators. The LFO contains a predefined set of frequencies ranging from 3.98 Hz to 72.2 Hz [150].

[16] See "Game Boy / Color Architecture" - Section 4.2.5 "Result"
[17] See "NES / Famicom Architecture" - Section 5.2.5 "Result"
[18] See "Sega Master System Architecture" - Section 5.4 "Video Output"
[19] See "Mega Drive / Genesis Architecture" - Section 4.5 "Video Output"
[20] See "Mega Drive / Genesis Architecture" - Section 5.1.1 "Yamaha YM2612"
[21] See "Mega Drive / Genesis Architecture" - Section 5.1.1 "Yamaha YM2612"
[22] See "Mega Drive / Genesis Architecture" - Section 5 "Audio"

Figure 7.15: *The Yamaha YM2610 paired with the YM3016 below. Both chips are needed to output audio.*

Now, even though the YM2610 is known for its FM synthesis, it houses additional functions that did not go unnoticed by music composers [151]:

- A **Software-controlled Sound Generator** (SSG): This is Yamaha's name for a Programmable Sound Generator[23] (PSG). In essence, the chip bundles a legacy Yamaha YM2149 inside, this can generate **three square waves** with optional **noise**. It also comes with an envelope control.
  - The original YM2149 came with an interface called 'I/O ports' to transfer data between the CPU and another component [152]. Since this is now irrelevant, the embedded variant in the YM2610 doesn't include it.
- Seven **ADPCM channels**: Enables to play **samples** using the 4-bit ADPCM format. These channels are split into two groups:

[23] See "NES / Famicom Architecture" - Section 6 "Audio"

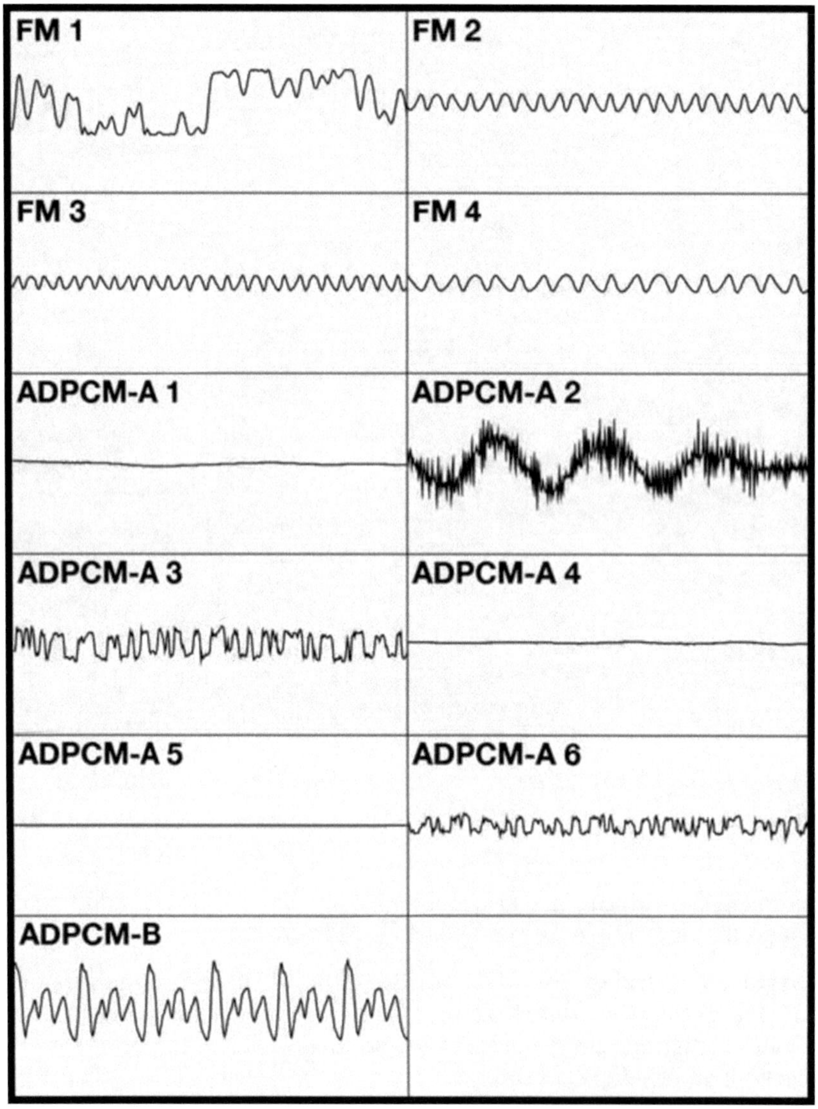

Figure 7.16: *Oscilloscope display of Metal Slug 2 (1998), showing the FM and ADPCM channels used for music.*

- ADPCM-A: Consists of six channels, providing a sample resolution of **12 bits** and a sampling frequency of **~18.5 kHz**.
- ADPCM-B: This is the remaining channel, with a **16-bit** resolution and a sampling frequency of up to **~55.56 kHz** (better than CD quality).

The YM2610 is connected to two memory chips in the cartridge called **V ROMs**. These store the ADPCM samples, with one V ROM per ADPCM group.

All in all, the audio subsystem is a combination of the 3rd, 4th, and (then unreleased) 5th generation of consoles. However, unlike the CD medium[24], Neo Geo cartridges can only store so much, so the ADPCM channels are mainly bottlenecked by **storage limitations**. In any case, some games found clever arrangements for ADPCM while leaving FM as a secondary constituent [153].

Finally, the YM2610 is paired with another chip to work: the **Yamaha YM3016**. The latter is a dedicated 16-bit **Digital-to-Analogue Converter** (DAC), which takes the digital signal output from the YM2610 and converts it to analogue audio (that speakers understand).

7.5.1 The conductor

For the audio chip to do anything meaningful, the Z80 must command it properly. So, the Z80 runs a program stored in yet another distinct chip called **M1 ROM**. This is found inside the game cartridge, particularly, within the CHA Board. The program for the Z80 is often referred to as the **sound driver**, and there were many implementations [128].

On a similar note, the Z80 is paired with a proprietary controller called **NEO-D0**; the latter acts as a memory bank and I/O controller.

[24] See "Sega Saturn Architecture" - Section 7.1 "The Compact Disc (CD)"

Figure 7.17: *The Zilog Z80, NEO-D0, and surroundings.*

7.6 Operating system

There is a **128 KB 'System' ROM** found on the motherboard [154]; this serves as the typical **BIOS**, providing:

- A **bootloader** to initialise the hardware, perform a self-test, and bootstrap the splash animation.
- A **configuration shell** (only on MVS models).
- Various **system routines** that abstract hardware operations.

7.6.1 The visual services

After powering on the console, the user will notice a splash screen known as the **Eyecatcher** [155]. Its code is stored in the System ROM, but the graphic assets (the Neo Geo logo and other labels) are fetched from the cartridge's C ROM and S ROM.

Alternatively, the P ROM header may contain a flag instructing the System ROM to delegate the splash routine to the cartridge [156]. This only works on the AES variant [148], yet later games adopted this to display different text.

Figure 7.18: *The Eyecatcher implemented by the System ROM. It still relies on tiles supplied by the cartridge. The official implementation displays the characteristic 'Max 330 Mega' subtitle, as a way to show off the theoretical storage capacity of Neo Geo cartridges. Later games, through the use of the flag, render 'Giga Power' instead.*

The MVS system also provides a **Test Menu** to configure the cabinet (e.g., adjust the calendar, test the components, etc.). This menu is triggered by flipping one of the DIP switches of the MVS (inaccessible to the end user). Consequently, its motherboard bundles an S ROM that stores the Fix tiles for this menu.

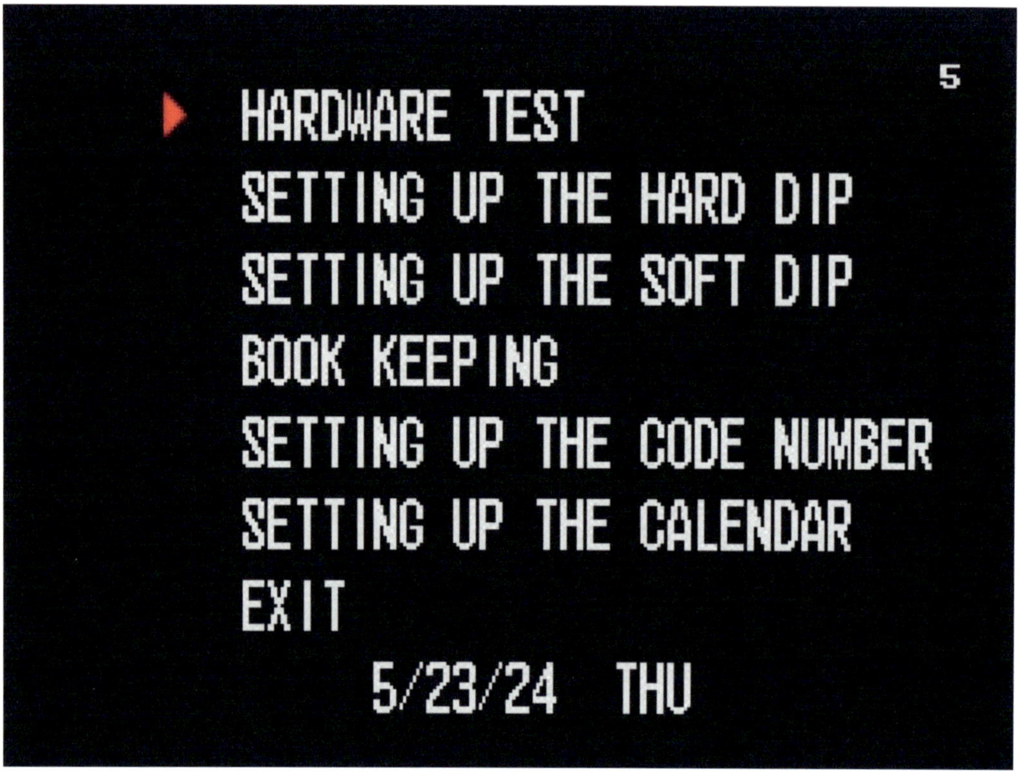

Figure 7.19: *The Test Menu, showing many maintenance functions required to set up the arcade cabinet.*

7.6.2 The System routines

Apart from the visual aspects, the System ROM provides software routines to operate the hardware. This includes:

- Reading button presses from the controllers and, in the case of the MVS, the coin slots.
- Accessing the Memory Card.
- Initialising VRAM with the proper structure for the sprite blocks and the Fix tile map.

Interestingly enough, system routines may, in turn, call game routines to continue some operations. This means games are also tasked with implementing certain calls [157] [158]. For instance, the System ROM may request the following from games:

- Show the custom Eyecatcher animation (if the required flag is set).
- Show the game's boot animation.
- Start the game demo. This is what you see before inserting a coin.

- Play the 'coin inserted' sound.
- Begin the game after enough coins are inserted.

As you can see, most of the low-end I/O is delegated to the System ROM; games instead focus on providing their unique content.

7.7 Games

To start with, games are written in **68k** and **Z80 assembly**. It is only with the next generation of consoles (and the arrival of new CPUs[25]) that programming languages become part of the toolbox.

7.7.1 Distribution medium

Following the trend of the 4th generation, the Neo Geo relies on cartridges as its sole medium for games.

Nevertheless, I must say, Neo Geo cartridges are the largest I have seen for a home console. This is due to the amount of dedicated chips housed within. Unlike the Super Nintendo[26], whose games could optionally expand[27] the capabilities of the console, Neo Geo games are strictly required to bundle a considerable amount of circuitry.

I have already mentioned some parts of the cartridge system in previous sections, but let me give you a quick summary so you get a proper overview of how this system works.

As you may know, Neo Geo cartridges are made up of **two boards**. The first is called **PROG Board** and houses the following ROM chips:

- **P ROM**: Stores the program the 68000 executes. It is connected with a 16-bit data bus and up to **2 MB** can be addressed (more will require a mapper).
- **V ROM**: Stores ADPCM audio samples read by the YM2610.

By contrast, the second board is the aforementioned **CHA Board** and embeds the following:

- The **C ROMs** and **S ROM**. These store sprite tiles and Fix tiles, respectively.
- An **M1 ROM**: Stores the Z80 program. As you may know, the addressing capabilities of the Z80 are very limited[28] (in this case, the ceiling is **62 KB**). So, M1 ROM access is interfaced by a dedicated mapper[29] called **NEO-ZMC** (found in the cartridge), which enables up to **512 KB** of memory to be addressed. This may be expanded by adding

[25] See "PlayStation Architecture" - Section 3.1.1 "A bit of history"
[26] See "Super Nintendo / Famicom Architecture"
[27] See "Super Nintendo / Famicom Architecture" - Section 6.1.1 "Beyond convention"
[28] See "Sega Master System Architecture" - Section 4.2 "Memory available"
[29] See "NES / Famicom Architecture" - Section 4.3.3 "Going beyond existing capabilities"

Figure 7.20: *Generic cartridge for the Neo Geo [3]. Notice the two boards sticking out.*

extra mappers to the CHA Board, or by adopting the NEO-ZMC2 (which enables up to 4 MB).

7.7.2 Keeping progress

As a home-arcade hybrid, SNK provided a rudimentary accessory to keep track of scores and progress: a proprietary **Memory Card**

The Memory Card worked on both AES and MVS models. Options ranged from **2 KB** to **16 KB** of battery-backed SRAM [159], though in all cases the battery was unserviceable.

The save data was structured as 64 B blocks distributed across five segments, while the System ROM provided I/O routines to operate it.

Having said that, whether arcade cabinets were actually 'prepared' for Memory Cards... That was another story.

I knew about the Memory cards from magazines, but official Neo Geo cabinets were rare in my town. Instead, we had plenty 'Video Sonic' cabinets supplied

Figure 7.21: *The Memory Card [3].*

by Segasa. Some lacked all the buttons required to play properly, let alone a Memory Card slot!

– Proud Neo Geo connoisseur from Jerez, Spain

7.8 Anti-piracy & Homebrew

Both consoles and games were targeted by unauthorised parties, many of whom ended up producing their own replicas [160]. Bootleg hardware was made using a combination of off-the-shelf and reverse-engineered chips, aiming to offer a cheaper alternative to SNK's hardware.

Thus, on one side, you've got SNK trying to fend off bootleggers. On the other, game studios were enforcing that their code only ran on a genuine console and cartridge.

7.8.1 Combating fake consoles

Neither SNK nor game studios favoured running on bootleg hardware (whether it was a Neo Geo clone or a bootleg cartridge). Hence, many games bundled routines that fiddled with very particular areas of the motherboard (e.g., status flags, the real-time clock, the Watchdog, etc.) in an attempt to spot any defects in clone boards [161]. Whenever any of these checks failed, the game would display a warning message and refuse to proceed.

7.8.2 Fighting fake cartridges

Considering cartridges housed an exceptional number of integrated circuits, games implemented creative measures to combat piracy.

Starting with the common techniques, the System ROM contains a portion of data called **Security Code** that is compared side by side with the cartridge's P ROM during boot [162]. The bootloader will proceed only if both areas match.

Additionally, games like *Fatal Fury 2* also interact with their companion 'PRO-CT0' chip (a multiplexer for the CHA Board) to ensure the program is residing in an official cartridge [163]. Otherwise, it assumes it has been cloned, triggering many anti-piracy **unpleasantries** (such as making the opponent invincible).

Later on, newer entries also stored **encrypted data** in the C ROM, designed to be seamlessly decrypted by the 'NEO-CMC' (found on the CHA Board) [164]. This chip contained a set of unusual XOR functions to deobfuscate the graphics data before it reached the VDC [165]. The NEO-CMC also acts as a multiplexer for tile data within the C ROMs, allowing manufacturers to omit the inclusion of S ROM chips altogether.

For more extreme measures, games like 'Metal Slug X' bundled specialised ICs in their PROG board, which complicated matters further [166]. This is reminiscent of Nintendo's CIC system[30], which required constant game-chip communication (albeit significantly distinct in terms of goals and architecture).

All in all, this shows that the anti-piracy battle was just another cat-and-mouse game. However, in this case, SNK was trying to steer both home and arcade owners away from cheaper knock-offs.

7.8.3 Post-market utilities

Once the lifecycle of this console had reached an end, a new phase emerged: **Homebrew** (running homemade software and/or hardware). At the time of writing (June 2024), the most common practices are **hardware modifications**, **firmware replacement** and **flashcarts**.

Thanks to its enthusiastic community, there are many online resources available that teach how to correct and/or modify MVS and AES hardware. These include converting MVS models to work outside cabinets (the so-called **consolisation**), while others focus on addressing deficiencies in particular models. For instance, the AES model I own had its video encoder bypassed, improving the quality of the RGB output.

On the firmware side, there have been developments like the 'UNIVERSE BIOS'/UniBIOS. This is the equivalent of a **custom firmware** made to replace the original System ROM.

[30] See "NES / Famicom Architecture" - Section 8 "Anti-piracy and region lock"

Behind the scenes, the UniBIOS is made of an MVS System ROM modified to provide the following additional abilities [167]:

- Switch between 'MVS' and 'AES' mode. This is very useful for AES systems, as games have a hardcoded number of coins/lives, and switching to MVS mode enables to increase this amount arbitrarily.
- Change the region. Some games are censored depending on the region they run on.
- Activate cheats.

Finally, to run arbitrary code in this console, stores are selling third-party flashcarts which can reprogram itself to replicate any past CHA and PROG boards. Due to their complexity, they are not exactly affordable, but that is another product Neo Geo owners have available nowadays.

7.9 That's all folks

Curiously enough, the last Neo Geo game was released in 2004, almost 14 years after its release. That's quite an achievement for a household/arcade console, and I hope that this analysis has helped you understand these outcomes from a technical perspective.

From my side, I found it engaging to return to a 2D console after typing so many words for the Nintendo 3DS article[31], this helped me revisit the 'classic' writing structure that I adopted during the website's beginnings in 2019.

Thinking about the follow-up articles, I've still got two avenues to explore: Continue the modern hardware timeline after the Nintendo 3DS[32], or proceed with another 2D console: The Pippin. The latter would help me introduce the PowerPC CPU, while modern hardware would enable me to talk about the ARMv7 and the ARMv8. We'll see!

Until next time!
Rodrigo

This article was originally published on June 19, 2024 and last updated on June 7, 2025. See the online repository[33] for the complete changelog.

[31] See "Nintendo 3DS Architecture"
[32] See "Nintendo 3DS Architecture"
[33] https://github.com/flipacholas/Architecture-of-consoles

Figure 7.22: *My Neo Geo AES. I bought it out of curiosity because the seller was offering a complete set with a flashcart and two controllers. Half a year later, it became a good excuse to write an article about it.*

8

Epilogue

I hope you enjoyed this edition!

If you liked what you read and would like to help out, you can suggest changes through the Github repository[1], provide translations through Crowdin[2] or get more books[3].

8.1 Acknowledgments

I want to give a big thanks to the following people for their past donations[4], which contributed to this release:

- All of the generous book & eBook readers
- Adam Obenauf
- Adrian Burgess
- Alberto Cordeddu
- Alberto Massidda
- Alex Christensen
- Alexander Perepechko
- Alí El wahsh
- Andreas Kotes
- Andrei Zbikowski
- Andrew Woods
- Angus MacMullen
- Antonio Bellotta
- Antonio Vivace
- AT13C
- BBQ Inc
- Ben Morris
- Bitmap Bureau
- Brandon Arnold
- Brenden Kromhout
- Cameron
- Carlos Díaz Navarro
- Chiang Yi-Ta

[1] https://github.com/flipacholas/Architecture-of-consoles
[2] https://crowdin.com/project/architecture-of-consoles
[3] https://www.copetti.org/writings/consoles/materials/book
[4] https://www.copetti.org/support

- Christopher Henderson
- Christopher Starke
- Cirilla Rose
- CLEMENT frederic
- Colin Szechy
- Colin Weltin-Wu
- CyberpunkDre
- D
- Daniel Cassidy
- David Bradbury
- Dávid Major
- David Portillo
- David Sawatzke
- Dillon A
- Dominic Wehrmann
- Dudeastic
- Duncan Bayne
- Eli Lipsitz
- Elizabeth Isley
- Elizabeth Parks
- Eric Haskins
- eurasianwolf
- Gerald Mueller-Bruhnke
- Grady Haynes
- Guillermo Angeris
- Hadlee Simons
- Hazel Boston
- Ian Shaw
- Ifeanyi Oraelosi
- Jack Wakefield
- Jacob Almoyan
- Jaerder Sousa
- James Kilner
- James Knowler
- James Montgomerie
- James Osborne
- James William Jones
- Jan Straßenburg
- Jason Strothmann
- Jerre van der Hulst
- jmi2k
- João Baptista
- Joe Pugh
- Johannes Baiter
- John Mcgonagle
- Josh Enders
- Julius Hofmann
- Landon Carbenia
- ltlollo
- Luke Groeninger
- Luke Wren
- Manish Sinha
- Marc C.
- Marek Vybiral
- Matthew Butch
- Max Robertson
- MCE
- Mia
- Michael Chi
- Michal Borsuk
- Nathan Castle
- Neil Moore
- Nicholas T.
- Nick T.
- Oleg Andreev
- Olivier Cahagne
- Owen Christensen
- Parker Thomas
- Paul Adamson
- Paul Gerver
- Payam Ghoreishi
- Pedro Henrique Martins Garcia
- petey893
- Phil Stevenson
- Piergiorgio Arrigoni
- quantaq
- Racri
- Red Wolf
- Rene Wolf
- RetroReversing
- rocky
- Rodrigo Groppa
- Roger Bolsius
- Samuel Shieh
- Sanqui
- Sara Sinback

- Sariya Melody
- Scott Munro
- Sebastian Brand
- Sébastien Lethuaire
- Shoaib Meenai
- Simon Pichette
- Stephane Dallongeville
- Stephen Molyneaux
- Str33tz
- Stuart Hicks
- TadeusTaD
- Thomas Finch
- Thomas Lanner
- Thomas Peter Berntsen
- Tim Cox
- Tobias Gruetzmacher
- Tomas Arriagada
- Ulrich Bogensperger
- znix

9

Licensing and Copyright

Just like the contents on the website, all of my writings and multimedia assets authored by me are available under a permissive Creative Commons license. This edition, in particular, is available under the Creative Commons Attribution-NonCommercial 4.0 International License[1].

9.1 External materials

The following tools and resources were used for the production of this volume:

- Pandoc
- R Markdown and Bookdown
- LuaTeX
- draw.io
- Node.js

[1] https://creativecommons.org/licenses/by-nc/4.0/

Acronyms

AES Advanced Entertainment System. 185

ALU Arithmetic Logic Unit. 22, 126

APU Audio Processing Unit. 41

BCD Binary-Coded Decimal. 23

CGRAM Colour Graphics RAM. 164

CIC Checking Integrated Circuit. 59

CRAM Colour RAM. 70, 71, 131

DAC Digital-to-Analogue Converter. 211

DDA Direct D/A. 108

DMA Direct Memory Access. 35, 141, 159, 195

Famicom Family Computer. 13

FDS Famicom Disk System. 56, 58

FM Frequency Modulation. 142

GUI Graphical User Interface. 125

HDMA Horizontal DMA. 159

LFO Low-Frequency Oscillator. 108, 208

LFSR Linear Feedback Shift Register. 78

MDR Memory Data Register. 160

MMU Memory Management Unit. 97

MPR Mapping Register. 97

MVS Multi Video System. 185

NES Nintendo Entertainment System. 13

OAM Object Attribute Memory. 30, 34, 41, 164, 169

PPU Picture Processing Unit. 28, 161

PSG Programmable Sound Generator. 41, 77, 107, 143

ROM Read-Only Memory. 30

S-PPU Super PPU. 161

SCB Sprite Control Blocks. 206

SMS Sega Master System. 61

SRAM Static RAM. 23

SSG Software-controlled Sound Generator. 209

SVP Sega Virtua Processor. 146

V-Blank Vertical Blank. 36

VCE Video Colour Encoder. 100, 105

VDC Video Display Controller. 98, 192, 195

VDP Video Display Processor. 70, 127, 128

VRAM Video RAM. 30, 131, 164

VSRAM Vertical Scroll RAM. 131

Sources

The contents of this document could not have been possible without the research and expertise provided by the works listed here. Some were carried out for commercial purposes while others were entirely volunteer-driven.

[1] Nerdly Pleasures, “Official variations of the nintendo 8-bit NES/famicom console hardware.” [Online]. Available: http://nerdlypleasures.blogspot.com/2017/06/official-variations-of-nintendo-8-bit.html

[2] Nesdev contributors, “Cartridge connector.” Nesdev Wiki [Online]. Available: https://wiki.nesdev.org/w/index.php?title=Cartridge_connector

[3] E. Amos, “The vanamo online game museum.” [Online]. Available: https://commons.wikimedia.org/wiki/User:Evan-Amos

[4] Nesdev contributors, “CPU.” Nesdev Wiki [Online]. Available: https://wiki.nesdev.org/w/index.php?title=CPU

[5] Radio Electronics, “Radio electronics magazine - december 1977 issue.” p. 86 [Online]. Available: https://worldradiohistory.com/Archive-Radio-Electronics/70s/1977/Radio-Electronics-1977-12.pdf

[6] Babbage, “Motorola’s pioneering 8-bit 6800: Origins and architecture.” [Online]. Available: https://thechipletter.substack.com/p/motorolas-pioneering-8-bit-6800-origins

[7] Babbage, “Leaving arizona.” [Online]. Available: https://thechipletter.substack.com/p/leaving-arizona

[8] Retrocomputing Beta, “How much did the 6502 and Z80 cost?” [Online]. Available: https://retrocomputing.stackexchange.com/questions/2760/how-much-did-the-6502-and-z80-cost

[9] Radio Electronics, “Radio electronics magazine - august 1981 issue.” p. 76 [Online]. Available: https://archive.org/details/radio_electronics_1981-08/page/n75/mode/2up

[10] Nesdev Forums, “Difference between 6502 and 2A03 CPU core.” [Online]. Available: https://forums.nesdev.com/viewtopic.php?f=9&t=9813

[11] Nikkei Trendi, “Nintendo ”famicom” was born in this way.” [Online]. Available: https://web.archive.org/web/20141017171734/http://trendy.nikkeibp.co.jp/article/special/20081002/1019378/
[12] T. Fahs, “The secret history of donkey kong.” Gamasutra [Online]. Available: https://www.gamasutra.com/view/feature/134790/the_secret_history_of_donkey_kong.php?print=1
[13] VisualChips, “Visual6502 - 6502 binary-coded decimal (BCD mode).” [Online]. Available: http://visual6502.org/wiki/index.php?title=6502DecimalMode
[14] Wikipedia contributors, “Semiconductor chip protection act of 1984.” Wikipedia, The Free Encyclopedia [Online]. Available: https://en.wikipedia.org/wiki/Semiconductor_Chip_Protection_Act_of_1984
[15] Tepples, “Sample RAM map.” Nesdev Wiki [Online]. Available: https://wiki.nesdev.org/w/index.php?title=Sample_RAM_map
[16] Nesdev contributors, “CPU memory map.” Nesdev Wiki [Online]. Available: https://wiki.nesdev.org/w/index.php?title=CPU_memory_map
[17] Nesdev contributors, “Open bus behavior.” Nesdev Wiki [Online]. Available: https://www.nesdev.org/wiki/Open_bus_behavior
[18] Kinopio, “Super mario bros. - NesCartDB.” NES Cart Database [Online]. Available: https://nescartdb.com/profile/view/2459/super-mario-bros
[19] Nesdev contributors, “NROM.” Nesdev Wiki [Online]. Available: https://wiki.nesdev.org/w/index.php?title=NROM
[20] bootgod, “Super mario bros. 2 - NesCartDB.” NES Cart Database [Online]. Available: https://nescartdb.com/profile/view/268/super-mario-bros-2
[21] Nesdev contributors, “MMC3.” Nesdev Wiki [Online]. Available: https://wiki.nesdev.org/w/index.php?title=MMC3
[22] Nesdev contributors, “Overscan.” Nesdev Wiki [Online]. Available: https://wiki.nesdev.org/w/index.php?title=Overscan
[23] R. Bagmanov, “Writing NES emulator in rust - emulating PPU registers.” [Online]. Available: https://bugzmanov.github.io/nes_ebook/chapter_6_1.html
[24] LilaQ, “Cartridge loading, pattern tables and ppu registers.” [Online]. Available: https://emudev.de/nes-emulator/cartridge-loading-pattern-tables-and-ppu-registers/
[25] NeoGeo Development contributors, “Palettes.” NeoGeo Development Wiki [Online]. Available: https://wiki.neogeodev.org/index.php?title=Palettes
[26] Nesdev contributors, “PPU nametables.” Nesdev Wiki [Online]. Available: http://wiki.nesdev.com/w/index.php/PPU_nametables
[27] Nesdev contributors, “PPU attribute tables.” Nesdev Wiki [Online]. Available: https://wiki.nesdev.com/w/index.php/PPU_attribute_tables
[28] Nesdev contributors, “PPU object attribute memory (OAM).” Nesdev Wiki [Online]. Available: http://wiki.nesdev.com/w/index.php/PPU_OAM
[29] Nesdev contributors, “PPU registers - PPUSTATUS.” Nesdev Wiki [Online]. Available: https://wiki.nesdev.org/w/index.php?title=PPU_registers#PPUSTATUS

[30] ChibiAkumas, "Hit me with your sprite 0 bit!" [Online]. Available: https://www.chibiakumas.com/6502/platform5.php

[31] dougfraker, "Sprite zero." [Online]. Available: https://nesdoug.com/2018/09/05/18-sprite-zero/

[32] Nesdev contributors, "The frame and NMIs." Nesdev Wiki [Online]. Available: https://wiki.nesdev.org/w/index.php?title=The_frame_and_NMIs

[33] Nesdev users, "Things in PPU that can change outside VBlank." Nesdev Forums [Online]. Available: https://forums.nesdev.org/viewtopic.php?p=80278

[34] Retro Game Mechanics Explained, "The nintendo entertainment system's loading seam." Youtube [Online]. Available: https://www.youtube.com/watch?v=wfrNnwJrujw

[35] N3S, "N3S - how it works." [Online]. Available: http://web.archive.org/web/20190523120018/https://n3s.io/index.php?title=How_It_Works

[36] T. Worthington, "RGB / s-video upgrade for nintendo NES." [Online]. Available: https://etim.net.au/nesrgb/

[37] Nesdev contributors, "Color 0D games." Nesdev Wiki [Online]. Available: https://wiki.nesdev.org/w/index.php?title=Color_$0D_games

[38] Nesdev contributors, "APU." Nesdev Wiki [Online]. Available: https://wiki.nesdev.org/w/index.php?title=APU

[39] Retro Game Audio, "NES audio: Review of the sound channels." [Online]. Available: https://retrogameaudio.tumblr.com/post/18843375536/nes-audio-review-of-the-sound-channels

[40] Nesdev contributors, "APU pulse." Nesdev Wiki [Online]. Available: https://www.nesdev.org/wiki/APU_Pulse

[41] Nesdev contributors, "APU triangle." Nesdev Wiki [Online]. Available: https://www.nesdev.org/wiki/APU_Triangle

[42] Nesdev contributors, "APU noise." Nesdev Wiki [Online]. Available: https://www.nesdev.org/wiki/APU_Noise

[43] B. Taylor, "2A03 technical reference." 2004 [Online]. Available: https://retrogameaudio.tumblr.com/post/18843375536/nes-audio-review-of-the-sound-channels

[44] J. Stolet, "Complex periodic waveforms." University of Oregon [Online]. Available: https://pages.uoregon.edu/emi/10.php

[45] J. Stolet, "Harmonics." University of Oregon [Online]. Available: https://pages.uoregon.edu/emi/11.php

[46] J. Stolet, "Square and rectangle waves." University of Oregon [Online]. Available: https://pages.uoregon.edu/emi/14.php

[47] J. Stolet, "Triangle waves." University of Oregon [Online]. Available: https://pages.uoregon.edu/emi/13.php

[48] J. Stolet, "Sawtooth waves." University of Oregon [Online]. Available: https://pages.uoregon.edu/emi/12.php

[49] Nesdev contributors, "Family computer disk system." Nesdev Wiki [Online]. Available: https://wiki.nesdev.org/w/index.php?title=Family_Computer_Disk_System

[50] Nesdev contributors, "FDS audio." Nesdev Wiki [Online]. Available: https://wiki.nesdev.org/w/index.php?title=FDS_audio

[51] Nesdev contributors, "FDS BIOS." Nesdev Wiki [Online]. Available: https://wiki.nesdev.org/w/index.php?title=FDS_BIOS

[52] Nesdev contributors, "CIC lockout chip." Nesdev Wiki [Online]. Available: https://wiki.nesdev.org/w/index.php?title=CIC_lockout_chip

[53] J. Takiff, "Video games gain in japan, are due for assault on u.s." The Vindicator [Online]. Available: https://news.google.com/newspapers?id=QBhcAAAAIBAJ&sjid=MlUNAAAAIBAJ&pg=2846,1271636

[54] thristian, "The japanese famicom didn't have a CIC." Hackernews [Online]. Available: https://news.ycombinator.com/item?id=1059686

[55] C. Rivett, "Christopher rivett - computer and video game enthusiast." [Online]. Available: https://christopherrivett.co.uk/

[56] smspower.org, "Registers." [Online]. Available: https://www.smspower.org/Development/Registers

[57] smspower.org, "Memory map." [Online]. Available: https://www.smspower.org/Development/MemoryMap

[58] Texas Instruments, *TMS9918A, TMS9928A, TMS9929A video display processors data manual*. 1982 [Online]. Available: http://www.bitsavers.org/components/ti/TMS9900/TMS9918A_TMS9928A_TMS9929A_Video_Display_Processors_Data_Manual_Nov82.pdf

[59] Sega, *Service manual schematics*. [Online]. Available: https://www.smspower.org/Development/SegaMasterSystemServiceManual#Schematics

[60] NEC, *D4168 data-sheet*. [Online]. Available: https://pdf1.alldatasheet.com/datasheet-pdf/view/129898/NEC/D4168.html

[61] codeslinger.co.uk, "VDP info." [Online]. Available: http://www.codeslinger.co.uk/pages/projects/mastersystem/vdp.html

[62] C. MacDonald, "Sega genesis VDP documentation - version 1.5f." 2000 [Online]. Available: http://jiggawatt.org/genvdp.txt

[63] smspower.org, "Collision detection." [Online]. Available: https://www.smspower.org/Development/CollisionDetection

[64] smspower.org, "SN76489." [Online]. Available: https://www.smspower.org/Development/SN76489

[65] Texas Instruments, *Texas instruments SN76489*.

[66] Sega, *Sega Mk3 hardware reference manual - Rev1*.

[67] smspower.org, "Pause button." [Online]. Available: https://www.smspower.org/Development/PauseButton

[68] B. Clark, "65C816 opcodes." [Online]. Available: http://www.6502.org/tutorials/65c816opcodes.html

[69] MagicKit, "PC engine hardware." [Online]. Available: http://www.magicengine.com/mkit/

[70] NEC, *HuC6280 - CMOS 8-bit microprocessor hardware manual.*

[71] ChibiAkumas, "Hardware sprites on the PC engine (TurboGrafx-16)." [Online]. Available: https://www.chibiakumas.com/6502/platform4.php#LessonP33

[72] NEC, *HuC6270 - CMOS video display controller manual.*

[73] NEC, *HuC6270 - CMOS video color encoder manual.*

[74] NEC, *HuC6280 - CMOS programmable sound generator manual.*

[75] "ADPCM demo PC engine." Youtube [Online]. Available: https://www.youtube.com/watch?v=jdWYOHPV6Uw

[76] Game Station X, "The PC engine exp connector." [Online]. Available: https://gamesx.com/misctech/pcebp.php

[77] Game Station X, "TurboGrafx/duo/PC-engine controller data." [Online]. Available: https://gamesx.com/controldata/turbocont.htm

[78] shu.sheldows.com, "Memory map." [Online]. Available: http://shu.sheldows.com/shu/download/pcedocs/pce_memory.html

[79] hardwarebook.info, "HuCard pinout." [Online]. Available: http://www.hardwarebook.info/HuCard

[80] nfggames.com, "101 secrets of the PC engine." [Online]. Available: https://nfggames.com/games/pce/

[81] pc-engine.co.uk, "Accessories catalogue." [Online]. Available: http://www.pc-engine.co.uk/?section=accessories

[82] Okqubit, "Motherboard." [Online]. Available: https://www.okqubit.net/machines/gamecons.html

[83] Motorola, "M68000 8-/16-/32-bit microprocessors user's manual." [Online]. Available: https://www.nxp.com/docs/en/reference-manual/MC68000UM.pdf

[84] MegaDrive Development Wiki, "Main 68k memory map." [Online]. Available: https://wiki.megadrive.org/index.php?title=Main_68k_memory_map&oldid=251

[85] MegaDrive Development Wiki, "Z80 area." [Online]. Available: https://wiki.megadrive.org/index.php?title=Z80_Area&oldid=469

[86] Stealth, "Sonic megamix is not sonic CD!" [Online]. Available: https://hcstealth.tumblr.com/post/13505293669/sonic-megamix-is-not-sonic-cd

[87] Plutiedev, "Using the Z80." [Online]. Available: https://plutiedev.com/using-the-z80

[88] A. Keil, "Sega genesis/mega drive VDP graphics guide - v1.2a." 2017 [Online]. Available: https://megacatstudios.com/blogs/press/sega-genesis-mega-drive-vdp-graphics-guide-v1-2a-03-14-17

[89] Plutiedev, "Changing screen resolution." [Online]. Available: https://plutiedev.com/screen-resolution

[90] Nemesis, "Double-screen?" SpritesMind.Net [Online]. Available: http://gendev.spritesmind.net/forum/viewtopic.php?t=1034#post_content14396

[91] djmips, "Mega drive: Corrections around audio and VDP clarification plus IP thoughts." Github [Online]. Available: https://github.com/flipacholas/Architecture-of-consoles/issues/54

[92] MegaDrive Development Wiki, "VDP ports." [Online]. Available: https://wiki.megadrive.org/index.php?title=VDP_Ports&oldid=275

[93] Plutiedev, "Sonic water." [Online]. Available: https://plutiedev.com/sonic-water

[94] Wikipedia contributors, "Yamaha YM2612." Wikipedia, The Free Encyclopedia [Online]. Available: https://en.wikipedia.org/wiki/Yamaha_YM2612

[95] jsgroth, "Emulating the YM2612: Part 1 - interface." [Online]. Available: https://jsgroth.dev/blog/posts/emulating-ym2612-part-1

[96] nukeykt, "Nuked-OPN2." [Online]. Available: https://github.com/nukeykt/Nuked-OPN2/blob/335747d78cb0abbc3b55b004e62dad9763140115/ym3438.c#L435

[97] Plutiedev, "Programmable sound generator." [Online]. Available: https://plutiedev.com/psg

[98] cvghivebrain, "Sonic the hedgehog (mega drive) disassembly." Github [Online]. Available: https://github.com/cvghivebrain/s1disasm/blob/main/sound/music/GHZ.s#L467

[99] ChibiAkumas, "Lesson P21- FM sound on the genesis via the 68000." [Online]. Available: https://www.chibiakumas.com/68000/platform3.php#LessonP21

[100] GameHut, "Toy story's hardware defying music - how we did it." Youtube [Online]. Available: https://www.youtube.com/watch?v=x3m3JrVImmU

[101] GST Channel, "The sound capabilities of the SNES." Youtube [Online]. Available: https://www.youtube.com/watch?v=dtK0t8k6akg

[102] notaz, "Notaz's SVP doc." [Online]. Available: https://notaz.gp2x.de/docs/svpdoc.txt

[103] Plutiedev, "I/o ports." [Online]. Available: https://plutiedev.com/io-ports

[104] Yaca2671, "Motherboard." [Online]. Available: https://commons.wikimedia.org/wiki/File:SNES-CPU-RGB01_01.jpg

[105] Computer History Museum, "Oral history of william david 'bill' mensch, jr." [Online]. Available: https://archive.computerhistory.org/resources/access/text/2015/06/102739969-05-01-acc.pdf

[106] wiki.nesdev.com, "CPU (6502 unofficial opcodes)." [Online]. Available: https://wiki.nesdev.com/w/index.php/CPU_unofficial_opcodes

[107] Super Nintendo Development Wiki, "65816 reference." [Online]. Available: https://wiki.superfamicom.org/65816-reference

[108] ChibiAkumas, "Learn multi platform 65816 assembly programming... For ultimate power!" [Online]. Available: https://www.chibiakumas.com/65816/

[109] S. W. contributors, "Multiplication." [Online]. Available: https://snes.nesdev.org/wiki/Multiplication

[110] S. W. contributors, "Division." [Online]. Available: https://snes.nesdev.org/wiki/Division

[111] Nintendo of America, *SNES development manual.* 1993 [Online]. Available: https://archive.org/details/SNESDevManual

[112] D. Piepgrass, “Qwertie’s SNES documentation plus DMA revision 6 - 2.1, non-profit use only.” 1998 [Online]. Available: https://media.smwcentral.net/Ersanio/SMWCstuff/Advanced%20documentation/qsnesdoc.html

[113] Nesdev users, “65816/SNES open bus/MDR mystery, (re: The latest RGMEx video).” Nesdev Forums [Online]. Available: https://forums.nesdev.org/viewtopic.php?t=24536

[114] A. Keil, “Super nintendo graphics guide.” 2017 [Online]. Available: https://megacatstudios.com/blogs/press/super-nintendo-graphic-guide

[115] Jademalo, “4:3 -> 8:7 aspect ratio correction for SNES.” [Online]. Available: https://videogameperfection.com/forums/topic/43-87-aspect-ratio-correction-for-snes/

[116] F. Sanglard, “Designing the super nintendo video system.” [Online]. Available: https://fabiensanglard.net/snes_video/

[117] F. Sanglard, “How the SNES graphics system works.” [Online]. Available: https://fabiensanglard.net/snes_ppus_how/

[118] Retro Game Mechanics Explained (Alex ”Dotsarecool” Losego), “Super NES features.” Youtube [Online]. Available: https://www.youtube.com/playlist?list=PLHQ0utQyFw5KCcj1ljIhExH_lvGwfn6GV

[119] A. Keil, “SNES sprite engine design guidelines.” 2018 [Online]. Available: https://megacatstudios.com/blogs/press/snes-sprite-engine-design-guidelines

[120] Snarius, “Super NES programming/DMA tutorial.” [Online]. Available: https://en.wikibooks.org/wiki/Super_NES_Programming/DMA_tutorial

[121] S. W. contributors, “Color math.” [Online]. Available: https://snes.nesdev.org/wiki/Color_math

[122] Retro Game Mechanics Explained (Alex ”Dotsarecool” Losego), “Color math - super nintendo entertainment system features pt. 03b.” Youtube [Online]. Available: https://www.youtube.com/watch?v=zcoU6-9_fDM

[123] Retro Game Mechanics Explained (Alex ”Dotsarecool” Losego), “Lag & blanking - super nintendo entertainment system features pt. 06.” Youtube [Online]. Available: https://www.youtube.com/watch?v=Q8ph2OVqZeM

[124] pinouts.ru, “Nintendo SNES pinouts.” [Online]. Available: https://pinouts.ru/dev/Nintendo/SNES/

[125] Nintendo, “Super nintendo - manuel d’instructions (france).” 1992 [Online]. Available: http://www.ffviman.fr/switch-snes/notice-eur-p-iii-iv.html

[126] vgmpf.com, “S-SMP.” [Online]. Available: http://www.vgmpf.com/Wiki/index.php?title=S-SMP

[127] Snarius, “Super NES programming/SPC700 reference.” [Online]. Available: https://en.wikibooks.org/wiki/Super_NES_Programming/SPC700_reference

[128] A. Stante, “Neo-geo programming manual.” [Online]. Available: http://furrtek.free.fr/noclass/neogeo/NeoGeoPM.pdf

[129] Retro Reversing, "SNES (super famicom) software development kit (SDK)." [Online]. Available: https://www.retroreversing.com/super-famicom-snes-sdk/

[130] Retro Reversing, "SNES (super famicom) development kit hardware." [Online]. Available: https://www.retroreversing.com/super-famicom-snes-development-kit/

[131] Wikibooks, "Super NES programming/SNES memory map." 2022 [Online]. Available: https://en.wikibooks.org/w/index.php?title=Super_NES_Programming/SNES_memory_map&oldid=4072115

[132] M. Bazzinotti, "SNES LoRom memory model." [Online]. Available: https://web.archive.org/web/20190311181601/https://www.cs.umb.edu/~bazz/snes/cartridges/lorom.html

[133] Super Nintendo Development Wiki, "Registers." [Online]. Available: https://wiki.superfamicom.org/registers

[134] Bucket Mouse, "The SNES cartridge, briefly explained." [Online]. Available: https://mousebitelabs.com/2019/05/18/custom-pcb-explanation/

[135] Snes9x DSP Team, "DSP1 gamepaks." [Online]. Available: https://web.archive.org/web/20110610122211/http://users.tpg.com.au/advlink/dsp/dsp1.html

[136] NeoGeo Development contributors, "JAMMA connector pinout." NeoGeo Development Wiki [Online]. Available: https://wiki.neogeodev.org/index.php?title=JAMMA_connector_pinout

[137] NeoGeo Development contributors, "MVS board types." NeoGeo Development Wiki [Online]. Available: https://wiki.neogeodev.org/index.php?title=MVS_board_types

[138] NeoGeo Development contributors, "Z80." NeoGeo Development Wiki [Online]. Available: https://wiki.neogeodev.org/index.php?title=Z80

[139] A. Clements, "Exception handling in the 68000, part 1," *Microprocessors and Microsystems*, 1986.

[140] NeoGeo Development contributors, "68k/Z80 communication." NeoGeo Development Wiki [Online]. Available: https://wiki.neogeodev.org/index.php?title=68k/Z80_communication

[141] NeoGeo Development contributors, "Watchdog." NeoGeo Development Wiki [Online]. Available: https://wiki.neogeodev.org/index.php?title=Watchdog

[142] NeoGeo Development contributors, "Coin lockout." NeoGeo Development Wiki [Online]. Available: https://wiki.neogeodev.org/index.php?title=Coin_lockout

[143] NeoGeo Development contributors, "Frame size." NeoGeo Development Wiki [Online]. Available: https://wiki.neogeodev.org/index.php?title=Frame_size

[144] NeoGeo Development contributors, "L0 ROM." NeoGeo Development Wiki [Online]. Available: https://wiki.neogeodev.org/index.php?title=L0_ROM

[145] NeoGeo Development contributors, "Fix layer." NeoGeo Development Wiki [Online]. Available: https://wiki.neogeodev.org/index.php?title=Fix_layer

[146] NeoGeo Development contributors, "Fix bankswitching." NeoGeo Development Wiki [Online]. Available: https://wiki.neogeodev.org/index.php?title=Fix_bankswitching

[147] NeoGeo Development contributors, “Sprites.” NeoGeo Development Wiki [Online]. Available: https://wiki.neogeodev.org/index.php?title=Sprites

[148] freem, “Neo-geo assembly programming for the absolute beginner.” [Online]. Available: https://www.ajworld.net/neogeodev/beginner/

[149] NeoGeo Development contributors, “VRAM.” NeoGeo Development Wiki [Online]. Available: https://wiki.neogeodev.org/index.php?title=VRAM

[150] NeoGeo Development contributors, “FM.” NeoGeo Development Wiki [Online]. Available: https://wiki.neogeodev.org/index.php?title=FM

[151] freem, “Yamaha YM2610 application manual II.” [Online]. Available: https://www.ajworld.net/neogeodev/ym2610am2.html

[152] Yamaha Corporation, “Yamaha YM2149.” 1987.

[153] C. Covell, “Alpha denshi (ADK) NEO-GEO MML music driver - dissection and Z80 disassembly.” [Online]. Available: https://www.chrismcovell.com/ADKMML.html

[154] NeoGeo Development contributors, “System ROM.” NeoGeo Development Wiki [Online]. Available: https://wiki.neogeodev.org/index.php?title=System_ROM

[155] NeoGeo Development contributors, “Eyecatcher.” NeoGeo Development Wiki [Online]. Available: https://wiki.neogeodev.org/index.php?title=Eyecatcher

[156] NeoGeo Development contributors, “68k program header.” NeoGeo Development Wiki [Online]. Available: https://wiki.neogeodev.org/index.php?title=68k_program_header

[157] NeoGeo Development contributors, “USER subroutine.” NeoGeo Development Wiki [Online]. Available: https://wiki.neogeodev.org/index.php?title=USER_subroutine

[158] NeoGeo Development contributors, “SYSTEM IO.” NeoGeo Development Wiki [Online]. Available: https://wiki.neogeodev.org/index.php?title=SYSTEM_IO

[159] NeoGeo Development contributors, “Memory card.” NeoGeo Development Wiki [Online]. Available: https://wiki.neogeodev.org/index.php?title=Memory_card

[160] NeoGeo Development contributors, “Bootleg MVS boards.” NeoGeo Development Wiki [Online]. Available: https://wiki.neogeodev.org/index.php?title=Bootleg_MVS_boards

[161] NeoGeo Development contributors, “Slot check security.” NeoGeo Development Wiki [Online]. Available: https://wiki.neogeodev.org/index.php?title=Slot_check_security

[162] NeoGeo Development contributors, “Security code.” NeoGeo Development Wiki [Online]. Available: https://wiki.neogeodev.org/index.php?title=Security_code

[163] NeoGeo Development contributors, “Fatal fury 2.” NeoGeo Development Wiki [Online]. Available: https://wiki.neogeodev.org/index.php?title=Fatal_Fury_2

[164] NeoGeo Development contributors, “NEO-CMC.” NeoGeo Development Wiki [Online]. Available: https://wiki.neogeodev.org/index.php?title=NEO-CMC

[165] Mame contributors, “Prot_cmc.cpp.” Github [Online]. Available: https://github.com/mamedev/mame/blob/master/src/devices/bus/neogeo/prot_cmc.cpp

[166] NeoGeo Development contributors, “PROGEOP.” NeoGeo Development Wiki [Online]. Available: https://wiki.neogeodev.org/index.php?title=PROGEOP

[167] ConsoleMods contributors, "UNIVERSE BIOS (UniBIOS)." ConsoleMods Wiki [Online]. Available: https://consolemods.org/wiki/Neo_Geo:UNIVERSE_BIOS_(UniBIOS)